A POETIC ORDER OF EXCESS

A POETIC ORDER OF EXCESS

ESSAYS ON POETS AND POETRY

José Lezama Lima

Translated from the Spanish, Edited, and Introduced
by James Irby and Jorge Brioso

GREEN INTEGER
KØBENHAVN & LOS ANGELES
2019

GREEN INTEGER
Edited by Per Bregne
København / Los Angeles

Distributed in the United States by
Consortium Book Sales & Distribution / Ingram Books
(800) 283-3572 / www.cbsd.com

First Green Integer Edition 2019
Published with permission from Agencia Literaria Latinoamericana
English-language Translation and Introduction copyright ©2019
by James Irby and Jorge Brioso
Back cover material ©2019 by Green Integer
All rights reserved

Book design: Pablo Capra
Cover photograph: José Lezama Lima

LIBRARY OF CONGRESS CATALOGING IN PUBLICATION DATA
José Lezama Lima [1910-1976]
A Poetic Order of Excess: Essays on Poets and Poetry
ISBN: 978-1-892295-98-9
p. cm—Green Integer 209
I. Title II. Series III. Translators: James Irby and Jorge Brioso

Green Integer books are published for Douglas Messerli

Contents

Introduction

Jorge Brioso

I.

DESPITE being one of the most influential Latin American writers of the twentieth century, José Lezama Lima's (1910-1976) work has had limited translations into English. His novel *Paradiso* was the first of his texts that was translated to English when in 1974 Farrar, Straus and Giroux published Gregory Rabassa's translation. This translation coincided with the great reception that the Latin American Boom writers had in North American culture and the academy during this period. Even though Lezama Lima is not, strictly speaking, a member of what the publishing industry came to call the "Boom generation," his novel *Paradiso,* published in 1966, was contemporaneous with other novels that marked an important milestone in Latin American narrative: *La ciudad y los perros* (1963) by Mario Vargas Llosa (*Time of the Hero*, 1966), *Rayuela* (1963) by Julio Cortázar (*Hopscotch*, 1967), *Cien años de soledad* (1967) by Gabriel García Márquez (*One Hundred Years of Solitude*, 1970), etc. It was the narrative innovation associated with the Boom, a general interest in Latin America and the Cuban

Revolution, and the Latin American Neo-Baroque that marked the reception of Lezama Lima's first translation to English.[1] However, *Paradiso* is different from all the other Boom novels in each one of the above categories.[2]

Unlike the other authors cited here, Lezama is, first and foremost, a poet. In some notes for a lecture about his novel *Paradiso* that he never actually delivered, Lezama writes about the relationship that exists in his work between the novel and poetry, poetry and prose:

> Poetry and the novel have the same root. The world made sense and simultaneously resisted interpretation like an immense poem… A phrase of mine that I have repeated: when my thoughts are obscure I write poetry; when I am more lucid I write prose. That apparent dichotomy got resolved in a unified manner in my novel. I thought it was clear because in it are my family, my mother, my grandmother, my circumstances; those things that are closest to me, the memory of the most immediate things. But quickly things began to get complicated.[3]

When the Cuban Revolution comes to power in 1959 Lezama supports it, as is evident in some of his texts from that period. However, his novel *Paradiso*, published in 1966, is characterized as decadent and pornographic due to the homoeroticism found in Chapter VIII. The situation gets worse in 1968 when Lezama is a member of the jury that grants the poetry prize "Julián del Casal" to the book *Fuera del juego* by Heberto Padilla, a poetry book that is highly critical of the revolutionary process.[4] The last two works that were published while he was alive, *Poesía completa* and *La cantidad hechizada*, appeared in 1970. From that year on, both his work and his person were condemned to silence and ostracism. It was not until the mid 1980s, many years after his death in 1976, that Lezama's figure was rescued from oblivion and his work was published again. In 1985 the Cuban publisher *Letras cubanas* published his *Poesía completa*, in 1987 they also published his *Cuentos*, an anthology of his essays in 1988, and his novel *Paradiso* in 1991.

With respect to the term neo-baroque that was used to try to define a good part of the new Latin American literature, Lezama also tried to distance himself from this characterization. He accepted the validity of that term to read his work, as he had demonstrated in many of his essays, especially in his book *La expresión americana*, but he did not consider it a valid term to understand the creative process of the other members of the Boom. In a letter to Carlos Meneses dated August 3, 1975, he stated the following:

> I believe that the term Baroque is beginning to stink, a product of habit and weariness. With the adjective baroque they try to express ways that deep down have very radical differences. García Márquez is not baroque, neither are Cortázar or Fuentes; Carpentier is neo-classical, Borges much less so. The manner in which our literature took Europe by surprise made

9

them use this old characterization. […]

A few of his poetic works and essays appeared in English after the translation of his novel *Paradiso* in different journals[5] but it is not until 2005 when the University of California Press publishes an anthology with his poetry in English in its collection *Poets for the Millennium*, edited by Ernesto Livon-Gossman, that another complete book of his is published in English. This anthology also includes three prose texts: an interview of Lezama, one of his letters to Severo Sarduy, and his essay "Confluencias," one of the few essays written by Lezama that had been published in English.[6]

We believe that in order to gain a full understanding of Lezama Lima's work, his essays are as essential as his poetry. Poetry and the essay are the two genres that Lezama Lima first worked in and these constitute the totality of his work, with the exception of a few short stories that he published between the 1930s and 1960s when he published *Paradiso*. He could not finish his other novel, *Oppiano Licario*, that was published posthumously in 1977.

Lezama Lima, along with Jorge Luis Borges and Octavio Paz, is perhaps one of the most important essayists in Latin American culture because of the originality of his thinking and language, and because of the cosmopolitan nature of his work, without it ever ceasing to be profoundly Latin American. Together with Borges and Paz, Lezama also occupies a central role in the creation of intellectual webs throughout the continent fomented by the various journals he edited such as *Verbum* (1937), *Espuela de Plata* (1939-1941), *Nadie Parecía* (1942-1944), and *Orígenes* (1944-1956). These journals published works by the most important writers in Spanish as well as translations and critical works of the most relevant contemporary artists. Octavio Paz called the journal *Orígenes* the most important journal in Spanish.

II.

This anthology tries to establish a dialogue among three of the scenarios from which a poet constructs his poetics. The first of these scenarios is structured around the moment the poet reflects about himself and his creative process when reading the work of a consecrated poet; a gesture through which he tries to construct his own literary genealogy and establish a critical distance from the poetic tradition that precedes him. The second of these scenarios is a self-reflection exercise, where an author indicates to us how to read his work and literature. The third scenario of reading is where the poet, through the rhetorical devices of his own poetry, performs his poetics.

When one speaks of poetics, we think primarily of the second one of the scenarios previously described or of a mix of the second and the third, trying to establish a dialogue between the expressive device of the poems and the reflections that the poet has about his own work.

However, we do not tend to grant the same importance to the moment when the poet we study confronts the work of another poet. This erasure probably occurs because it is associated with imitation, to the copy of a model. In the classic concept of the author, translation, gloss and commentary of others' texts were considered as important, if not more, than the "original" work of the author. It is not like this in modernity where, if we believe Octavio Paz, the only form of tradition that is perceived as legitimate is the radical and constant rupture with the past and where influences, if we believe Harold Bloom, provoke more anxiety than anything else. And yet, there is a detail that cannot be ignored, especially when studying a poet, and it is that when poets compile their work, they include their own texts as well as any translations that they made. The act of appropriating another's language into one's own, of trying to resolve with one's own language what another said with his language and in a foreign tongue, constitutes a decisive moment in the formation of every contemporary poet, perhaps because this act constitutes an anti-modern gesture without which it would be impossible to conceive of the singular and marginal space that the poet occupies in modernity.

Having said that, why is the study of that moment when a poet reads another poet so important? It is because this way we discover not only his affinities but also his phobias. Upon confronting the work of another writer, with another vocabulary, he not only discovers a positive form of expression but the poet also measures himself against a creative danger. When a poet situates himself in relation to another, he sees it first and foremost as a creative problem. How does a poet confront and try to resolve the problems that he broaches in his work? In which areas does he succeed or fail? A poet confronts another one that he considers a milestone in culture while at the same time perceives him as an exemplary failure, an expressive form that has brought tradition to a dead end, an *aporia*. And it is this milestone-aporia that allows and incites the creative gesture that inaugurates his or her own work. One writes because one thinks that others did not succeed at saying what had to be said. Below, I include an example of one of the most well-known writers in Spanish, Jorge Luis Borges, as well as the most debated poet in the Spanish language whose work has generated more phobias and *philias* than any other, Luis de Góngora.

Jorge Luis Borges' challenge to the homage being paid to Luis de Góngora on the European side of the Atlantic in 1927 is emblematic of the visceral reaction that another writer's work can provoke: "I, too, am ready to remember Góngora once every 500 years...." Góngora is a constant preoccupation for Borges during the 1920s and '30s; in fact, it was his great preoccupation as a writer. Góngora is perhaps the writer most quoted in Borges' essays, although it was always to revile him. What would become of a writer without his counter examples, without those forms of writing that he rejects, without his phobias? Can we understand a writer who wrote *A Uni-*

versal History of Infamy without his art of insult? At the moment when Borges was convinced that literature was just a syntactic act,[7] Góngora's *Soledades* constituted one of the greatest challenges since it is one the most anomalous syntactic acts produced in Spanish. The most curious thing is that Borges inverts the reproach that many of Góngora's critics posit. Borges reprimanded Góngora for not daring to accept that literature is only played out in the syntax, in the prosody, and for continuing to pretend that it also has to be a mystery, even if it is a mystery made only of rhetorical tricks. Towards the end of the 1930s and the first years of the 1940s, the notion that Borges has of what makes literature changes radically, as does his perspective about Góngora. In *Los Conjurados* (*The Conspirators*), his last book, he dedicates a beautiful poem to Góngora. The poem merges Borges' and Góngora's voices. The two enemy-poets end up by speaking as if they were one and the same. He directs the final appeal of the poem to both of them: "I wish to return to the common things: water, bread, a jug, some roses."

The poets that Lezama dedicated the most attention to during his literary career were: Luis de Góngora, Stephane Mallarmé, Paul Valéry, and the Cuban poet Julián del Casal.[8] One cannot study French or Spanish literature and thought without understanding the great influence that Góngora's and Mallarmé's writings had in their languages. Góngora and Mallarmé, each in his own language, are the poets that have generated the greatest tradition of exegetes, perhaps because they are considered the most hermetic poets in their respective languages. One could do a history of French thought, from Valéry to Quentin Meillassoux, by studying the different ways in which thinkers have positioned themselves before Mallarmé's poetry. Góngora, who was the most discussed poet of his time, the seventeenth century, was also extraordinarily influential on both sides of the Spanish Atlantic during the early twentieth century until 1950. His influence, whether because of great admiration or rejection, on figures such as Rubén Darío, Alfonso Reyes, Juan Ramón Jiménez, Jorge Luis Borges, many of the Spanish poets from the Generación de 1927 (Gerardo Diego, Dámaso Alonso, Jorge Guillén, Federico García Lorca), Octavio Paz, and Lezama is decisive.

The dialogue that Lezama maintained with Mallarmé's work could be synthesized in the following question-problem: Why does the destiny of a poem depend on being able to learn how to think with propriety about the place that paradoxes have in thinking, the deviations in morality, and islands in culture and geopolitics? Lezama through his confrontation with Góngora faces the following creative dilemmas: Can the literal meaning of a work constitute its principal mystery? Can we speak of a cosmovision of a poem when all its dilemmas dissolve into its form? Can the surprise, the shock that modern poetry produces, transform into a collective experience, into one of the factors that configure the *sensus communis*, "the unanimous" as Lezama calls it?

Paul Valéry was still alive and productive when Lezama began to publish in the 1930s and was one of the most influential figures in Latin American and Spanish poetry in that moment. Valéry's influence and the study of the poem "Le cimetière marin" saves the young Lezama, according to his own words, from many of the temptations of Modernism and the Avant-garde: "Studying that poem put an end to the following things: To poetry as a copy of pictures traced by dreams. Proust's nightmare. To facile pastiches of folklore in the Spanish style.... To the superficial accumulations of surrealism" ("Conversation about Paul Valéry"). But Paul Valéry's work is also a challenge for Lezama. What happens to the poem if inspiration and poetic furor are dismissed. These two are the mechanisms with which tradition tried to explain the transition from possibility—the "before" of a work, its "outside"—to the act, the very work. What happens with that void, with the threshold that separates the work understood as an entity realized and finished and with a vocation of totality from the materials, the fragments, the pieces with which it is configured? What happens, as is the case with Valéry, when the "before" of a work becomes the creative space *par excellence*? Julián del Casal was the nineteenth-century Cuban poet about whom Lezama wrote more perhaps because he was a highly controversial figure and because through his work it was possible to think through one of the great dilemmas that organized the Latin American tradition at least until Lezama's generation: How does one build traditions in Latin America where the failure of the attempt to appropriate/rewrite a foreign model is constitutive and also the driving force of tradition itself?

Due to space constraints in this introduction I cannot expound on all the problems outlined above. I am going to concentrate on some of the relevant aspects of Lezama's reading of Góngora's work. I will conclude this brief introduction with a short section where I discuss the topic that, in my opinion, provides structure to all of Lezama's work and lends its name to this anthology: a poetic order of excess.

III.

Alfonso Reyes compares the exegetical passion that Góngora's work awakened to the passion aroused by contemporary authors such as Robert Browning or Stéphane Mallarmé. This passion went to such an extreme that the work of these authors was "translated" into their own language, even by some of their contemporaries. Jules Lemaître translated Mallarmé's work into French and Góngora's critics did the same with his work. But what type of rhetorical, semantic, syntactic, prosodic, and lexical estrangement must a work of art have in order to be translated into a simplified version of its own language? When this occurs, what is in question, above everything else, is the literal meaning of the work. Everything is up for discussion: the mythological allusions, the allegorical or moral meaning of the text, the polysemy of its symbols, its possible interpretations; but the process always begins with a dispute about the literal meaning of the words and the way in which they display on the page. It seems as though the obscure, the mysterious, in Góngora begins with the materiality of the letter, the lexicon chosen, and the syntactic order.

Lezama tells us in his essay "Serpent of Don Luis de Góngora" that a poet like Góngora—who dislocates the syntax of Spanish to the point of making it unrecognizable—forces his critics to always begin with a debate about the literal meaning of each verse; what is in question is not what he wished to say but what he actually said. Góngora's language tries to establish a single meaning for the poem after all other previous meanings through which reality is organized have been discarded. As Bastasar Gracián tells us in his book *The Critic (El criticón*, 1657), in a world like the Baroque, where everything is ciphered and where the immediate meaning of things has become inaccessible (*"one can no longer understand bread as bread, but rather as earth, nor wine for wine, but rather as water, to the extent that even the elements are ciphered in the elements"*), the task of the poet is to attempt to reinvent a single meaning, reinvent the face value of things.[9] But this literalness is of a new type because it is only subject to the artifice of language. Góngora's critics, more than hermeneutists, as I have already stated, are translators: they attempt to fixate, reveal the mystery of the letter. Góngora's obscurity is not because no one could allegorize like him, or that his language unveils the great mysteries of the world, but rather, as Lezama points out at the end of his essay as he quotes Góngora: no one heard what he said because no one had ever seen a world like that.[10]

The question that sustains Lezama's reflection about Góngora centers around the weight that form has with respect to mystery and whether a mystery, that holds itself up only through form, and that is divorced from collective beliefs, is sustainable. Can the poetic work propose its mysteries, its enigmas, only as formal problems or does it need a philosophical substratum, as is the case with Sor Juana Inés de la Cruz in her poem *Primero Sueño* (*First Dream*), or religious ones as is the case with Saint John of the Cross and all mystical poetry? What is the viability of two of the great utopias imagined for the work of art: the possibility to write a book about nothing as Flaubert imagined, where everything that happened occurred in its form, or the possibility to write an absolute book that can replace the world as Mallarmé proposed? These are two positions that approximate each other because what they attempt to do is to separate the work of art from reality either because the work refuses to reproduce any content that is imposed on it or because the work tries to impose its own rules on the world. This issue leads us to another question: Can a mystery that lives only in the form overcome its condition of shock, of pure surprise, of whim?

The tradition of Spanish-language poetry, according to Lezama, has seen itself trapped in two models for the work of art that do not manage to resolve the dilemma that the modern work of art confronts: how can you invent a cosmology for the work after we have learned that the great belief systems that organized reality, what Lezama calls the unanimous, have fallen into crisis and we accept that the innovations that the work of art has realized at the level of form cannot subsist without some type of dialogue, however precarious, with the plural systems of belief that abound in our contemporary world? The two models at hand failed for different reasons: the mystics' model dared to defy all existing meanings with the goal of finding a transcendent certainty that lives outside of language and was shared by its contemporaries. But in the modern world there is no certainty either inside or outside language that we all share. Góngora's model, through a radically immanent notion of the work of art, destroys all existing meanings and constructs a single meaning for which there does not exist any cosmology that corresponds to it. But a cosmology cannot be created just with the experimentation at the level of the form and the modern work of art cannot survive without it.

Góngora was able to find a solution to this aporia but gave it up. The landscape that could have saved him—the poetry that turns its back to cosmology dwells in a wasteland—was the American landscape. But Góngora's poetry, so daring in almost all other things, preferred to stay in the hackneyed aquatic metamorphoses of Greco-Roman mythology. Góngora's America whose flora and fauna turn out to be fraudulent announces the vision that

Hegel would propose in his *Lectures on the Philosophy of World History* about the American continent three decades later: "America, then, is a nature that has fallen into original sin, into a paradoxical unresolvable illness between nature and spirit" (*La expresión americana*). It will be from this territory that lived so many centuries outside of Western books, outside the *Geist*, of the Western civilizing project, where Lezama will try out his project to create a cosmology for the modern work of art that he will denominate *las eras imaginarias (the imaginary eras)*.

It is in his book *La expresión americana* (1957) where Lezama attempts, for the first time, to replace the study of cultures for the study of imaginary eras. Before defining what these imaginary eras are, Lezama is interested in distinguishing them from Spengler's *Morphologie der Weltgeschichte* (*Morphology of World History*) and from T. S. Eliot's mythical-critical method. Spengler in *Der Untergang des Abendlandes* (*Decline of the West*) proposes studying the different civilizing processes as if they were biological cycles; he attempts to find analogies (affinities in form) and homologies (affinities in function) between cultural phenomena from different historical epochs. Eliot takes as a point of departure the impossibility of modern poets to emulate ancient ones due to their inability to create new myths. The modern work of art for Eliot can only aspire to be a gloss to foundational texts: "creation was realized by the ancient poets, for us contemporary poets what we have left is combinatorial play" (*La expresión americana*). If the modern era lacks myths, Lezama thinks it is largely because modern poets have not created them. It is the poets that have to direct the energy of the modern to that zone of gestation, of possibilities where myths are created. It is not about trying to find the mythical in the *arjé*, the fundaments, nor in what is encased in darkness, what is previous to any causality. Every myth is a theater of metamorphosis. The origin is no more than a moment inside becoming, the moment that Lezama defines as difficult ("only that which is difficult is stimulating") because it is what incites creation: "a becoming of a form in which a landscape goes to its meaning" (*La expresión americana*). More than proposing finished forms, a myth designs an itinerary for the transformations. All compilations of myths ought to carry the title that Ovid gave to his: *Metamorphosis*. Imagination, like myths, does not bring the tablets of the law but instead unfolds a map of possible paths for the mutations, the changes, for the metamorphoses.

The metaphorical subject, who is in charge of configuring the *imaginary eras*, was not only anchored in a concrete space (the American space) but also turns his gaze to a specific time (the past). But not to the past that was sealed to us because of its definite and irreversible character. The task of the metaphorical subject was to discover new meanings in the past. But how can one discover new meaning, the potentiality in the past? New potentialities in the past are activated when two images that originated in two different historical moments and with no previous relationship between them are counterposed, contrasted. The metaphorical subject revives these images by offering them a causality that is totally different from the one imposed on them by their own culture and releases these images from the regulated itineraries, the limits that their own historical moment prescribes for them. An afterlife is gifted to an image. There are many affinities between the *Imaginary Eras* of Lezama and the atlas of images that Aby Warburg titled *Mnemosyne*. The topic of Aby Warburg's atlas[11] was also the afterlife, the posthumous life (*Nachleben*) of the image. Warburg, like Lezama, created a science of intervals (*Zwischenraum*) a cartography of the discontinuous life of the image between different historical moments. *Mnemosyne* like *las eras imaginarias* tries to follow an itinerary of an impulse, a seed endowed with the power to create new forms, capable of transcending different times and cultures. These two projects, Warburg's *Mnemosyne* and Lezama's *Eras Imaginarias*, try to invent a mythology for an era that lacks them.

IV. A POETIC ORDER OF EXCESS

The other concept that structures this anthology of Lezama's, where we see together with the other two scenarios of reading that we emphasize in this anthology, is the one included in the title of this anthology and that constitutes, at least in my opinion, one of the central axes of Lezama Lima's poetics: "A poetic order of excess." Lezama thinks about form from its limits and from its margins. Therefore, the concepts through which he approximates this problem are contours and formlessness. The Cézanne phrase "contour escapes one" that Ambroise Vollard quotes in his biography of the French painter constitutes, perhaps, the unit-idea of Lezama's poetics. The battles that Lezama proposes against the classic order of representation should never be reduced to simple transgression-subversions or absolute negations as occurred in a great deal of Modernism and the Avant-garde. As Cézanne's phrase rewritten by Lezama states in a categorical fashion, it is the contour that escapes us. Things have ceased being inside the safety and the intelligibility of their limits; the contours have lost their solid and definitive nature, they are full of holes and perforations. Between the inside and the outside, between the form and formlessness, it is not possible to establish decisively clear boundaries.

"Coronation of Formlessness," a short essay that Lezama wrote on January 2, 1955, is the text where he best explains the order that begins with excess, that aspiration to a norm that we can only access when all the contours have escaped from us. This essay takes as its point of departure a Goethe quote where he affirms: "The most elevated, the most excellent in man is formless and we must prevent ourselves from configuring it in any way that is not a noble feat." The quality of man, Lezama continues in his commentary about the phrase, comes from the sacramental dose of mystery and non-conformity that it is capable of carrying. The hero, the model of excellence that Lezama's text proposes following Goethe's quote, is distinct from the classic hero where individuality (the concrete) and the concept (the paradigm) coincide, as well as from the modern hero that only understands his originality in terms of how he or she is different from the rule. The Lezamian-Goetheian hero becomes excellent by allowing that that portion of the cosmos, of formlessness that inhabits his soul, be what constructs a new model or feat, what proposes the paradigms. A colossal heroism: order of excess, triumph over formlessness: "For the primitive Greek, colossus does not mean size, but figuration, a little doll could be colossal if it achieved its figuration, if it triumphed over the formlessness. A superior order of excess, a new creationist order of man and of the gods" ("Homenaje a René Portocarrero," 1962). To conceive formlessness, according to Lezama, means following the trace of becoming that goes "from a nebula to the cosmos." More than imposing a form on the formlessness, a sense of finality, we must crown it, capture it without stopping it, and allow it to reach its best sense at the moment it escapes.

Translators' Note:
In Praise of Fidelity and Hospitality

James Irby and Jorge Brioso

How is it possible to ignore or defy the taboos of knowledge, the "you will not write this way" professional... commandments?

JULIO CORTÁZAR.
"Para llegar a José Lezama Lima."

There is no problem as consubstantial with letters and their modest mystery as the one that translation proposes...What are the many *Illiads* of Chapman to Magnieu if not diverse perspectives on a moving event, if not an experimental gamble of omissions and emphases?

JORGE LUIS BORGES.
"Las versiones homéricas."

TO think about translation is to think about accuracy and faithfulness. There are as many translations and theories about translation as there are versions of faithfulness. However, unlike being as Aristotle conceived it, faithfulness is said in only one way. What complicates everything is that each one has his own style, his way of saying things, his unique way to be faithful. Pierre Klossowski, for example, according to Michel Foucault in his article "Les mots qui saignent," attempts to be faithful to the *Aenead* word for word, respecting the placement of each word in Virgil's original Latin without caring too much about the violence that this principle exerts on French syntax. Pierre Joris, in his introduction to the poetry of Paul Celan entitled *Breathturn into Timestead*, defines the language of the author of "The Meridian" as "a truly invented German" and disqualifies any attempt to try to "naturalize" his poetry when it is translated into English in the following terms: "any translation that makes a poem more accessible than (or even as accessible as) it is in the original will be flawed." And he continues, "...another problem... concerns what I like to call the present episteme of American poetry... which demands that the language of poetry be as close as possible to the spoken, colloquial language of today...[and which] can all too often induce the temptation to oversimplify the original poem... in a doomed attempt to make the language sound 'natural.'"

Any theory about faithfulness that does not include a reflection about hospitality remains mutilated. If we go by the previous examples, absolute faithfulness to the original does not have much consideration for the language it is getting translated to, nor to the modes of reading that characterize it. Hospitality establishes an intense dialectic between the native and the foreign, between the starting point (the original language) and the point of arrival. Thanks to hospitality, customs, uses, and meanings in a culture are permeated and stirred by the contact with the other. But this commotion does not only occur in the place that welcomes the stranger that arrives, the text that travels, it also becomes necessary to transform its customs, meanings, and uses.

To make Lezama's prose and verse suitable to English is not an easy feat. Nor is it easy to force English to fit this writer who makes his own mother tongue sound like a foreign language. Difficult, if not impossible, is the task to do justice to the "density" of José Lezama Lima's texts, they possess an extraordinary force—in both poetry and prose—by virtue of their radical deviations from usual norms and expectations, their compacted and at the same time expansive verbal mass. In their unpredictability, they resemble surrealist texts, but their vocabulary is far more varied, and their notion of the oneiric emerges as radically different.

Lezama's texts recover the organic-vital sense of the work as an organism that the Romantics gave to this concept. But it would be more accurate in his case to speak of texts like dense bodies or a convergence of many such bodies, displacing or interpenetrating one another; cf., the repeated motif of physical bodies traversing spaces amid other bodies in the ten prose poems of *La fijeza*, which both enact and discourse upon alternative kinds of physics. Texts that, as they advance, often move away from their initial elements into seemingly unrelated aggregates. Texts that flow rather than cohering into unified wholes.

Central to the difficulty that Lezama's texts present is their indomitable originality. Originality that even dares, as Cortázar's quote at the beginning of this section tells us, to enter territory that high culture considers in poor taste,[1] or as pure and simple grammatical and cultural error. This uncivil Lezamanian originality forces us to question what the limits that separate innovation from error are, the discovery from the nonsensical. This trait of his writing, of course, did not just get him praise. The most influential public intellectual of republican Cuba, Jorge Mañach, in a letter dated September 25, 1949, complained about the inhospitable obscurity that he detected in the poems of the book *La fijeza*[2] of which he said: "I don't even understand the grammar." This makes faithfulness to the original even more agonizing for us as translators. Is the unintelligible translatable? Can you be faithful to that lack of polish, that indocile, plebeian side of Lezama's poetry and prose?

It is no small feat translating into English Lezama's syntax which, on many occasions, borders on the ungrammatical. The radical ambiguity of his use of pronouns is impossible to reproduce in English. His predilection for compound words also presents difficulties. But we have already said in this section of our introduction that the passion for faithfulness, near and dear to every translation, has to be completed with an equal appreciation and attentiveness to the language that welcomes the work. In order to do justice to both needs (fidelity and hospitality), we have forced English to speak in Lezamanian but we have also forced Lezama to acclimate to the English language. It is a double fidelity that can be interpreted as a double betrayal. That is the ironic destiny of translators: their passion for fidelity has earned them the fame of traitors. Traduttore, traditore.

One last word about how the translations were done. The process was always the same.

James Irby would do a first version in English that we would then exhaustively revise together.

A NOTE ABOUT THE TEXTS IN THIS ANTHOLOGY

Of the 15 texts included in this anthology, 11 are totally new translations into English. The following texts have been previously published and you can see below the places where they have been published:

1.—"Diez poemas en prosa," translated by James Irby
   a. *Sulfur* Vol 1. 3, California Institute of Technology, 1982, 40-52
   b. *Selections*. José Lezama Lima. Ed. Ernesto Livon-Grossman (*Poets for the Millennium*), California University Press, 2005, 37-55

2.—"Pensamientos en La Habana," translated by James Irby
   a. *Sulfur* 31, 1992, 70-80
   b. *Selections*. José Lezama Lima. Ed. Ernesto Livon-Grossman (*Poets for the Millennium*), California University Press, 2005. 22-31
   c. *The Whole Island: Six Decades of Cuban Poetry*. Ed.

Mark Weiss, University of California Press, 2009, 59

3.—"Confluencias," translated by James Irby
   a. *Sulfur* 25, 1989, 155-175
   b. *Selections. José Lezama Lima*. Ed. Ernesto Livon-Gross-
      man (*Poets for the Millennium*), California University
      Press, 2005, 99-122

4.—"Interview with José Lezama Lima by Armando Alvarez
   Bravo," translated by James Irby
   a. *Sulfur*, 24, 1989, 173-183
   b. *Selections*. José Lezama Lima. Ed. Ernesto Livon-Gross-
      man (*Poets for the Millennium*), California University
      Press, 2005, 122-138

The texts that had been previously published have
been meticulously revised. At least one of them, "Pensamientos en La Habana," changed radically compared
to a previous version. All the texts in prose have been
exhaustively annotated to aid in their reading. In the poems, we avoided using footnotes to prevent the critical
apparatus from interrupting the typographical and prosodic structure.

ACKNOWLEDGEMENTS

JAMES IRBY.—First of all I want to express my
gratitude to my late brother Kenneth Irby, my wife Mar-
ta Peixoto, and my friends Arcadio Díaz Quiñones and
Paul Firbas for their keen literary insight and constant

encouragement over many years. In Cuba in 1978 I benefitted from conversations with Cintio Vitier, Fina García Marruz, Eliseo Diego, and José Rodríguez Feo, all of whom had been close associates of Lezama. And my special thanks to Jorge Brioso for the literary sensitivity, intellectual rigor, and enthusiastic diligence of his collaboration.

JORGE BRIOSO.—I want to thank, first of all, my parents, Jorge Brioso and Caridad Bascó, without whom this adventure of translating Lezama Lima's work into English would not be possible. I also want to express my gratitude to three of my Carleton College students who helped me with different elements of the edition of this text: Winona Rachel, Ellie Zimmerman, and Rae Tennent. My gratitude also to Carleton College for providing funds that made possible my many trips to Princeton to work with Jim and for the funds that made this publication possible. When this project was in danger of a shipwreck, Modesto Milanés Soria, Sandra Rossi Brito, Lena Burgos, Licia Fiol-Matta, and José Quiroga offered a friendly hand. For that, my gratitude. My great friend Paul Firbas introduced me to James Irby and always encouraged both of us during this long process. For all of that, my gratitude. Without the love and support of Yansi Pérez, my wife, neither this translation nor anything that is good in my life would be possible. And last but not least, my special thanks to James Irby, whose passion for and knowledge of Latin American poetry has no parallel.

I.

AN AUTOBIOGRAPHICAL ESSAY
AND AN INTERVIEW

Confluences[1]

I used to see the night as if something had fallen upon the earth, a descent. Its slowness kept me from comparing it with something descending a stair, for example. A tide upon another tide and so on, ceaselessly, until it came within reach of my feet. It would blend the falling of night with the sole expanse of the sea.

The headlights of the cars threw their beams in zigzags and the shouts of "who goes there?"[2] began to be heard. The voices leapt from one sentry box to another. The night began to be populated, to feed and grow. From a distance, I could see it crisscrossed by ceaseless points of light. Subdivided, fragmented, riddled by the shouts and the lights. I was a long way off and could only sense the signs of its activity, like some secret parley in the depths of the night. Distant and voluble, mistress of its own hesitations, the night would penetrate into the room where I was sleeping and I could feel how it spread through my sleep. I would rest my head on a succession of waves that reached me with their elusively slight ripples. I could feel myself resting on smoke, on a cord, between two clouds. The night made me the gift of another skin, it must have been the night's own skin. And I would turn about in that vast skin that stretched back, as I turned, to the mossy beginnings of time.

When I was a child, I would always wait for the coming of night with undeniable terror. Terror, for me, of course, was also the room that can't be opened, the trunk with a lost key, the mirror where someone else suddenly appears beside us, a form of temptation. It was never a provocation to adventure or a fascination on the horizon. I never rode on the back of the night as it withdrew, nor did I have to reconstruct for my other period of sleep during the day the fragments of myself that the skin of the night had left scattered separately over my bed.

The enormous skin of the night would leave me with innumerable ways of sensing for innumerable kinds of evidence. The dog that during the day had passed by me many times with my hardly noticing him, now, at night, lay beside me drowsing, and then I stared at him with the most unwavering attention. I evidence the wrinkling of his skin, the way he moves his tail and paws trying to scare off non-existent flies. He barks in his sleep and bares his teeth angrily. In the night he has invisible enemies who still harass him. The angry reactions he had before do not depend on anything homologous to his daytime motivations. At night he doesn't depend on motivations, but rather, unwittingly, he engenders innumerable motivations on the skin of the night that covers me.

The night has become reduced to a single point, which then grows until it becomes the night again. This reduction—which I evidence—is a hand. The placement of the hand in the night gives me a sequence of time. A time in which this can happen. The night was for me the territory where the hand could be recognized. I would say to myself: that hand can't be waiting for anything, it doesn't need any evidencing from me. And a weak voice, which must have been very far away from some small fox-like teeth, would say to me: reach out your hand and you'll see how the night and its unknown hand are there. Unknown because I could never see a body behind that other hand. Hesitant in my fear, and then inexplicably certain, I would slowly start putting out my hand, as if moving anxiously over a desert, until I found the other hand, that otherness. I would tell myself: this isn't a nightmare, go more slowly, because you may be hallucinating, but finally my hand would evidence the other hand. The conviction that it was there lessened my anguish, until my hand went back once more to being alone.

It is only now, almost half a century later, that I can clarify and even separate into different moments my nighttime quest for that other hand. My hand would fall upon it because it was waiting for me. If it hadn't been there, my failure, which would have meant another fear, of course, would have been greater than the fear engendered because the hand was there. One fear hidden inside another. Fear because the hand is there and possible fear that it might not be there.

Later, I learned that hand is also found in Rilke's *Notebooks of Malte Laurids Brigge*,[3] and later still I learned it is found in almost all children, in almost all textbooks on child psychology.

So there already was the becoming and the archetype, life and literature, the river of Heraclitus and the unity of Parmenides. Take my hand away? Belittle my terrible experience because someone else had already suffered it too? Turn a decisive and terrible experience into a simple play of words, into literature? The time that went by taught me a solemn lesson: the conviction that what happens to us, happens to everyone. That experience of my hand upon the other hand will go on being extremely valuable, no matter whether all hands held out were to meet all the hands of the invisible.

It was such a decisive experience that, even though it may be found in child psychology, there are still nights with that other hand, the hand that appears. There will always be a night when the other hand comes and other nights when my hand remains rigid and unvisited.

I waited not only for the other hand, but also for the other word, the word that is always forming in us a continuum that for a few moments is created and then destroyed. A flower that forms another flower when a dragonfly comes to rest on it. To know that for a few moments something comes to complete us, and that by breathing more deeply we find a universal rhythm. A breathing in and breathing out that form a universal rhythm. Things hidden are things that complete us and make a plenitude in the length of their waves. The knowing that is not ours and the not knowing that is ours form for me true knowledge.

The word in the moments of its hypostasis, the complete body behind the word, the syllable, the wrinkling of someone's lips or the unexpected irregularity in someone's eyebrows. The residue left in each word by the vast dimensions of the stars became a momentary mirror. A fine sand that left letters, indications. A solitary word that became a prayer. Words were a hand excessive in its perspiration, an adjective was someone's profile or head-on look, eyes upon eyes, with the tension of a deer's perked up ears.

Every word was for me the innumerable presence of that fixity of the hand in the night. "It's time for a bath," "let's have lunch now," "off to bed," "someone's at the door" were for me like inscriptions that engendered ceaseless evaporations, unchanging and obsessive sketches for novels. They were larvae developing into metaphors in continuous chains, like a farewell and then another visit.

Waiting for the hand and having it come would start the verbal chain, or in that unending development the nighttime hand would be found. Sometimes waiting for the hand was fruitless and that would disproportionately separate one syllable from another, one word from its traveling companion. It was a momentary void because of the distance, which could engender things either in an anxious time of waiting or in the paradoxical emptiness of some good advice. It was like a move made in a game that fell, or I should say *collapsed*, upon some unknown board. A disturbing verbal move, because something advanced and then something in return offered a challenge and sent out its call over a net that brought up only one single fish eager to befriend all others.

In this way, I found in every word a germ that sprang from a union of the most distant stars with the deepest and most hidden things inside us, just as, at the end of time, the pause and expansion of each moment of our breathing will be occupied by an irreplaceable and unique word. In each word there will be a germ planted in the communicating vessels of the sentence, but in that world the verbal germ, as in the succession of visible and invisible spaces in breathing, produces the astonishment natural to man at a coordinate in time. The realm of the stars, that realm the Taoists called the silent sky,[4] required the transmutations in man's deepest flesh, the fires of his innermost organs, his most secret inner changes, for the purposes of which the mysterious pineal eye perhaps existed, the extinct inner mirror reconstructed by the Greeks as "being," like the *moi haïssable* of Pascal,[5] like the "unified self"[6] of the Alexandrines, which later will attain its highest expression in Saint Augustine's *logos spermatikos*,[7] the participation of each individual word in the universal word, the participation that includes a breathing that joins the visible and the invisible, a metamorphic digestion and a spermatic processional that changes the germ into a universal word, a complementary protoplasmatic hunger that engenders the participation of each and every word in an infinite, recognizable possibility.

But man not only germinates, he also elects. I would

stress the similarity between these two phenomena, which are for me equally mysterious, because when we elect we start a new germ, but, since this germ stands in a more direct relation to man, we will call it an "act." In the dimension of poetry, to carry out an act and to elect are like a prolongation of the germ, because that act and that election come within what is known as the tactile consciousness of the blind, though, even as I venture to call it that, I know I only slightly approximately what it is.

It is an act that takes place and an election that occurs in a ciphered form beyond nature, in supernature. The answer to a question that cannot be formulated, that floats in infinity. A ceaseless answer to the terrible question posed by the demiurge: why does it rain in the desert? Act and election that take place in supernature. Cities that man reaches and then cannot reconstruct. Cities slowly built over thousands of years and then struck down and leveled in the blink of an eye. Made and unmade with the rhythm of our breathing. Sometimes unmade by the sudden descent of the stars and other times made like a row of instantaneous columns rising out of the earth.

What is "supernature"? The penetration of the image into nature engenders supernature. In that dimension I never tire of repeating the words of Pascal, which were a revelation for me: "True nature has been lost, everything becomes natural";[8] the terrible affirmative force of those words made me decide to put the image in the place of the nature that has been lost. In that way, man replies to the determinism of nature with the total freedom of the image. And the pessimism of lost nature is answered with the invincible joy in man of the reconstructed image.

Do they live in some ruins? Are they actors on vacation? Is there a painter there? We are looking at Goya's painting *La gruta*, one of his best but one of his least considered. In the background, the purple sky and accumulated clouds of El Greco, contrasting with the calm flight of the doves. Covered by the tablecloth, or underneath the table, they hide so the doves will come closer. A coliseum in ruins, a deserted square, the collapsed wing of a convent. In front of that desolation they have set up a stall to sell food, where an apparition covered with a tablecloth pecked by the pigeons engenders expectation and humor. It is an unknown space and an errant time that have no place on earth. And yet, we walk in this here and elapse in this now, and we succeed in reconstructing an image. That is supernature.

Supernature is revealed not only by man's intervention in nature: man and nature both, each at their own risk, join together in supernature. Among the Tartars, dead children marry. On fine paper, drawings are made of the warriors who attend the wedding, the musicians, the family members bearing pitchers for the libations. All those present sign their names and the signatures are kept in well-guarded archives. Both families of the dead children try to keep each other company, living in the same neighborhood. They share their property and celebrate all ritual feasts together. Here we have life bustling around the dead and the dead children as a couple penetrating into life. This is a reply to what the morphologists of the Goethean school have claimed, that all species in becoming more perfect engender a new species, in the same way that nature, when enlarged by the image man provides, attains to the new realm of supernature.

In the mastabas[9] of ancient Egypt, a door was always left open to receive the magnetic winds of the desert. Genetic winds that the dead continue to receive. The penetration of the pyramids northward into the parched lands caused the queen's chamber to be constructed with the most favorable orientation possible for receiving the magnetic winds of the genesial desert. Hence my belief that the construction of the pyramids was meant to create not only a lasting space for the dead but also a genesial chamber for the kings to procreate with the concurrence of the magnetic winds of the desert. In this way a true lineage of both dead and living kings was attained. One after another the pyramids advanced into the parched lands, into the region of the dead, just as the humus, the muddy lands, were inhabited by the living, and so, at the very edge of death, the genesial chamber of the queen received the plenitude of the magnetic winds, to which Baudelaire's elastic phantoms,[10] the cats considered godlike by Egyptian culture, are so sensitive.

For the Egyptians, the only talking animal was the cat, who could speak the word "like" that could join together the two magnetic ends of its whiskers.[11] These two magnetic points, infinitely relatable to one another, lie at the basis of all metaphorical analogies. It is a genesial, copulative relatedness. Join together the magnetic points of a hedgehog with those of a shepherd's pouch, an example we are very fond of, and a chestnut is engendered. The magnetic "like" also awakens new species and the realm of supernature.

Supernature has little to do with the *proton pseudos*,[12] the poetic lie of the Greeks, since supernature never loses the primordial substance from which it comes, because it joins the one to the non-dual one,[13] and since man is image, it participates in the world as such and in the end encounters a total clarification of the image. If the image were denied him then he would have no knowledge whatsoever of resurrection. The image is the unending complement to what we can only partly see and hear. Pascal's fearful *entredeux*[14] can only be filled by the image.

Horror vacui is the fear of being left with no images at all, in times when the pessimistic combinational finitude of separate particles prevailed over the demiurge's spiraling movement to break away. In numerous medieval legends there are mirrors that do not reflect the image of a damaged or demoniacal body, because when the mirror does not speak, the devil sticks out his slimy tongue. That innate conviction in man of knowing that our key can open the door of another house, our sword can lead another army in the desert, our cards can play another game in another place. Everywhere there is the reminiscence of something unconditioned and unknown to us, a reminiscence engendered by a causality in what we can see, which we sense like a lost city we recognize anew. Actually, everything the image is based upon is hypertelic, goes beyond its finality, rejects that finality and offers the infinite surprise of what I have called "the ecstasy of participation in the homogenous," a point, an image, wandering in space. It is a tree, a reminiscence, a conversation strengthening a river by tracing a line with our finger.

Germ, act and then potency. Possibility of act, act upon a point and point that resists. The point is an Argos, a lynx, and leaves its track among the stars. Its traces, endowed with an invisible phosphorescence, are lasting. In all this there is a finite possibility that potency interprets and develops. A man's act can reproduce a germ in nature, and make poetry permanent by a secret relationship between germ and act. It is a germ-act that man can accomplish and reproduce. The howling, penetrating unity of a hunt, the cry of exultation, the permanent response of an orchestra in time, the warriors in the shadow of the walls of Ilium, the *Grande Armée*, what I have called imaginary eras and also supernature—all these form by an interaction of germ, act and potency, new and unknown germs, acts, and potencies. Planting a germ or seed on earth also means planting it among the stars, and following the course of a river also means walking one's way through the clouds, just as in Chinese theater a certain movement of the legs signifies riding on horseback.

When potency is applied to a point or when it acts in space, it does so always in company with the imago, the deepest unity we can know between the realm of the stars and the earth. If potency were to act without the image, it would be only a self-destructive act having no participation, but every act, every potency, is an infinite growth, an overriding excess, in which the stars reinforce the earth. The image, by participating in the act, produces a momentary visibility, which, without the image as the only recourse available to man, would be an impenetrable excess. In this way, man takes possession of that excess, makes it come forth and reincorporates a new excess. All *poiesis* is an act of participation in that excess, a participation of man in the universal spirit, in the Holy Spirit, in the universal mother.

Man as germ points to that development in his surroundings, and a broad strong basic trunk equates it with a fervor for establishing foundations, though we will never know, looking only at nature, what causal series produce splendor or decay, nor at what moment the unconditioned will irresistibly penetrate into those causal series. In some Asian cities, when people move from life into death, the dead are not taken out through the door, but instead a wall is torn down, as if the dead were being prepared for a new order of causality. In other Asian cities, at the moment of cremation, drawings on paper made by friends and jewels and food are also put into the flames, as if to provide the deceased with protection and company during a voyage presupposed to be into a new space.

In a few chosen vessels,[15] as they are called in the Bible, their development in life goes forward along with a prodigious anticipation of that other space. From the stark plains of Castile comes the foundation established by Saint Teresa as an oblique experience that is later reproduced in Martí, for whom the paradoxical germ of exile takes the place of the desert. After his imprisonment, Martí must have felt a kind of rebirth in the image of resurrection, just as later, after his death, he comes forth again in the flesh. The desert and its new symbolic appearance in exile become equivalent. Hence, in *Paradiso*, in order to prepare the way for his last encounter with Oppiano Licario, in order to attain to the new causality, to the Tibetan city, José Cemí has to go through all the occurrences and recurrences of the night. The placental descent of night, the balancing point of midnight, appear as variants of desert and exile. All the possibilities of the poetic system have been set in motion, so that Cemí can keep his appointment with Licario, the Icarus, the new attempter of the impossible.[16]

In *Paradiso*, world outside time becomes equivalent to supernature, since time is also lost nature and the image is reconstructed as supernature. Liberation from time is the most unrelenting constant of supernature. Oppiano Licario wants to provoke that supernature. Thus he continues on its quest through ceaseless labyrinths. Chapter XII, negation of time: inside the glass urn the dead boy and the dead centurion ceaselessly exchange faces. But in Chapter XIV, at the end, the one who appears in the urn is Oppiano Licario himself.[17] Negation of time achieved in sleep, where not only time but also space disappear. I move the enormity of an ax, I reach infinite velocities, see the blind men in the markets at night talking about the pictorial qualities of strawberries, and finally the Roman soldiers playing dibstones in the ruins: I attain the *tetractis*, the number four, god.[18] Chapter XIII attempts to show a *perpetuum mobile* in order to break free of spatial conditioning. The sheep's head turning on a pinion attains that freedom and in that dimension of Oppiano Licario's, the dimension of supernature, the figures from a childhood past return. It is a cognitive infinity acquired in Licario's presence, but in a different Pythagorean rhythm: from the systaltic, violent rhythm of the passions, there has been a movement to the hesychastic rhythm of tranquility and contemplative wisdom.

Licario has set in motion the vast coordinates of his poetic system in preparation for his last encounter with Cemí. It was necessary for Cemí to have his last encounter with Licario's words. "The spider and the image in place of the body"[19] says one of the statements he is given on the last night. Licario's sister Inaca Eco Licario appears and delivers that poetic statement as if it were a promised land. The shadow, the double, is the one who delivers the offering. The double makes the first offering, delivers the first image and Cemí ascends the sacrificial stone in order to put into effect his patronymic meaning of "idol" or "image." Let us suppose a starry Pythagorean night in 1955. I have spent several hours listening to Johann Sebastian's *Art of the Fugue*, absorbed in the interweavings of the *fuga per canon*. Infinite relationships are attained in the spirals of the night. The constructions and dilations of the rhythm are repeated in each of our steps and we grow as we walk. We go down one of those streets that have swollen like the rivers of paradise. The lights of the funeral parlor shining in the night, unknowingly, have to startle and halt the person walking by. The repeated music of a merry-go-round sustains and hastens the person on a nighttime stroll. The house in its vertical dimension, like a demented tree, thrusts at us the temptation of its last terrace, where, under the protection of the priapic god Terminus,[20] two buffoons are playing chess. Here there is something like the repetition of a circular movement. At the very edge of death, the coordinates of the poetic system thrash about desperately; with nature now exhausted, supernature subsists; with the earthly image now shattered, the unending stellar images begin. There, in the most unattainable distance, where the Pythagoreans located the soul of the stars.

The surprise is the house with its blinding lights, which the man interprets, while his saliva thickens and the circulations of his lymph and blood flow together. A *maestoso* and a *vivace* form a new unity which moves forward like a chessman into the invisible. In the merry-go-round there is also a circular repetition which breaks into spirals, into a shower of stars in the Babylonian night, into the comet that precedes and announces the death of Julius Caesar.[21] A black cat of enormous size that goes from one crowd of people to another, as an announcement of death. The searching orange spheres in Van Gogh's night, cast like stones into the belly of the whale. It is the secret conversation at the entrance to Toledo in El Greco. It is the infinitely repeated music of the merry-go-round, between the blazing house of death and the infinite vertical polyhedron, where the image would like to set up its winter quarters. It is the indomitable urge to reach the Tibetan city of the stars, where man converses with the white buffalo, where vegetal shadows penetrate into our sleep. One day I heard one of our *decimistas* say, as he recited an octosyllable: "the soul grows in the shade" (*el alma se da en la sombra*). An intuition that concurs with a theologian who tells us that man has to feel like plants, think like angels and live like animals. Perhaps, at the other end of the cord occupied by the angel, what we have is not the beast, but rather that happy coincidence of humanism's *otium cum dignitate*[22] and the grazing of beasts, both of which are manifestations of the Taoist's contemplation of the silent sky. The day we can establish a mutual clarification between human leisure and animal grazing, true nature will again be inhabited, because in both activities there is an expectation of the realm of the stars, of the world of infinite openness, because the complete relationship between animals and their surroundings has not yet been deeply understood and we are still ignorant of how the interrelationships of the universal word are established, but some day the world of *gnosis* and the world of *physis* will be univocal.

A surprise in the course of the seasons. Rain and more rain. When we go to bed, the cold linen offers its first rebuff, we have to press the pillow closer to our cheek to feel the delight of resting against something, a sensation like sailing into a resistance that can be overcome. Our sleep, as it continues, occupies new fragments of the night. Wool at night, slowly and secretly, comes to prevail over daytime linen, and the goat goes on dancing, but no longer in the sunbeam. All that is hidden, closed off, put away, opens its doors and offers the quiet new sumptuousness of a new marketplace. Cotton coins that make no metallic sound acquire magical fabrics. Shapeless bundles that had been kept in the storehouse now move toward the four bonfires blazing at the four corners of the marketplace and turn into clusters of faces. All that is hidden and dark, as the new season arrives, takes on figure and shape, becomes the child who leaves his house every morning in Whitman's poem.[23] And he comes back and tells his tale. And he gets lost and goes on with his tale: can you hear him?

In the big house on the army base, I used to watch the coming of winter. The kitchen, the dining room and the bedrooms became more subtle in their differences, their silences made a more inward sound, conversations turned more to whispers. My grandmother would visit us more often. Our preparations for her visits were very extensive and careful, it seemed as if she were coming to spend the whole winter with us, but the day after she arrived, at breakfast we would hear her say: "I don't like to abandon my house on the Prado," using the word "abandon" the way a queen refers to a castle that has been abandoned or the way we refer to a neighbor who has abandoned her children. An abandonment and neglect grandmother found intolerable. She would spend a very happy day with us, but by late afternoon she was already getting ready to go back home. I would spend the rest of the day in the sadness of that farewell. I would wander much too slowly through every room in the house. I would linger as I went from the living room out to the backyard and see there, hung up for airing, the bedspreads that were going to inaugurate the winter. Somebody would come and start bearing the dust out of the bedspreads with some long branches. And the dust flying up would turn into showers of sparks that enlarged or blotted out the faces that would come out of the fabric until the branches made them disappear. On misty winter days I liked to watch those faces that only my imago projected and that then faded away, sneezing from the dust.

Those faces I attempted to fix in a poem:

Golpea el pastor con su cayado
las más delgadas telas,
después del inútil ruido del azoro,
otra llamada, que ya no está, nos viene.

Ese ruido, naciendo en otra puerta,
se deshace en las preguntas de una muerte.
Ruido de otro total se perdería,
si no fuese universal la carne de la tela.
Nadando en nuestro instante alguien viene
a brindar su cuello por regusto o sucesión
y aunque el cayado se aplaque por las venas,
saca, saca las caras de la tela.
El golpe no es el que corresponde a cada cara
y cada cara se pierde por la tela.[24]

The shepherd knocks with his staff
the thinnest fabrics,
after the useless noise of the fright,
another call, not there any more, comes to us.
That noise, arising at another door,
dissolves into the questions of a death.
Noise of another total would be lost,
if the flesh of the fabric were not universal.
Swimming in our instant someone comes
to offer his neck in aftertaste or succession
and even though the staff is placated in the veins,
it brings, brings out the faces from the fabric.
The knock is not the one that corresponds to each
        face
and each face is lost in the fabric.

But the poem was also imparted by a kind of daring. Its title taken from esoteric Pythagorean thought and symbolic mathematics was pervaded by another adolescent naiveté. The poem was accompanied by another memory, not the clouds of autumn, but the operations of algebra. Things hidden behind the full moon of the zero. A negative quantity coming to strengthen another growth in memory. In that winter fabric, behind those clouds of dust, there were chubby-faced angels or bony heads nodding and oozing tar and pitch. Remember that figures appearing in showers of sparks, billowing dust or clouds, display obvious traces of pitch on their teeth, their fingertips or their earlobes: are these perhaps the signs of their origin or derivation? Unknown affinities with the world of carbon and flames are betrayed at times, and this makes the figures recognizable, because of their blackheads or the dust left on them from their conversations with María la Luna.

Hidden in the minus zero, in the layers of dust, the faces kept on disappearing. When the branches began to beat the bedspreads, the signs would dig their nails into the negative quantities in order to hang on to a few faces, a few intersecting lines, until finally the fabric was alive with conversations, with after dinner talk, with interchangeable faces. It seemed as if the masks were kept in huge wardrobes with three mirrors and came back from one season to another.

The house offered not only that expected metamorphosis, but also continuing hidden marvels. The colonel's study. Tables with maps and drawings, weapons hanging on the wall, diplomas, medals, armillary spheres, Mercator projections. That was located on the other side of our parents' bedroom, beyond which we never went. The "beyond" was the study, where the colonel spent most of his afternoons and evenings. If we ever penetrated into that room, through some furtively opened door, we would then run away in fright, like someone who has entered an atmosphere that refracts him. We would go in slowly, looking at a corner or a shadow or a creaking piece of furniture, and then run out like arrows shot from a bow.[25]

That room was also a gift from the course of the seasons. It would be opened up to the curiosity of the other inhabitants of the house in the muffled passage from summer to winter. There you could see a piece of black and green marble, comparative drawings of daggers from Florence and Berlin, an obsidian chess set with men as large as your hand. It would be opened up simply to be aired out, but for us it was a kind of magic spell, a challenge, something that invited us to commit some exceptional act and then withdraw in concealment. Those figures appearing in the changes of seasons, those fleeting sallies beyond what we ordinarily knew, occurred slowly, as if lingeringly and apart from any repetition. Insistence did not seem to be part of their nature. They were fleeting, barely glimpsed, shadowy, but how deeply they satisfied us, and now that they are separated from us by the dusty sands of time, it seems as if they had been repeated over and over again, as if innumerable faces kept coming out of the fabrics, as if we had made whole sojourns out beyond the Pillars of Hercules.

From that room, library, storeroom, resting place for

wayward things, I would later unravel the magic that I have sensed in all dwelling places of men, like the protectiveness of a snail that offers its defensive labyrinths to the assaults of the ocean's waves in the darkness of night.

It was the conviction that there, in the remoteness of what was right at hand, could be found all the sparks of an unseen forge. All the inhabitants of the house were asleep, but in that room that was unlike the others, we could perceive the difference with all the secret involutions of our being, there were movements so slow as to extend over thousands of years or centered on a wheel spinning with dizzying speed. There life took on indecipherable movements, remnants of some liturgy in a deserted forest or dense filterings down into some underwater cave, but the sleepers would come holding their tiny seashells to listen to the stars and broad lecterns would allow the intoning of psalms.

The conviction that the dragon, what is there and not there, what appears and disappears, needs a place of protection out beyond the Pillars of Hercules, also had at its disposal the library as supernature. There, in solitude one seeks company, and more specifically in public libraries, where company seeks solitude. The struggle against the dragon had to take place in the ceaseless relationships between solitude and company. From the memory of the mysterious room, out beyond the pillars, on the army base, would come my conception of Chinese culture: the library as dragon. Lao Tse, he of the sense of the creative that is uncreated, was a librarian, and Doctor Kung Tse, the Confucius of the Jesuits, spent the last fourteen years of his life working on the *I Ching*, the book of changes, of the visible and the invisible, where the dragon takes up lodging in a book to speak with the dead and trace the coordinates between the insignificant and the vast excess of the stars. And, like making the legible more intense with fire, we can speak with the invisible.

In itself, the urge to bring to a book that which cannot be heard or seen, the urge to have the uncreated that creates take on meaning, tells us that the struggle with the dragon has to be out beyond the pillars, that it will be in an imaginary era, that it will have its place in supernature. And just as it is claimed in some medieval legend that the devil likes to sleep in the shadow of the bell tower, so the uncreated that creates likes to spend the day in the library, because the library has begun by being something unheard, unseen, and thus nature will be found again in supernature.

We have also lost the living sense of things so decisive for man as a bonfire, a glass of water, a mirror or a sword, or as the alphabet, that safeguard to keep caravans from being lost in the desert. Along with the memory of the house, the river, the planted fields, the bull, in the alphabet we find the five letters that poetry provides. These are signs that cannot be deciphered, they must not be signs of reminiscences of figures, but symbols of the persistence of the secret challenge concentrated in an alphabet. This is the offering made by poetry, five unknown letters, wayward analogue between the stars and the earth, of the cloud entering the mirror. These were the letters in the depths that leap out like fish when we drink water from our cupped hands.

I would look out into the backyard again and that distance between the limits of the house and the line of the horizon also became filled with unknown figures.[26] The presence of hand upon hand in the middle of the night would change into a column of army mules going down into the woods, into the darkness. I would watch them and see how, with the most invincible resistance, they moved into a destiny they knew nothing about. They plodded their way through Fall and Redemption, enduring total sorrow. The closer I got to them, the more clearly I could see the trembling of their skin. They would sweat, tremble and plod, on and on. They knew nothing of their destiny, but they resisted. They went down into their Fall as into their Glory, and their resistance lighted the way for the passage of great transports. One might say that in reply to the punishment they receive they offer the punishment of their resistance. They move unknowingly out beyond the pillars, breathe like bellows in supernature and move the broad foundations of imaginary eras. Their distances are occupied by the ceaseless transformations of poetry. The resistance of the mule sows its seeds in the abyss, just as the duration of poetry sows its seeds by a resurgence in the stars.[27] The one resists in its body, the other resists in time, and the incipient wings of each can be seen to seek their complements, unknown, known and again unknown.

Because of an unprecedented increase in collections of family photographs, I realized that I was moving from a blazing zenith, from the ways of the *splendor formae*, down into a deep darkness. When my mother died, her album of family pictures enlarged my collection. In hers the people most frequently depicted were those who had gone down into the shadows of Hades, whereas in mine it was my contemporaries, those who still enjoyed the realm of light. What I can now contemplate with apparent calm was for me then a very violent, desperate shock. It was as if old relationships, the most pathetic family stories, had become peopled anew, had come to the table after dinner and could quietly dialogue with us, without the slightest alarm on our part.

Amid all these dizzying trials, I found myself plunged into darkness. The more these pictures found their places in the reaches of the past, the more they took on for me the dim glow of words read under a gas lamp. These portraits regained their serene joy, their sumptuous presence. They were real ghosts, tangibly existing in the image that provided them with bodies to walk about in, with voices that could be heard and with deeply moving farewells. The image they had abandoned like an egg embodied them anew. They lived in the palace with the green windows, went about the city with a hundred doors, came to hear mass in the Cathedral of Havana. That exquisite and most refined group of people, never complaining, never hurried, did not need any help from me to reach the house where the dragon was lodged. I am the spirit befuddled by those apparently confused emigrants, I am the one who listens, seeks and brings together again the cotton and the scent of vanilla, the wavering lamp and the ancestral yellow of the lace. There stands Andresito, the child prodigy, holding his violin: he died in an accident in a benefit held to collect funds for the cause of Cuban Independence. He was playing that night in the tuxedo his father often wore. He fell from the elevator and was killed and my grandfather died soon after of grief. And my grandmother, telling the story of it all, would end with a kind of antistrophe from some Greek tragedy: and why did it have to be my son?[28] When I was a child I wanted to be that violinist, the one who would attain expression in exchange for a confrontation with the *fatum*. He was constantly configured in me, even across the distance of death. He was the absent one, gone with the best of the family into the darkness of Moira, occupying all our family *sympathos*, and I liked to hear my grandmother and my mother tell what his studies and the night he died were like. And the delicacy of my Aunt Queta, my father's sister, secretly in love with my Uncle Alberto, my mother's brother, who, beneath his exterior as the ne'er-do-well uncle that all families have, possessed the treasure of a style of conversation that I have always sought to have as the source of my own stories.[29]

In 1880, my maternal grandfather, who was very Cuban and went into revolutionary exile years later, made a trip to Spain. Around the same time, my paternal grandfather, who was a Basque and very Spanish, made his trip to Cuba. Years after that, both families entwined their destinies in such a way that whenever I have been called a *vasco criollo* I have always felt a special pride, but my true pride I need not even confess.

A few years before she died, my grandmother opened up a gigantic wardrobe that was located in the back room of her Prado house, and then my youthful years felt a great flood of memories rush over me. There were my grandfather's tuxedo, the one my Uncle Andresito died in, and the dresses that my grandmother had worn to all her daughters' weddings. There also was an enormous inkstand with an inkwell and some solid silver reindeers, and lying on top of the inkstand was an amber backscratcher of the kind often used in the 18th and 19th centuries. That innocent wave of recollections went into the second stanza of my poem "Oda a Julián del Casal," where, to suggest the title of one of Casal's own poems, I allude to the reindeer on the inkstand and an amber backscratcher. Sometimes I think with delight that on the day of farewells, that gigantic wardrobe will again open for me. We hear once more:

> *Déjenlo que acompañe sin hablar,*
> *permitidle, blandamente, que se vuelva*
> *hacia el frutero donde están los osos*
> *con el plato de nieve, o el reno*
> *de la escribanía, con su manilla de ámbar.*[30]

Let him be with us and not speak,
allow him, softly, to turn
toward the fruit bowl where the bears are
with the plate of snow, or the reindeer
on the inkstand, with its amber backscratcher.

It was a prayer I was saying for Casal and for myself.

Inside that magic wardrobe, Uncle Andresito's violin, protected from the dust in its tightly closed case, displayed the silent veins in its wood. Streaks of amber, small tomb of jasper, tiny graceful citadel erected by Amphion. In those parades in my poem "Pensamientos en la Habana," where I don't want to choose my shoes in a store window, where I indicate that the scratch on the lute deciphers nothing, where I conjecture that the first flute was made from a stolen branch, suddenly there comes "the violin of ice shrouded in recollection" *(el violín de hielo amortajado en la reminiscencia)*, which awakens the forest seraphine that ties and unbraids the strands of memory. And it is the violin that seems to exhale the poem's final orchestration: "my soul is not in an ashtray" *(mi alma no está en un cenicero)*.[31]

An ancient legend of India reminds us there is a river whose tributaries cannot be known. In the end its flow becomes circular and begins to boil. A tremendous confusion can be seen as it sweeps along, things totally unlike and trivial coexist with jewel-like symmetries and harmonious love. This is the Puraná, carrying everything in its waters, always seeming to be in confusion, with no analogue or likeness possible. And yet this is the river that leads to the gates of Paradise. Amid the reflections of its waves pass in procession the potter's vestibule, the tree of coral, the chain of the tiger's eye, the celestial Ganges, the malachite terrace, the inferno of the lances and the repose of the perfect man. Ceaseless contemplation of the river transmits its dualism, the adventure of the analogue and the couples who withdraw to their small islands. A tree before certain eyes, a tree of coral before the tiger's eye; the lances before the terrace, and then the infernal lances before the paradisiacal terrace of malachite. Blessed are we the ephemeral who can contemplate movement as an image of eternity and follow intently the parabola of the arrow until it is buried beneath the line of the horizon.

Interview with José Lezama Lima (1964)[1]

Armando Álvarez Bravo

AAB.—You are known and renowned as an enigmatic poet. For many you are the figure of obscurity *par excellence* in Cuban poetry. There is no doubt that your endeavor inaugurates a novel way of seeing things which delivers nothing easily to the reader and instead demands of him an alert attitude. After these twenty-five years, how do you consider what has been said and is still said about these characteristics of your poetry?

JLL.—I do not think that the contemplation of my poetry offers at present greater difficulty than that offered by the contemplation of any other poetic prism. It is true that our romantic and later our *fin de siècle* poetry had no elements that could be considered enigmatic. But this fact cannot serve to join together, as is customary, the concepts of the enigmatic and the obscure. These two concepts are not necessarily tangent. Once I was told that Góngora was a poet who made clear things obscure and that I, on the contrary, was a poet who made obscure things clear, obvious, radiant.[2] I have stressed the fact that it was among medieval minstrels that the *trobar clus* appeared, these being the minstrels who produced obscure poetry. Thus we see that even minstrelsy, which by definition was simple, had nothing to do with clarity, since already among the minstrels there were some who produced obscure or hermetic poetry. And in Nordic countries there were kings who were skalds[3] that in their own palaces cultivated obscure poetry, just as there were kings who performed as buffoons in their own courts. The verses of the skalds were always nebulous and difficult to understand. For example:

> I place the round serpent
> on the tongue of the falcon's perch
> beside the bridge of Odin's shield

What this means is that a ring is placed on the small finger of the hand. One needs to know that falcon's perch means the falconer's hand. The tongue is the small finger. And the bridge of Odin's shield is the arm from which the warrior's shield hangs. Is it told that a skald, a hermetic Nordic troubadour, invited a king to have some beer soup. The monarch accepted and the poet took him to the edge of the ocean, where he said: there's your soup; when you finish, you'll have your beer. I cite these examples taken from skalds so you can see that obscure poetry has nothing to do with the baroque, with the southern Baroque of Marino,[4] of Chiabrera,[5] of Góngora. There is obscure poetry and there is clear poetry. This is a fact that we have to accept simply, just as we accept the existence of the day and of the night, of the things that are done by day and the things that are done by night.

But you will understand, my friend, that, in short, neither obscure things are so obscure as to terrify us, nor are clear things so clear as to let us sleep in peace. But all this business about obscurity and clarity now seems to me outmoded, overworked. What matters is what Pascal called *pensées de derrière*.[6] That is, the eternally enigmatic other side of things, both of the obscure or distant and of the clear and immediate. The tendency toward obscurity, toward resolving enigmas, toward playing games within games, is as common to mankind as is our image reflected in the clear surface of the water, which can lead us with egotistical voluptuousness to the final blow, to our death. There is no need to seek obscurities where they do not exist.

AAB.—Image in your poetry is a motif, a theme, a concern. It arises as a defense against realities that become realities by their own momentum, but, at the same time it arises as a force. How do you establish the relationships between image and metaphor?

JLL.—In the terms of my poetic system of the world, metaphor and image have as much in the way of carnality or living flesh within the poem as they have in the way of philosophical efficacy, external world or essential reason. One of the mysteries of poetry is the relationship between the analogue or connective force of metaphor, which advances and by so doing creates what we might call the substantive ground of poetry, and this advance through infinite analogies to a final point where the image is located, which image has a powerful regressive force, capable of covering all that substantiveness. The relation between metaphor and image can be likened to a horse that can both fly and swim and persists within a resistant substance, which is what we may consider the image to be. The image is a reality of the invisible world. Thus the Greeks placed images[7] as populators, inhabitants of the world of the dead. I believe that the marvel of a poem is that it manages to create a body, a resistant substance set between a metaphor that advances by creating infinite connections and a final image that assures the survival of that substance, that *poiesis*. In the same way that man has created orchestras, battles, soldiers sleeping in the shadow of palisades, great armadas, and homes in the bellies of whales, he has also created artificial bodies that are both caressable and resistant, like nature itself eluding and yielding to our touch. Once, when I was speaking of Martí[8] and trying to establish the mysterious laws of poetry (and don't forget that the first laws were written in poetic form), I made reference to the fact that for those prodigious laws of the imagination twenty years of absence are equivalent to a sudden vortex in death, just as, in an orchestra, a trumpet may be equivalent to twenty violins. The connections of metaphor are progressive and infinite. The "fire-covering" that the image forms over the substantiveness of poetry is as unitary and fixed as a star. That's why I state in one of my poems this deep paradox of poetry: that love is not made caressingly from pore to pore, but from pore to star, where space forms a suspension and the body plunges down and swims at length.

AAB.—When you reached your mature years you set forth a very personal conception of poetry, a poetic system. The formulation of this system began to take shape in a series of prose fragments included in your book of poems *La fijeza* [1949].[9] What we might classify as theory had its beginnings as poetry. Those first insights later took on a discursive form in essays and the bases of the system were nurtured from different sources. In spite of this later evolution, is it still correct to think that the driving force of the system is fundamentally poetic?

JLL.—That's correct. The driving force is essentially poetic. Some innocent people, terrified by the word "system," have thought my system is a philosophical study *ad usum* of poetry. Nothing could be further from my intention. I have always proceeded on the basis of elements proper to poetry, i.e. poem, poet, metaphor, image. When I began to come of age intellectually—and like all poets I have been a man of varied and voluptuous readings, following the tradition of La Fontaine, who postulated the poet as the *amateur de toutes les choses, le polyphile*[10]—, I came to understand that, by virtue of that hazardous and reversible play of metaphor and image, what seemed to be a dispersion in my readings was really an all-devouring urge towards integration into a unity, into a mirror, into a water both flowing and fixed. One day I was thinking about great periods of history that have had neither great nor powerful poets and yet were great periods for the world of poetry. It was a very important fact for me that, from Lucretius and Virgil down to the appearance of Dante, there had been no great poets in that immense expanse of time, no access to the poet as an expressive unity. And these were the times of Charlemagne, of the *Enchiridion*[11] or Magic Book, the cathedrals, the Holy Grail, the knights of King Arthur, the Crusades, the Golden Legend, Saint Francis, Saint Catherine.... This led me to study what I call the imaginary eras or eras dominated by an image, which I have expounded in several essays I believe are the most significant part of my work.

AAB.—I would like you to tell me more about those imaginary eras. And, within them, about how conceptions that are pagan from your own Catholic point of view can be integrated into Christian conceptions, producing thereby a denial of Heidegger's postulate of man as a creature destined for death and offering instead, as you do in your system, a postulate of man as a creature destined for resurrection by way of poetry. And also, how plant, animal and mythical elements do not collide with quotidian ones, but instead converge with them.

JLL.—For me it is both fascinating and difficult to speak about all that you suggest. The subject offers infinite possibilities. I see it all as a whole and it is impossible for me to express it in a moment, or perhaps even in an eternity, as such. Whenever I approach it I come up against this difficulty, but let us talk. There is an Idumaean period, or period of phallic fabulation, when the human being is still joined to the vegetal and when time, because of hibernation, does not have the meaning it later takes on for us. In each of man's metamorphoses, his dormancy creates a fabulous time. Thus, there appears the mysterious tribe of Idumea, in Genesis, where reproduction is not based on carnal dialogue by couples, on germinal dualism. The human being falls asleep on the cool river banks, beneath the broad foliage of the trees, and with graceful slowness a tree sprouts from his shoulder. The man goes on sleeping and the tree goes on growing, thickening its bark and roots and moving closer to the secret mobility of the river. This new creature of the germinating tree detaches itself in the propitious season of summer and smilingly begins to sing its rowing songs in the dawn of the rivers. This is how man lived, close to primitive nebulas and the trees, which, as they grew, gained perspectives with no need to be submissive in a movement. This is the great period when the evidence of beauty is immediate. But there are others. We can refer to the presence of the image in the siege of Ilium, whose reality is preserved by poetry in the face of its dark destruction. Or the relationship between the mysteries of the priest kings and Fou Hi (2697 B.C.) preserved in texts like the *Tao Te Ching*, a title whose closest translation might be "The Book of the Creative Uncreatedness," where the Taoists meditate on the luminous egg, on the mirror, on primitive androgyny. I should like to make a reference at this point to the way a culture may give greater depth to concepts taken from another very distant culture. For example, for the Greeks and the Romans the poet was the *puer senex* or aged child, but for the Taoists the name of Lao Tzu meant old-wise-child. We see how in the fifth century B.C., in the period of classic China's great religious upsurge, there appears a more profound concept of the Greco-Roman esteem for the poet.

AAB.—Almost an intuition.

JLL.—Quite so. When I was delving deeper into the imaginary eras, studying the great moment of the Etruscans, with their priest king Numa Pompilius,[12] the creator of bronze, of the vestals' cult of fire, and of the king's copulation with the nymph Tacita, I encountered the word *potens*,[13] which, according to Plutarch, represented in priestly Tuscan the "it is possible," the infinite possibility we later observe in the *virgo potens* of Catholicism—or, how to engender a god by supernatural means—and I came to the conclusion that it was that infinite possibility that the image must embody. And since the greatest of infinite possibilities is resurrection, poetry—the image—had to express its most encompassing dimension, which is, precisely, resurrection. It was then that I gained the perspective which I set against the Heideggerian theory of Being-toward-Death, proposing a concept of poetry that establishes the prodigious causality of being-for-resurrection, of being that triumphs over death and over the Saturnian realm. So, if you asked me to give a definition of poetry, which would be for me an almost desperate predicament, I would have to do it in these terms: it is the image attained by the man of resurrection. Then I discovered or moved on to another concept: kings as metaphors, and by this I refer to monarchs like Saint Louis, who signed himself *Roi de Tous les Français*, Edward the Confessor, Saint Ferdinand, Saint Elizabeth of Hungary, Alfonso X the Learned, in whom the person came to be constituted in a metaphor that progressed toward a concept of the people as emanating a grace and penetrating into the valley of splendor, into the path of glory, in anticipation of the Day of Resurrection, when everything, even the scars of the saints, will glow with the glow of a stellar metal. This phenomenon appears not only in history, but also in particular choral situations. It can be seen in men, in the warriors who sleep in the shadow of the walls they are about to assault. Like those who formed what was called in Napoleon's time the *Grande Armée*, who marched across all Europe. A body of men who in victory or defeat attained to a unity in which the metaphor of their connections took on the totality of an image. In other words, man, a nation, different situations that form certain groupings, may rise to a poetic plenitude. This conception of poetry may even group the animal kingdom into an arrangement of direct poetry with regard to man. A bit more boldness here, and we can take a step further. We are on a farm and suddenly we see what the Oriental masters call the elemental invisible, which turns into a white butterfly. We see how a dark corner is reanimated into a moving shape. It is the spider coming closer to become intoxicated with the music surrounding man. And just as a tree does not walk because it has a an aerial perspective, the spider in its web has a wider ambience than man does. A stay at the beach sadly comes to an end. The crab has shared a space with man and at the end of the season we see it leaving its marks along the highway man takes back to his boredom. We see the frog, in its ancestral position at the mouth of a well, maintaining its statuesque mien as a prince transformed. It shrieks with a trembling of its legs, as if it were about to give birth once more to the prince hidden within its body. Also there are simple human positions that attract a mysterious dialogue in a propitious image, as in some silent sacrifice. A ship plows the waves. A traveler comes to the railing and his cigarette burns with a slowness that becomes as magnetic as a desert wind. If we close our eyes and then open them, the traveler is no longer alone. By his side, in the night, a shape has been reanimated, similar to that vertebral consciousness that holds together the flight of birds in their autumn migrations. All this is very strange, but…. As you can see, there is much to see and try to decipher.

AAB.—In the system you have generally outlined, you borrow certain expressions from various authors and historical periods and give them meanings somewhat different from the ones they had in their original contexts. Was that change or expansion necessary in order to integrate them into your system?

JLL.—It was. Knowledge, repeated encounter with those expressions and meditation helped me enter into the ways of their possibilities. My poetic system unfolds, as is logical to suppose, within the history of culture and of the image, and not within some kind of wild frenzy. Thus, I inscribe at its threshold a series of maxims having very deep resonances. The first is from Saint Paul and says: *caritas omnia credit.*[14] "Charity believes everything." Next to it I place another from Giambattista Vico: the impossible credible.[15] In other words, man, by virtue of being a believer, of dwelling in the world of charity, of believing everything, comes to dwell in a supernatural world filled with gravitational forces. At this point I move on to that vast world extending from Saint Anselm to Nicholas of Cusa, who said in his book *De Docta Ignorantia*: *The greatest things are understood incomprehensibly*, meaning that the steps rising up to God, The absolutely Maximum, are understood without comprehension. This can be clarified, on the one hand, by thinking that one can comprehend without understanding. But there is a moment when this comprehension and this understanding come together, and that moment is provided by an acceptance of the absolutely maximum concept. To close this series, I will allude to a statement by Pascal which clarifies his argument that, since true nature has been lost, everything now can be nature. The statement is: "…He must not see nothing at all, nor must he see sufficiently for him to believe he possesses it; but he must see enough to know that he has lost it. For to know of his loss, he must see and not see; and that is exactly the state in which he naturally is."[16] I have given you four expressions scattered about in these writers' work without implying that they have there the explicit intention I give them in my system. Expressions that in my poetic world are points of reference forming a contrapuntal projection to reach their unity in this new conception of world and image, of enigma and mirror.

AAB.—In developing your poetic system, you have indicated, at different times, that with it you aim to arrive at a purely poetic methodology. Would you tell me something about that methodology?

JLL.—I try in my system to destroy Aristotelian causality by seeking a poetic state of unconditionality. But the marvelous thing, which we outlined earlier in relation to metaphor and image, is that this poetic unconditionality has a powerful gravitation, has its bases and its adamantine points of reference. Hence it is possible to speak of poetic ways or a poetic methodology within that unconditional realm formed by poetry. First, we will cite the Stoics' concept of *occupatio*, that is, of the total occupation of a body.[17] In referring to the image, we have already seen how it covers the substantive ground or resistance of the poem. Next we will cite a concept that seems to us of enormous importance, which we have called "the oblique experience." This is as if a man, without realizing it of course, were to create a waterfall in Ontario just by turning the light switch in his room. We can offer a very obvious example. When Saint George plunges his lance into the dragon, his horse falls down dead. Observe the following: the mere causal relation would be knight-lance-dragon. The regressive force we could explain by the other causality: dragon-lance-knight; but notice that it is not the knight who falls dead but his horse, according to which the relation is not causal but unconditional. This is the kind of relation we have called "oblique experience." There is also what I have called "the sudden flash," which we can consider as opposite to the Stoic *occupatio*. For example, if a student of German encounters the word *Vogel* (bird), then comes upon the word *Vogelbauer*[18] (birdcage), and then encounters the word *vögeln*, suddenly *[de súbito]*, as the causality bird-birdcage snaps into light like a match, he encounters the unconditional *vögeln*, which gives him the meaning of the bird penetrating into the cage, i.e. copulation. There is also what we might call "the hyper-telic way or method" *[el camino o método hipertélico]*, in other words, that which always goes beyond its final-ity by overcoming all determinisms. Another example. For a long time it was believed that a certain kind of cili-ary worm would pull back only as far as the tide reached. But it has been observed that even when there is no tide they pull back the same distance. There are animals like the white-headed dipteran that while copulating kill the female. That hypertelic way that always goes beyond its immediate finality, as in this case, is essentially poetic. I see I need again to quote some words, this time from Ter-tulian, who says: "The son of God was crucified, that is not shameful because it is shameful, and the son of God died, that is all the more credible because it is incredible, and after his burial he returned to life, that is true because it is impossible." From these words we can derive two poetic ways or methods: what is credible because it is incredible (the death of the son of God) and what is true because it is impossible (resurrection). I think I have answered your question.

AAB.—You have spoken repeatedly of a return to origins (with regard to poetry, of course), and, in that return, of an elimination of dualism. What can you tell us about that view?

JLL.—Already in my introduction to the first issue of *Orígenes* [in 1944] I tried to stress that. I wanted the poetry appearing in that magazine to be the poetry of a return to magic spells, to rituals, to the living ceremony of primitive man. It's very curious that a poet like Mallarmé, who enjoyed the benefits of a great tradition, should have come in his mature years to long for the magical art of a tribal chieftain,[19] as if that essence of poetry he sought for contained both primitivism and the most extreme refinement. Similarly, we can stress that in his "Prose pour des Esseintes" he speaks of the *hyperbole de ma mémoire*, a position very close to that of Descartes when, as part of the methodical doubt of his intellectualist philosophy, he mentions what he calls hyperbolic doubt, repeating the famous argument that excessive doubt, the radical *dubito*, culminates in total hyperbolic affirmation.[20] Thus, what was involved for us was a problem concerning the incarnation of poetry, or, to put it in a language recalling that of theology, the hypostasis of poetry. What was involved was finding a foothold for poetry, an incarnation of metaphor and of image in historical temporality. Thus, metaphor was as much of a matter of metamorphosis as it was of *metanoia*,[21] or—what amounts to the same thing—of successive transmutations of body and soul, offering all the suggestiveness and fascination of metaphor as a *metanoia* that goes beyond simple metamorphosis to produce a transmutation of the *animus*. Since I've now spoken of metaphor, I'll make another reference to image. I should like what I mean in this dimension to be clearly seen. If we proceed on the basis of Pascal's claim that since true nature has been lost,[22] all can be nature, we can situate the image in a precise area of striking fascination. In the first place, image is a substituted nature. In the second place, image covers the frightful destiny of the house of Atreus, for only it can clarify for us that frightful destiny. It clarifies for us the poetic concept of the entire ancient world.

AAB.—And what about the modern world?

JLL.—I think that in the case of Baudelaire, there is a return to *areté* or poetry as destiny, as sacrifice, and to *aristeia* or Pallas' protection of Diomedes as it appears in book VI of the *Iliad*. You can see, therefore, why that image has to appear obscure. It is obscure, torn from the very darkness of night. But that darkness or obscurity seems to repeat Oedipus' memorable words: "Ah, darkness, my light." Of course, both that *areté* and that *aristeia* must entail an asceticism resulting from the prodigious accumulations bestowed by the joy of a lineage of the best. So the poet, by means of the image, makes himself master of nature and offers the most seductive of asceticisms, the only kind that can be tolerated, just as the basket makers of New Guinea were born with their umbilical cords wrapped around their necks or the kings of Georgia were born with the marks of their royal nature inscribed upon their left nipples.[23]

AAB.—Do you have any thesis regarding words used in a poetic sense?

JLL.—Already in ancient times, Pythagoras cast a great deal of light upon the different varieties of the word. There are simple words, hieroglyphic words and symbolic words. That is, words that express, words that conceal and words that signify. When today, guided by the latest discoveries of German philology, we speak of the meaning of poetry, we realize that already Pythagoras had told us about words that signify, about symbolic words.

AAB.—Of those varieties postulated by the philosopher, which have you preferred?

JLL.—The poet makes use of all of Pythagoras' words or varieties, but he also goes beyond them. He manages to express a kind of *supra verba* which is actually the word in all its three dimensions of expressivity, concealment and sign. I would say there is a fourth kind of word which is the only one for poetry. A word to which I will not give a name, but which, based on the progressions of image and metaphor and on the resistance of the image, strengthens the body of poetry. I want you to keep in mind that all these things we've been talking about take place in the realm of what the harmonious Greeks called *terateia*,[24] marvel, portent. You will recall that the whole atmosphere of *Prometheus*—of Aeschylus' *Prometheus*—takes place in the *terateia*. Aristotle clarifies this concept when he says that Aeschylus set about to achieve more of a marvelous surprise than an illusion of reality.

    AAB.—In that statement Aristotle posits two esthetic positions. Which do you believe is decisive?

    JLL.—I believe that contemporary man has attained to a position that surpasses that of the world of the Greeks. Scientific research concerning the structure of reality testifies to its symmetry and beauty. If we contemplate the staggered layers of sand left by a simoom, forming a kind of enormous colosseum, what we see combines marvel and surprise with a realistic illusion deriving from the laws of optics and our modern concept of perspective. But I'm going to pick up again the thread of what I was saying before, which I think will offer some clarification concerning your question. The Catholic lives in the supernatural realm and lends greater depth to the Greek concept of *terateia*, for he is imbued with the Pauline effort to give substance to faith, to find a substance for what cannot be seen, what cannot be heard, what cannot be touched, attaining, in poetry, to a world of full, valid signification.

    AAB.—And what about the non-Catholic, the atheist? What signification will he find? Where will it come from?

JLL.—Well, can you imagine the case of a man who writes poetry and doesn't believe in anything at all?

AAB.—I think all men believe in something. Since we are talking about poetry, what I would specifically like to know is how your poetic system accounts for the poetry written by a man who does not proceed on the basis of any religious conception. A man who is not a Catholic.

JLL.—Look, Robespierre himself spoke of the Goddess Reason, just as Lucretius, the atomistic genius of atheism, talked about whirlwinds and furies and other forces of nature and considered them as gods. Aside from the fact that a man cannot deny the great contributions of the Orient, of the Greco-Roman world, of the sum of all that *anteriority* which Catholicism assimilated with exemplary reason and intuition, in accordance with the Pauline maxim which reveals the meaning of being *indebted*: "to Greeks and Romans, ancients and moderns, to all I am indebted."[25] Though an atheistic poet may deny all these contributions, he cannot fail to turn within their ambience. I'll remind you of a contemporary example. We all know that Valéry always professed his atheism. But when he gave his definitions of poetry, he called it "the paradise of language." You see how this atheist uses the word "paradise" with all the resonance of a Catholic. Besides, we have his studies of Leonardo, where he praises the position derived from the Council of Trent about the soul and the body being intertwined,

81

forming a unity, and about there being a mystery of the body and a mystery of the soul that in man are ready for his transfiguration. With this concept of transfiguration, the Catholic world surpassed the Greek concept of metamorphosis, in which the memory of the previous stage is obliterated by sleep.

AAB.—This is Valéry's conception. But for many people, and I'm sorry to keep insisting, there is no soul, and yet that attitude does not prevent them from writing poetry. How do you reconcile these facts?

JLL.—My friend, I've always believed my poetic system is something beautiful in itself, but I've never been so arrogant as to believe it is something unique. Above it I place poetry, poetry as the most transparent of mysteries or, if you wish, as mysterious transparency. That ambiguity allows me to say to you that it is not I but rather time that must answer that question: time that makes poetry and poetry that makes in time. We both serve poetry and all those who do the same will agree with me when I say that in the end poetry will unify everything; it is already beginning to do so. I don't think there's anything else to say.

AAB.—Or everything's left to be said.

JLL.—Or both.

II.

ESSAYS AND POEMS ABOUT POETICS

X and XX[1]

X.—Start with a verse. *Tout en moi s'exaltait de voir / La famille des iridées / Surgir à ce nouveau devoir.*[2] An illumination for the family of the iridaceas: yellow saffron, pineapple, tiger lily. Even the most obscure and distant things have their duties. Thus, it's a matter of overcoming certain limitations into which the Greeks had fallen. The replies were no longer Apollo's, after his death the demons and the priestess of Apollo conversed in the cave.[3] The family of the iridaceas is not a gratuitous statement of Mallarmé's, but rather a linked causation of his reminiscences. His procedure of an illumination and a suspension, of a whiteness continued by an absent wave length, goes in pursuit: island, charged with sight and not with visions; flower, a flower so enormous that it becomes separated from its lucid surroundings; garden, but before that, another hyphen: lagoon, out there the desires.[4] Vegetables growing like our desires, arrows over the flamingos.

XX.—So as not to fall into symbolism and its increasingly well-known device: a word like a piece of metal, a suspension, and then, Easter Island, Paradise. Start with precise definitions. With painters' formulas. In an obese concert of certainties, Rubens proposes (*De Coloribus*) two-thirds half tints, only one third light and shadow in all.[5] But those formulas only serve—a blow-gun against André Lhote[6]—when they touch their delight; basically, they have a primitive fragrance, as of a magic charm or spell.

X.—Since you concede that I'm right, out of courtesy, I'm going to make a correction. We eliminated the Greeks too soon. The sunbeam has a divinatory capacity, in someone in whom this solar nature can clearly touch life or death. When Apollo isn't used against Jupiter, he has the sunbeam of presentiment. When he goes against Jupiter he's obliged to be a king of shepherds, to inspire moderation.[7] But out beyond Mallarmé's island, inserted between a phrase and a suspension, there is also the breeze. The Greeks conferred upon the breeze all its merits and extensions. The cold Zephyr, when it touches the open mouths of mares, engenders swift horses that live for a very short time. Exactly the same as Euphorion.[8] Uneven levels of temperature become creative because of the velocity of the wind they receive. As in Genesis: a great wind rippled the waters. That serves us in order to place at different elevations the poetic statements by the Greeks and those by later people. In the other tradition, which is no longer Greek, to call the wind a wrestling of youths is a baroque violence. But for a Greek, whose mythology bestowed upon him the twelve winds imprisoned at Jupiter's command, it was a graphic phrase, with no resonance at all.

XX.—Beyond symbolism and mythology, beyond reminiscence and the dull metal of each word, all we have left is the dream that skims past us, those stones that we feel are still wet when after waking we remember we had company in the dark homogeneity of those waters of possibly phosphorescent steel. So heavy and so gleaming! I'm carried along on an enormous bull. It's not a ride during some Sunday outing, nor is it the black bull of an impossible destiny. Because of its size it seems like I'm on a hippopotamus, but swifter; an enormous bull bloated not with some passing growth, but rather with an inflation that is calmly going to last for many years. My body, thrown forward toward its horns by the animal's frantic impulse, looks down into an abyss, somewhat cold, since the rocks seem like huge geometrical pieces of ice. I jump off right when the swollen bull plunges into the abyss, and not only do I find footing on cold but firm ground, but also coldly contemplate the animal's slow descent. Now it has all its body under water, and its mouth desperately seeks a window for air; it slowly settles itself, making its death more possible. I'm up above, cold and contemplative.

Now the bull begins to be surrounded by its own blood; the poor creature now accepts the facts. Once in a while I look down and it horrifies me that I too might take a plunge... The bull slowly becomes reduced to a point of bright blood that remains like an eye, a bestial witness or eternity.

That's all I've been able to retain from my last dream, which horrified me with a coldness that was one of the most accusatory forms of terror.

X.—Because of that dream you tell me, you ought, when awake, to use your time to read and reread Descartes.[9]

XX.—Following your advice, I'll tell you another dream (smilingly they've conveyed this oneiric humoresque that involves me). She and I are in the Sierra de Gredos, dressed as shepherds. I amuse myself by shooting arrows. She insults me, my marksmanship is awful. I shoot off clouds of arrows without ever hitting the target. I go on shooting arrows, without my marksmanship improving. One of the arrows sticks into the back of a lamb. Furiously, in desperation, she insults me. Guided by her shouts I try to pull the arrow out of the dying lamb. I keep trying but can't succeed, she goes on rebuking me.

Then another lamb passes by. It begins to rub up against the poor dying animal. It manages to pull the arrow out. The two lambs go off happily in a possible impossible dialogue.[10]

X.—I prefer, over an individual dream, an adventure we can't provoke ourselves, a dream of many, a cosmology. A soft colloidal tegument we can press momentarily with our fingers and then abandon ourselves. Poetry comes even to assist its enemies. When an Empedocles of Agrigento defines vision as the coincidence of the effluvium exhaled by the light and the igneous ray emanating from the fire contained in the eye.[11] Thus mathematical physics later acts upon the cosmologies and entire world of the Ionians, but then in their opportunity for delights, cosmologies act again upon sciences.

Autophagy, atoms like planets, hypertelia, at the center of mathematical physics.

XX.—Then you believe that in dreams a strange divinity spreads a cloth over us, ties us down and amuses itself by offering us fruits for the most obscure palates, but placing between our desires and their form a thick current that we can never get across. Whereas in cosmologies what intervenes is an oblique but extremely powerful will. Many people feel some invisible obligations, the point to which we take them is decided by one's will to penetrate in the form of one's person into that obscure body that is no longer our own body. Apropos of will, how can we not salute Julien Sorel? You'll recall his words on returning from London. He claims that what gives the English their self-assurance is that even the most prudent of them are insane for an hour every day. During that hour, they're always visited by the demon of suicide.[12] Without stopping to provide an obvious gloss on this, we can assert that even in the most exquisite of wills, there is a moment of dismay, of helplessness, but whether we may get out of this, whether in some form of innocence we may manage to take up again a thread we're gaining down to the end, will be proven by whether our sponge went into the liquid or rested on the sand. In the Tropics it all depends on the style of your siesta. And on the fact that during your siesta you think of suicide. Then you emerge from that siesta with your senses enlightened. Every day, during your siesta, as an exercise in asceticism, think about death. That will strengthen your sensualism, make it more authentic. It's in poetry, in its substance, that the will succeeds in manifesting itself with the greatest dignity, becomes totally invisible. It's there that there's a struggle between withdrawals and concordant numbers. A poem advances in the concordance of its numbers, in other words, its rhythm, but suddenly that gratuitous impulse hesitates and sees it just can't go on, because in order to await the birth of a word one has to isolate it with unusual violence from its prior impulse, from its echo and from the metal with which it shores itself up moments before being extinguished.

X.—But I think that before proceeding on the basis of Sorel's Pascalian will, a will that uses suicide as a point of departure and as a source of nourishment, or the withdrawal, also the Pascalian abyss, that is found alongside each word in order to launch the birth of another word amid tongs and dark puffs of air, I think that before falling into that we can touch the word in a more obvious form.

XX.—Your *falling into that*, expressed in that form, is painful. It seems as if we were pointing to a presence, someone advancing toward us. Falling into that is also an obscure expression, something we don't dare to touch. Words advance toward us with unusual obviousness and we don't dare name them. When that obviousness has passed through our body, when that joining together of two bodies has formed the dimension of the poem, the time that its extension lasts, what surrounds the one who's agitating the words until they shut their eye. But now I don't want to abandon myself to that development. Please continue.

X.—For the Greeks who see the dawn as a chariot, the horse is a sunbeam. The ephebes who tamed horses on the banks of the Eurotas or the Chrysorrhoas had a dual sensation, since they had joined the existence of the horse to that of a symbol, which was at the same time an existence weighing down upon their eyes. The reaction provoked in us by a horse, not leaping before our eyes, but leaping in escape from another word or sensation. And not just the word, but something more delicate, it's time that slowly burnishes the word with no possible pursuit, imbuing it with desires other than those of the first hand that governed it. Cervantes's manner poses to us the most subtle questions about the writer as an invariable product and successive ages as variable products. He has shown us how sentences free themselves, in time, from the first extension that traces them. Perhaps, among our greatest classics, it's Cervantes who most frequently offers this most curious miracle. He uses almost always sentences of medium originality and incorporates what surely in his time would be clichés. But how delightful the transmutation afforded by time to Cervantes's sentences. I find in his *Novelas ejemplares* sentences like this one, in his time a cliché, but today a difficult elegance: bebió un vidrio de agua fresca. That leads us to think about the range of meaning the writer confers upon each of his sentences. The hand slowly begins to lose control over its extension and this makes us wonder, because we can't tell exactly whether that was a deliberate, malicious sentence, or whether on the contrary it forces us to turn against time as the betrayer of the writer's initial will. Time as the ally of good writers, not in the respectful sense we always attribute to that idea, but rather by improving his sentences, putting into them a new meaning perhaps alien to them, surely this will engender a criticism of the most exquisite details, the historical vicissitudes of each sentence, of its death and resurrection.

In each of a writer's sentences its sense of belonging to him is obliterated, and the spectator, even when he's a contemporary, establishes distances and trajectories that preserve all the impedimenta for fixing the sense of words. The trajectory extending to us is reversible, if it's a contemporary we can anticipate the smile of his descendants and judge him as if he were a classic. In so doing our presumption is infinite, since no one can foresee the meanderings of taste. At the height of the 18th century, in the evaluations of learned salons, at the height of the Enlightenment's *flatterie*, Crébillon was preferred over Voltaire. If it's an ancient that doesn't frighten us, a Petronius or a Longus, we can situate him in the comic ordinariness of a swimming pool where coevals submerge their delights. That simplicity also conceals an unprecedented presumption, because in all literary counterpoints time slowly extracts the distinctions of an uneven instrument. And it's extremely risky in the crescendo of any literary organism to establish an arrest in order to isolate in a poem the face of an image, a pair of plurals or embody movement in a fortunate verb. Very soon this becomes an island resistant to the overall understanding of the text. "Vicetiple del húmedo pescado" is a line from a Gongoresque poet of Granada; for a long time, seduced by its special attraction, I was kept from concluding that in the weary baroque of a Soto de Rojas there was a return to the atmosphere of certain eclogues in the Italianate manner. At other times, in the *Epístola moral*, I would select my sweet toothed preferences for moments of verbal accomplishment, in a poem whose great aftertaste depends upon a total accommodation to its sense of incessant death and of nostalgia *cum dignitate*. Since that dignity is engendered because it has to die. From a man's irremovability extremely slow gestures become detached and have to be carefully emphasized until they acquire an engraved contour that we can reproduce by luxurious will and provoked creation. And when sensual recognition would linger over verses like: *usó como si fuera plata neta / del cristal transparente y luminoso*,[13] how we had to pay for their delight by obscuring those other verses that seemed swept along by the meaning of the poem in which our tastes wanted to extract or emphasize certain elements. Those verses kept us from savoring others: *¡Oh! si acabase, viendo cómo muero / de aprender a morir...*,[14] which are moments of unshakable evidence of the style with which a people approaches death. And these moments are impossible to isolate, like a current penetrating into darkness by joining together someone's sorrowful tread and meditative voice during the night of his vigil of arms.

XX.—While you were speaking of the new meaning that time bestows upon sentences, I was noticing a coincidence in which mystery becomes a delight and a game. Just think: the lips that approach the water, and the intermediary of the glass, where water and air have made a synthesis. Each person savors sentences according to the way of his own lips, or, at least, needs to allow time to become a sensation in his mouth.

X.—Of course, that echo, that resonance, is a survival of the symbolism of my adolescence. I have to make a deliberate effort to separate myself from the mist, from what the words regale us with, and, more than to their crystallographic evidence, they force me to a derivation or oblique mode. Not like some symbolists who, in order to allude to a horse, have to refer to a swan (Proust called a circus horse a swan of crazy gestures). But they always lead me to a suspension, to a withdrawal where I usually place a possibility that I no longer attain even as a word. Hyperbole of my memory, we might say, following the suggestions of the greatest of the symbolists.[15] When memory is not only the retained reproduction of the external world; when it goes beyond prenatal memory, beyond recalling things that never happened; when still excluded from those realms, memory goes on piling up its treasures. Memory, more than inopportune existence, more than the homogeneity without causation of the orientals, is the seed whose flower successively destroys itself as it passes from germ to form.

XX.—I prefer not to follow you. That memory that dispenses with the prenatal and wants to go beyond the recollection of things that haven't happened, I'm afraid may engender a barbarous rite, something on the order of a banquet in limbo for lambs because we feel annoyed. Excuse me. I'm afraid that the symbolism you allege is just a maneuver of yours so as to lay siege to the theme of islands with greater ease. When you presented that theme to one of the great poets of our time, he seemed to deny it. Everything is an island, he said, earth, moon, planets. Then he showed more interest.[16] Now that that theme only registers my fatigue, you want to turn islands into a new inquiry into culture. In other words, what is it that emerges when man provokes that emptying out? When extension as a coordinate for its own memory is broken? When the secret of the pauses seems to predominate over the certainty of the linkages of words, of memories or of glances? You were speaking of a hyperbole of memory, but actually it's a hyperbole of curiosity that decides, out of the conviction of its own pride, but not out of any constructive need, to accumulate risk upon risk, without lingering over any evidence, any land possessed. I go on being loyal to the classical manner, in other words, a discovery, a creation, and then a religion in order to turn that into a nourishment for us all. That's why I believe that when a poet achieves two successful metaphors in a row, the first success was very slight. The first success has to be a synonym and have the same extension as the rest of the poem. When I find a word, I don't have to put alongside it an abyss, but just another word.

X.—Minoan or insular civilizations make a synthesis of the Prince of Flowers and the Lady of Serpents.[17] Why this ugly word "synthesis"? Whereas on continents synthesis has to be overcome by the concept of feeling indebted, on islands the suspension one needs to overcome in order to reach them doesn't make a continental synthesis of white and black, but rather of dark, shifting and very slight roots; not of Orient-Occident, not of old world and new, but rather of the Prince of Flowers and the Lady of Serpents. The ancient world was devoted to situating out beyond the hyaline quality of a limit—among the Greeks a limit is always surrounded by a great clarity—a river whose mother is of carbon; out beyond some columns a dark swampy current seeks an uncertain destiny. But styles of imagination vary, only in Persian culture can an empress indulge her whim of sending out her hunters so they can offer her for lunch a bird that feeds only on dew. In the Renaissance man no longer sees out beyond a limit a darkness, but instead his effort is to inaugurate the will of his desire, and then where there's a limit, his appetite is heightened, his tensions are inflamed and out beyond what he knows he situates some islands.

XX.—But I see you're beginning to touch upon a design that's too obvious, and you had promised us the insular as a cultural theme. In other words, what in the realm of thought is called a paradox, what in the moral realm is an adventuresome deviation, in the terrestrial realm is called an island. The Greeks used custom as a backdrop, but they acknowledged the subject's faculty for deviation, for having an opinion that deviated with regard to his culture. In such a way that if they spoke of a theory of fish, in the sense of a procession, they alluded to the form of thought they most liked. But another of their forms of knowledge is the furious or erotic, in other words, when Socrates covers his head with a cloth in order freely to evoke Venus Urania.[18] That other paradoxical mode of thought is, more than people think, a source of certainty. It presupposes, in the first place, a solid mass of opinions, a custom whose opinions are signs of health. That deviation is constantly being refracted with regard to habit. As to that other deviation of carnal morality, I'm convinced that it's born of purity, of seeking purity as a birth. That adventure is a source in isolation, purity as an isolated product. Someone speaking of the Greeks emphasized that in them science appeared as knowledge of the real quantity of pleasure, which is a phrase that has a powerful gravitation.[19] It seems like an equation, *real quantity of pleasure*, but then it starts changing into a body, like the quantity of matter necessary for the delight of our vision. In order not to separate science from wisdom, nor wisdom from saintliness, it's well to keep in mind that knowledge acts upon a quantity that isn't simple extension, but rather extension of limited matter, a real quantity. And that pleasure is not like a shadow or shower that returns or falls upon the body. Thus, pleasure is not like an exception or sickness of the body, but rather the body turned into a magnitude and acting with the silent gravitation of things.

X.—Ah, I see you sympathize with doxa as the vertical weight of bodies. If paradox exists, or so your claims seem to imply, it's because in relation to a body, deviation erupts. If that possibility exists, it's because there also exists the impossibility of becoming transformed, of having a second corporeal birth, as long as the previous senses, the usual ones, remain invariable. There exists all that is not a self in relation to an instant, all that is cold spatial extension and cold temporal continuity. You see, in a temporal-spatial parallelism, that continuity is going to be constituted[20] as an historical substance; that continuity is being converted into a resistance. And the asymmetries and dissimilarities between our body and that extension—their approaches to one another are impossible because if in them the will to similarity can appear it's only as a voluptuous mask of death—constitute the great mass of continuity. It's a vicious continuity when the parallelism between our body and that extension is perfect. But what centuries after the Greeks we have to understand as health is to free oneself from the dead weight of the mass of that extension, a lightness in order to undertake the second birth. Thus our body when it enters into life and when it dies is surprised, its senses have not been lulled by a prior landscape. Thus paradox consisted in an adaptation to the familiar, to what had fallen and already begun to form a horizontal substance.

Of course, from that point of view adaptation is impossible, because the subject pulverized the object, or vice versa. Their approaches, the new approaches or rejections, constituted a vicious space in which the self tried to proceed with its back turned toward an extension that in becoming a continuity was changed into an historical substance. That's why a Spaniard can't be paradoxical, but only contradictory. A Spaniard believes that the increase or penetration intensified between self and extension that has been turned into substance is at odds with his acuteness for resistance. That's why Cervantes tells us: "no te asotiles tanto que te despuntarás."[21] He prefers that punctiform instrument with which he touches extension, in his resistance that knows that one's side has to be illuminated by the point of the lance.[22] He knows that the man of violence has to penetrate into the painful body. An act which he evidences with an obscure carnality, with an obscure violence. He doesn't attempt to prolong the opposition between self and extension, but only goes toward extension, just as a point has to go toward a fire.

XX.—That's why there's a moment when the continuum of the sphere, as a contemporary of Aristotle sensed that theme, coincides with the sphere that appears in the hand of the Divine Child. Of course, discontinuity has the same source as perfectible essence, it's only the tense bow. It's impossible to conceive of the current of becoming that clashes with discontinuity. *Poiesis* is the form or mask of that discontinuity, the only form of provoking the visibility of what is creative. One of the most obstinate essences grasped by Catholicism is to have delivered that becoming, that continuum, to the people so that they may have their joy, so that it may form the substance of unanimity. In the ancient world that discontinuity was operative in relation to becoming and to continuum. The illuminated world that takes its place, the supernatural Christian world, set the human creature within that consciousness of unanimity, but since its trajectory went from obscurity to peace, discontinuity had no need to be isolated, it was an indeclinable attribute of the person. But, in order not to fall into the *charmant* world of the theological, I'll take you back again to the symbolist poets we enjoy so much. I know that when you hear me there's no danger that the word "symbolist" will lose its power, since for you, as for me, symbolism is that great poetic current that flows from the power of Dante to the delights of Mallarmé. Valéry's phrase seems to me very apt, "discontinuous aristocracy," referring to Mallarmé.[23] Just as Plato couldn't reach in the Parmenides a definition of unity, we can go on thinking about the mysterious or what we might almost call the previously resolved continuity of poetry. Apparent discontinuity; difficult linkage of images. Continuity of essences; prolongation of discourse and incomprehensible solution of linkages, which make us think that, if the paper upon which they rest were to disappear, it would go on tracing the signs in the air and in that way, assert its necessity, its incontrovertible presence; is then the paper a net? But let's add this: does the thought that's caught in the net have to be a dead fish?[24]

Does poetry have to be a discontinuity or an entity? Is the most valuable part of it the moment when its rupture occurs? Is it possible for it to adapt to non-being and then be constituted as an entity? If perhaps there were an incessant proliferation of the discontinuous, we don't know whether we would have the sufficient optic energy and whether it could come forth with a coincident magnetization. Or perhaps we could integrate a body of similarities when one of its extremities is dipped into the most laborious dissimilarities. That's why we believe that someday the size of a poem may have an ontic justification. In other words, the time that the flow of poetry resists in words can become a substance established between two dissimilarities, between two parentheses, comprising a substantive being, which makes visible in momentary stasis a terrible flow, caught between the limits of the echo that is needed and a coincidence in non-being with the enemies of our body and of our consciousness, which are ready to destroy themselves in a noise as of crumbling sand, but this is the only cloud that can transport the stone in the river to the frightened mirror of our consciousness, awakened in the dawning of the unknown incorporated as a breath of air.

X.—Then it's difficult but also avidly existent, this relationship between the size of a poem and the form in which we fall into death. If poetry feeds upon discontinuity, there's no doubt that the most accomplished and gravitating discontinuity is death. People speak of a death of one's own, but that implies a Protestantism of emphasizing fragments. A sinister vanity that wants to halt the instants in order to extract from them an ear of grain. It's a morbid wind that leads us to call for a different death. We know we cannot constitute as a style the death of each of us. We know that in that act of death there is only the solitude of actor and spectator. It's true that Rilke had in his favor—when he spoke of a death of one's own[25]—the fact that he was pursuing the greatest possible differentiation between the proper flavor of death (the flavor of life or death was an expression much savored by the Stoics) and the disharmony of the destroyed being. If our self-assurance has been harmonious, the coincidence with non- being would like to create for us our own style of death. But the death one would like to be one's own is actually successive. The form in which death gradually traverses us remains unperceived, but as it moves it forms a substance that is equally coincident, acting as the space occupied like a poem, a space that very quickly becomes a substance, formed by the presence of the gravitation of the words and by the absence of the unforeseeable other side they engender. The size of a poem, as far as it is filled with *poiesis*, as far as its extension is a domain of its own, is a resistance as complex as the initial discontinuity of death. In other words, there is no poem of one's own, but rather a substance that suddenly invades and constitutes the body or the hapless disturbance. The form in which one must touch it or respect it, abandon it or possess it, discharges in what is immediate a quantity so ineffably contracted that it's impossible for the subject himself to review it. The poet is like a copyist who as he copies prefers to do so in ecstasy. When that peremptory state disappears and resolves a form of writing, it would then create alien styles in one's own hand. Whereas if he copies, it's as mysterious as reproducing a letter or a number. When he creates, when he attempts to do so, the discontinuity becomes so extreme that coincident potentiality is no longer possible.

XX.—Poe, who opened up the possibilities of symbolist imagination more than the geometrical coincidences of his protagonists, used a contrapuntal device for extracting from the forward movement of his narratives a very plastic moment that is quickly transmuted into an echo. Perhaps the passage of time may have obliterated for us the plot of Arthur Gordon Pym, but certain plastic devices are unforgettable by virtue of their power to transmit a substance that our senses evidence as it comes into being. Thus the vapors of whale oil, in the hold of the ship, are soporific, and that produces the distracted somnolence that keeps the Captain from anticipating the mutiny of his crew.[26] Augustus is hidden in the secret room: "I have scrawled this with blood—your life depends upon lying close."[27] Augustus, who is drunk, after the presence of the accursed ship, thinking he has been turned into a fish, asks for a comb with which to remove his scales before he disembarks.[28] The astonishment of Too-wit, the Eskimo chief, when he sees his image in the mirror run away just as he himself runs away.[29] On the island there's a kind of water that resembles gum arabic and shows itself as transparent only in waterfalls.[30] If those moments remain in our memory it's because the plasticity of their birth entailed a resistance so as not to become extinguished in time.

In general, I detest Poe's imagination, it reminds me of 1830, when in gastronomy swallows' nests were considered an exotic dish that could counteract one's excesses. In Canton a 133 pounds of first quality nests cost ninety dollars, he tells us in horror.[31] He was forgetting that already Montaigne, an old man with an exquisite palate, reminds us that Charles V, set upon pleasing the King of Tunis, used cloves to prepare for him a peacock and two pheasants, at a cost of a hundred écus, releasing balsamic clouds throughout the entire neighborhood.[32]

X.—Those effects, those emanations of white vaporosity, elude our vigilance and depend on the spectator's capacity to rearrange what's been received. The remoteness in which reminiscence is lodged keeps it from accompanying us when we need it. But if our will isn't decisive for penetrating into reminiscence, constituting a substance or a space propitious for illuminations, it is touched by special grace or receptivity for appreciating the details of our escape. How forgetful the realists were when they thought escape was a disgust for the object, an impediment to resting our eyes on it. Escape is a decision to penetrate to the other side of the weave, to the other face that doesn't exist on the medal that isn't touched. Almost always when we hear a voice we are escaping. But terror can only be a spiral in the innermost part of our capacity to receive temptation. By escaping we develop a space that certainly isn't illuminated, but, even though it doesn't answer to the visible demands of our will either, it does constitute in its carnality the only possible specification of our gravity and resistance. The gravity of someone who escapes, of someone who is afraid and seeks a clarity that will provoke for him an ambience of company, is forming a substance which is externally devouring, but which transports the need for silence in order to prepare the change of expectation into the straightforwardness that arouses itself and recovers its functionality for the senses. No life in potentiality has transmitted to its expectation a depth as symbolic as did the lives of Simeon and Anna the prophetess. They had lived by nurturing their spirit with the Son, sensing him through a dense covering of prayer. They had lived in prayer for the Encounter: the silence was realized. Simeon speaks with Anna; Joseph and Mary with Simeon and Anna the prophetess. The Greeks had their day of encounter; but in Catholic dogma, it is the Purification of the Virgin, the Day of Candles, when the body of the Son is for a long time thrown from Simeon to Anna, to Mary and to Joseph. According to Cardinal Bérulle, quoted by Héllo, the Ceremony of the Candles is the feast of the secret of God.[33]

Just as the expectation, so the resistance and the escape, for the escape doesn't nourish its memories, but turns them into a point with which cosmic fear acts again. An innumerable attack and defense at that point of fear that fortunately always appears so as to lead us to gain the best space for the escape.

XX.—We must avoid an irreconcilable antithesis between what is foretold and its fulfillment. An impossible acedia is the consequence of gratuitous stages *ante rem*. Of course, it's not just a question of registering the presence of things, but we shall not abandon ourselves to absences without having a sense for them. It's no luxury for the intelligence to launch some ships in order to contemplate untrodden sands. May our demoniacal will to the unknown be of a size sufficient to create the need for some islands and their fruition so we may reach them. A demiurge takes pleasure in fabricating the refined coincidence of a nominalism with the stealthy evaporation of what we have to overcome after reminiscence. Already for us what arises from the most brutal discontinuity is the only initiation in order to evidence the real need for the size of a poem; the legitimacy of a substance that after a calm liquid pause has to reappear. Discontinuity is the only way for us to approach incessant reappearance. If our impulse decides to be more concerned about its own splendor than about its finality, then at least let this impulse occupy a distance capable of moving the most desperate of our tensions. Among us, to be lost means to die. I've lost him… perhaps that's an expression created by not wanting to die, and enduring it as a loss. Remember Pedro Antonio, the chocolate vender, a character of

Unamuno's, when faced with the death of his son.[34] He means to tell us that among us the most decisive discontinuity, death, is like losing one's way, as if we had decided to go *au fond de l'inconnu*,[35] but at the same time an irresistible impulse to reappear, in order to design islands after the paradox that is for us the most costly, but which is the only form that can prelude the second death.

Coronation of Formlessness[1]

SOME ill-advised people take comfort in claiming that the classical spirit excludes what is formless, rejects it, even to the point of abhorrence. For them, the shapeless would be like copper threads in a piece of gold ore. A residue meant to be overcome by means of successive filters, in a process of centuries-long decantation. But perhaps those outlines of classic countenances may turn out to be for us a like a glove with a hole in it, bitten by fish in a nightmare, on the other side of which we may find only a few truths. The first among these is that the classical spirit that doesn't see the formless as a prime enemy to be overcome, having necessarily had to go out and struggle with the dragon whose countenance is like a huge ball of fire, can shield itself only behind its own parody. If it refuses combat, it becomes exhausted, sobs in its withdrawal, since by abandoning its enemy, the formless, it loses, along with a justification for the passage of time, the fever of summer in its blood. Goethe an enemy of the formless? We should begin with this phrase of his: "That which is most elevated, most excellent, in man is formless and one must avoid configuring it in any way other than by a noble feat." From this utterance leap forth, like splendid Siberian foxes, two subordinate assertions encompassing a wide optic field. Quality in man comes to us from whatever sacrificial dose of mystery and formlessness he can endure. A high dosage of the formless, a possible spiritual parable of extreme richness, a shuddering little personage leaping through the chapters of a fictionalized summation, carried along by the rapid powder trail of the "chosen vessel."[2] A small dosage of the formless, rosy-cheeked equivalence of good taste, chess player adjustments of the spirit of finesse. Then, in Goethe's phrase it is openly declared that the feat has to be a resounding one, that the configuration amounts almost to being the battle of a man who gains laurels from the gods; maturity as the reappearance of an impregnating Hercules, surrounded by pails of grapes and centuries old goats, tenacious readers of Hesiod.

At times, Gide has striven to find the veritable melody of the classical spirit. He has traced the different incarnations that formless has had in the world. He tells us (*Journal*, p. 1,164) that Montaigne uses the word formless more in the sense of "unbeautiful" than in that of "having no form." He adds that Virgil and Horace use it more in the sense of "unbeautiful" than in that of "having no contour."[3] One may observe, we add, in the confused usage of that word by our contemporaries, the influence of the plastic arts. For which, the formless is what cannot be seen, it separates the concept of visibility from that of becoming. The formless for a large number of painters is what cannot be reduced to visibility. Forgetting that that irreducible monster, that formlessness that doesn't offer its neck to the lance, extends the overall coordinates of its senses when these feel themselves invaded by form-lessness. For that contemporary plastic spirit, the form-less consists in shuffling disparate elements, piling up the most surprisingly heteroclite elements, but the flow of becoming that moves from nebula to cosmos is amus-ingly unknown to it.

The classical spirit desires and surrenders to the sin-gular touch. What confluences or reencounters offer a basis for the happily singular touch? Amiel, for example, situates the unique touch in the area of the indubitable, to attain it we have to reject doubt.[4] Amiel, a loser, a min-iaturist of inhibition, who would hide a glass of water in a tossing of clouds, recommended the audacious stroke, the sudden seizing of the invariable turn. Gide, the vo-luptuary of the somatic, the continuator of the Greek spirit given over to the external world, is irritated with Amiel, since he believes that the unique touch doesn't depend upon the sense of verbal rapture that the writer may have, but rather, on the contrary, he seeks a "consent to sacrifice." Here we have the play of antitheses leaping from the darkness of a person. The timid long for audac-ity, but the audacious seek out possibilities for sacrifice. And it all comes down to Gracián's dictum: we concert ourselves with the disconcerting.

The true classical spirit doesn't refuse the serpent's bite. It finds its basis in the nebula of the obscure so as to configure it. The formless appears as a becoming at the point of being grasped, at the point of achieving its coronation. Form can no longer be defined as the final stage of matter, but rather as the most efficacious instant for movement to be grasped without being halted. In the death of Archemorus, son of kings, we can clarify that persistence of struggles against the formless, which centers the classical spirit. While he shows a king the discursive continuity of a river, the serpent bites his son and kills him.[5] Between the outline of a river, its dialectical arrest and the unassimilable introduction of the serpent, the classical spirit balances towers upon defensive white elephants. Stopping a river, without a serpent biting our children, is its good fable. But sometimes the formless turns into the unstoppable filtered, a murmur that slips under our arms as we dream. Between the consciousness of a medulla, which pours the instant onto a point, and the marrow of an ox, elusive formlessness lets us pat it on the back. As this caress is prolonged and the beast lingers within our reach, with the sting of its muscular phosphorus lulled, the classical spirit has greater sway over the formless or over decapitated trembling little worms.

January 2, 1955

Complex and Complicated[1]

RACINE is complex, Gide is complicated, a subtle distinction concerning levels of profundity that one malicious annotator has let fall like insignificant ash. Then, between the two companion terms, almost always tumbling in a cascade of adjectives in good company, there can be inserted, rather than the classic thinness of an onion skin, the complex play of a bull's horns. Perhaps the first difference between the complex and the complicated we find in tandem with the antipodes of command and insinuation. The complex is alert to the commands of the angel; the complicated drowses in surrender to the insinuations of the serpent. Between the indifference or interregnum of the pauses, amid the emollient fronds of the siesta or during the vulturous tensions of midnight, the complicated senses a low-lying caterpillar inching along with its lethal venom. That's its insinuation, as it slips away or strikes with treacherous opportunity during one's neglect or laxity. In empty moments we sense how it slowly gobbles its syllables one by one. It brings us, along with a flattery that lulls, those voluptuous morsels within the circle enclosed by our ego. But the insinuation is subdivided, given over to the cheap glitter of its fragments, and we recognize it by the fact that, if it appears syllable by syllable, it obliges us to obey it in disarray and reluctance. At the end of the siesta or the beginning of midnight, insinuation sets up its winter quarters, and the serpent, in satisfaction, gleams. Then, the complicated licks his lips.

If the insinuation seems such that we discover it slowly, the angel's command we immediately recognize. His commands plunge us into participation, transport us to the land of our mission. His commands have no harshness, nor can they find in us any discordant refraction, for they begin to touch us by the *cantabile* of his wings rubbing together. What the articulate angel says has nothing to do with an insinuation that fades at moments but instead transmits a continuum of vision or fulfillment and, since it addresses the full mystery of our body, we feel a joy at being engulfed in his voice. We hear that voice without opposing any antithesis, a voice which doesn't even require our response, but rather our recognition, since at that moment our appetite for knowledge has become transparent, has been touched by a theological light. Then, the complex has set himself in motion.

Now let's see insinuation addressing one of the most prodigious listeners ever, Friedrich Nietzsche, condensing almost in the clipped form of aphorisms, for he is endowed with such organs of apprehension for the swift lightness of insinuation, that no sooner it begins its slippery movement, it seems as if it were releasing for his grasp the winged worms of his epigrams. To the subdivided serpent of insinuation, he adds the serpent's tail of his aphorisms turned into arrows. "If there are gods, why

am I not to be one of them?": here we find insinuation
making Nietzsche tremble and spreading over the entire
foliage of Lutheran culture.[2] An insinuation of vast extent, tempting a man of great style, grafted onto a culture
that has drunkenly oscillated between power and word.
Now comes Vossler with a valuable nuance in our support. It was his opinion that Psalm 45: *Vacate et videte*,
can be interpreted broadly in two ways in the Western
tradition.[3] One, in the manner of Petrarch and Catholic
humanists of the period of freedom, as saying "free thyself and deliver thyself to contemplation." But, in the
other, Renaissance way, according to Luther's gloss on
that psalm, as saying "Calm thyself and acknowledge
that I am a god." Here we have the lightness of an insinuation capable of clustering at the core of a culture
and constituting itself as a deviation, as the source of
its pride and individualism. Capable of heightening its
energy to the infinite and plunging it into an irritability of
unfulfillment. Insinuation moves freely in a large sector
of Lutheran culture, to the point of producing desperation. "I should like to die in desperation," "I love only
what devours me": phrases of Gide's that make him akin
to Nietzsche. Desperation that comes only when the substance of things that don't exist has lost its gravitation
and makes us spin like the stormy blades of a windmill.

Quite other is the fate and fortune of the complex. We
come upon Racine strolling through the well-groomed
woods of the Tuileries, with their rocks covered with exotic dwarf plants and the conceptual refinement of their

fountains extending their jets into the light of artifice. He seems to speak and respond to the trees, seeking in echoes the rhymes needed for his couplets. The artisans begin to laugh at him as if he were a madman, while he is finishing his *Mithridate*. He thus establishes the first law of the complex: repeated, fixed eternity, plus a derived enigma. The unanimity of the eternal plus what comes to him as derived in the mirror of his enigma.[4] But in such a case the complicated refuses and insists on the opposite which subdues him: instant plus sensation. He attempts to bring together what is alien in the instant and what is proper to sensation, and then he begins to become magnetized in an alienated circle. The complex likes to repeat after Goethe: I don't make myself, I have been made. He knows in what form he is being retouched by the artisanship of the angels. The complicated falters, seeks, in the labyrinth bathed in the enchantment of dwarfs and sirens, the diversity of adventure, in which he believes that his instant and its sensation are strengthened and trace signs inexhaustible and lucid in their incitations.

The complex prepares the humility of his exercises. He knows that each adventure houses monotony and desperation, and prepares himself to receive, in the apparent monochrome of *askesis*, of exercise, the annunciation that will set him in motion in order to capture the response to the voice that awakened him for all time.

What an irradiation in the complex, in which the slowness of emanations is equal to the rapidity of the most magical equivalences! It casts, like a tree, a disturbing shade, where in dreams it seems as if the soul were bathing secretly in a river. But see now the complicated passing by with his attributes of sadness and tedium: he has forgotten that man is not made for the exceptions of adventure, but rather for a faithfulness to the course of the seasons and for discovering the splendor of creatures.

August 14, 1954

Joyful Night[1]

THE hut by the seashore has kept for one night the naked body of the solitary fisherman. Sleep has been rest-
less, but that unabandoned reality of the lynx-eyed paint-
brush accompanies him like a cloak of dew. His turnings
on the accompanying quilt were due to the bright stages
of moving fire, which even in sleep assured the supreme
dignity of movement. When his eyes flashed, his body
was already rising from the bed: a good way to answer
the ray of light with a movement of the body. Now his
body is amid the waves and the sinister lantern of the
enemy shore undulates like the whims of the enemy
beast. In successive conversations with the sleeping fish
his body advances, laughing at its reflections. An arm,
a leg, but always the body as a pursued sign ends in a
perpetual dignity. How could the body in emerging from
sleep and the hut already be prepared for the trembling
definition of the current? When he arrives the earth is
still silent and nocturnal, but the pilgrim touches it with
his forehead and his pursued sign, and in a rhythmical
curve his body now prepares to pursue the lantern of the
shore left behind. The silence of his body accompanied
by the song of the fish, by the curled-up blood of the coral accordions and by the trees of fireflies that come down

to the shore to touch the body of the solitary fisherman. And the trees seem to greet both a man and the friendly fragrance of the dye bark. He has again penetrated the hut on the shore, but now he has found it all illuminated. His body transfused in a light sent from elsewhere seems to show forth in a Participation, and the Lord, just and benevolent, smiles an exquisite smile. But the fisherman does not interrupt his joy in the Presence; he spurts out a curved stream of water, reminiscence of love for the enemy shore and the benevolent hut, and says to us, *What has passed through here?*

Fabulous Censures

QUICKLY, the water is reabsorbed nervously into the corpuscle; slow it is, like the invisible splashing of lead. The crevices, the dry protuberances are pulled to the same level by the whale-like passage of the water. It covers Tartaruses, Barathrums, and Depths, and does not sleep in its extension because of the hum. Who hears? Who pursues? The very rock, previously a freezing, cooks in the straight decisive swift corpuscle sent by the light, the new bodies of the dance. The receptacle creaks sluggishly, and the shark—slow breadth of silver in the accelerated breadth of lead—gradually shows his smile, his leisurely and total frenzy. A shred of veined copper stays over his tail, a laughing dolphin hovers on the dorsal fin. The slow column of impelled horizontal lead has fulfilled its role of closing off the deformities and nobilities, the gentle silver and the corrugated iron. The smoke of secreted evaporation has gesticulated in the rocky casserole, which thus afflicts the stone with the very brief touch of a thread torn loose from Energy. The shark that has been able to breathe in the column of lead, matching the stream he has breathed with the color of his skin, in all later years has continued in the water with the muscular jubilance of a star outside the window. The breeze was a guide: testimony of each pore used by the opal, the

119

scorpion, and the hoopoe. The body of the shark forced the chorus of rocks surrounding his neck, while the light like an oxyhydrogen torch painted animals and flowers on his venerable face. Applying himself then to the innermost part of the rocks, he provoked the dynasty and destiny of the roots spreading out in galleries where the perverse flow of lunar liquid had circulated. The rock is the Father, the light is the Son. The breeze is the Holy Spirit.

The Adhering Substance

IF we left our arms in the ocean for two years the tough-
ness of our skin would be strengthened until it bordered
on the greatest and noblest of animals and on the monster that comes at the call of soup and bread. Crude lath-
erings with the tegument of a horse. Chew a crab and
breathe it out through our fingertips while playing the
piano. Qualities that come and are repulsed with slowness, with displeasure and propriety. With celestial disgust. With celestial scorn for inconstancy and the errant,
wayward stamp, the submerged arm dignifies its cramps
and its absent whiteness; it endures the sleep of the tides
first, and the miserable jewels that drill through its flesh
until they are blessed by a rosy doubling void, perhaps
to make with them a region of sands like eyes, where
the hollow pincer, the shameful foot are transported with
the natural swiftness of air thickened by a hard silver
light. The submerged arm, as it is turned into a chamber
for centerings and bubbles, indocile hump for resolute
informers, finds itself circled by the insect like a flying
point; while the snail like an instant point, frantic yet
very very slow, becomes encrusted on that portion, flesh
and earth, pounded with masterly craft by the renewed
numbers of the waves. Thus that submerged fragment,
secured by the trial period of peace, is returned by echo

and reflux as a superhuman, very very white mystery. As the years go by, the submerged arm does not become a marine tree; on the contrary it returns a larger statue, with an improbable yet palpable body, a similar body for that submerged arm. Very very slow, as from life to sleep; as from sleep to life, very very white.

Fifes, Epiphany, Goats

CLARITIES became dark. Until then darkness had been a diabolic sloth, and clarity a contented insufficiency of the creature. Unchanged dogmas, clear darknesses, which the blood in spurts and in continuity resolved, like the butterfly caressing the shepherd's forehead while he sleeps. A birth that was before and after, before and after the abysses, as if the birth of the Virgin were prior to the appearance of the abysses. *Nondum erant abyssi et ego jam concepta eram.* The delectable mystery of sources that will never be resolved. The rejected uncooked clay now cooked, already leaping outside origins for grace and wisdom. The Book of Life that begins with a metaphor and ends with the vision of Glory is all filled with You. And Yours is the tremendous punishment, the sudden decapitation: You can erase from the Book of Life. Eternal Life, which arches from man clarified by Grace to the nocturnal tree, can declare mortal, strike down, release the spark. Once the erasure is made, a new name comprising a new man occupies its place, which thus does not even leave behind the shadow of its hollowness, the scandal of its ashes. Tremendous drought now erased by the goats of familiar contentment, by the pipes of overturnings and colors. Herd together, stumble, understand yourselves, more deeply if one is disposed to be born, to march toward the youthfulness that is becoming eternal. Until the arrival of Christ, Pascal said, only *false peace* had existed; after Christ, we may add, true warfare has existed. The warfare of partisans, of witnesses killed in battle, the hundred and forty and four thousand, offered as the first fruits unto God and to the Lamb (Revelation, 14:3 and 4): And they sang as it were a new song before the throne. Herd together, stumble, goats; begin at last, pipes, God and man are now alone. Tremendous drought, blaze of sun: I go toward my forgiveness.

Weight of Flavor

SEATED inside my mouth I attend the landscape. The great white tuba establishes non-spiraloid mumblings, bridges, and linkages. In that tuba, the paper and the large drop of lead fall slowly but without causality. Although if we withdraw the mat of our tongue and suddenly confront the palatine vault, the paper and the drop of lead could not resist the terror. Then, the paper and the drop of lead downward are like the torture upward but without ascending. If we were to withdraw the mat…. Thus the flavor that tends to become pointed, if we were to tear out its tongue, would multiply in perennial arrivals, as if our door were continually attended by bulldogs, Chinese beggars, angels (the order of angels called Thrones, who rapidly place things in God), and long-tailed crustaceans. When the mat is sliced, turning the void into an inquisitive though eyeless fish, the vocal cords receive the flow of dark dampness, beginning the monody. A dark lurch and the echo of the vocal cords, the night thus pursuing the night, the waning cat's back pursuing the dragonfly, obtaining the necessary amount of whiteness so the messenger can go through the wall. The sheet of paper and the drop of lead go toward the luminous circle of the abdomen that extends its fires to receive the visitor and keep away the speckled agony of the pitiful tiger. The weightiness of the palatine vault grinds up even the breath, deciding that the luminous ray must advance amid the colloidal states formed by the revolutions of the solids and liquids in their first inaugural fascination, when the beginnings revolve, as yet unable to detach the ages. Later, the successions will always maintain a nostalgia for the limited single specimen, the white peacock or the buffalo that hates mud, but with proximity forever communicated and attained, as if we could only walk on the mat. Seated inside my mouth I notice death moving like the motionless fir submerging its icy glove in the trash of the pond. An inverse custom had made for me the opposite marvel, in dreams during afternoon naps I thought it a consummate obligation—seated now in my mouth I contemplate the darkness surrounding the fir—for the scribe to wake up day after day as a palm tree.

Death of Time

IN a void velocity dares not compare itself, can caress
the infinite. Thus a void is defined and inert as a world
of non-resistance. Also a void sends out its first negative
graph so it can be like non-air. The air we were accustomed to feel (to see?): soft as a sheet of glass, hard as
a wall or a sheet of steel. We know by an almost invisible stirring of the non-existence of an absolute void that
there cannot be an infinite unconnected to a divisible
substance. Thanks to that we can live and are perhaps
fortunate. But let us suppose some implausibities so as
to gain some delights. Let us suppose an army, a silk
cord, an express train, a bridge, rails, air that constitutes
itself as another face as soon as we draw close to a window. Gravity is not a tortoise kissing the ground. The
express train always has to be halted on a bridge with a
broad rock base. It impels itself—like the impulsion of
smile to laughter, to raucous laughter, in a feudal lord
after his garnished dinner—, until it decapitates tenderly,
until it dispenses with the rails, and by an excess of its
own impulsion slips along the silk cord. That velocity
of infinite progression borne by a silk cord of infinite
resistance comes to feed upon its tangencies that touch
the ground with one foot, or a small box of compressed
air between its feet and the back of the ground (lightness,

angelisms, nougat, larks). The army in repose has to rest upon a bridge with a broad rock base, impels itself and comes to fit, in hiding, behind a small poplar, then in a worm with a backbone grooved by an electric time. The velocity of progression reduces the tangencies; if we suppose it to be infinite, the tangency is pulverized: the reality of the steel box on the archetypal rail, in other words the silk cord, is suddenly halted, the constant progression derives another independent surprise from that temporal tangency, the air turns as hard as steel, and the express train cannot advance because the potency and resistance become infinite. There is no fall because of the very intensity of the fall. While potency becomes ceaseless impulsion, the air mineralizes and the moving box—successive, impelled—, the silk cord and the air like steel refuse to be replaced by a crane on one foot. Better than substitution, restitution. To whom?

Procession

THE parade of numbers took place in the tedium of its invincible fall, a malaise tolerated as proof of its comfortable succession. Within the numbers there were successions and meanings: if the former motivated their friendly groupings, the latter motivated the challenging fluidity of their rhythms. The parades of the binary of war, the elusive sequence of fish, forgot their origins and their ends, their impulsion and their extenuated frenzy, in order to give us in the muscles of the leopard the finest geometrical progressions, in navigating magnets a ridiculous and unforgettable limitation. The fascinations of those archetypal groupings, of the magnetizing that convokes in order to flee from a whirl that must be reduced to the law of its structure, gradually brought about the end of the cynic, the atomist and the pre-Augustinian Alexandrine. *The vendor of words.* Man propagates and injures his substance, God superabounds, the encounter takes place in His generosities. But the beginning, at false and visible moments, seemed to be separated from the Other. From then on, men will form two groups: those who believe that the generosity of the One engenders duality, and those who believe that it leads it to Darkness, to the Other. Thus the procession which in emerging from Form is prolonged until it passes through and is submerged by ultimate Essence, is saved yet again by being filled with the symbolic and concupiscible figure that encloses the already illuminated substance. And thus where the Stoic thought that he leapt out of his skin into a void, the Catholic situates the procession in order to awake in his body as a limit, the adventure of the same real and richly possible substance in order to awake in Him. When he dies, the Procession has become so excessive that the plasticity of the chorale is replaced by an echo that seems to turn back again toward us, already holding out its hands, walking another cross. In the snow, in the defile, in the chosen mansion, the procession of men goes on dividing by similarity, occupying, betraying or communicating the same body, the blood and the oils.

Tangencies

AFTER inventing the zero, Prince Aleph-Zero proceeded
on horseback until sleep was put across his path, throw-
ing him from his horse toward the grass that covered
soft spongiform rocks. The horse's arrow is his nose. He
placed his knife between the ground and himself, and then
placed his shield over the knife with malicious inclination,
since through there his sleep was going to pass. As the
knife moved over the ground, the fountain gushed forth,
but the seed was dying. In the first shipwrecks of sleep, he
had leaned with his somnolent bow on the vertical thrust
of the recent fountain, in such a way that the bow resting
on what he could glimpse was hardened horizontally; as it
increased its potency, the jet of the fountain touched both
the man detached from the air and his sleep so lightly that
he could keep himself horizontal without giving up the
sleep that had detached him from his horse. Sleep ampu-
tated him from his horse, making him feel that as he abandoned it he abandoned himself, so that then he could regain the impenetrable hardness of the same sleep crossed
upon the clock inside the fountain. Again the horse throws
its hyaline crewman through sleep. The horse that savors
arsenic rejects tortoise shell powder. The cargo thrown by
the horse into the fountain keeps his forehead softly resting on the edge of the window. He is not the inventor of
the zero, he is the inventor of the sling and seed, the one

who waits until the water putrefies so that the planetary memory of the seed may begin. The marvelous man, on the contrary, at the corner of his garden of triangular and lozenge-shaped flagstones, squats on his legs and stretches out his arms like a swan fed with diorite cotton. Even at night, a tribune gymnast, losing his memory, retrospective acidity with a patina, hemmed in by his rhythmic, copious, trembling scratches. At midnight, the man of the seed with his face cut drops his head softly on the edge of the window, which also supports the two feet of the man in the green, orange and gray tights of steel mesh, taking the corner of his garden like a rope in a port. Each separated by the edge of the window, the man of earth lifts his eye more to listen than to discover, while the gymnast, in the same midnight of startled normality, raises and lowers his legs in a rhythm that seems like the memory of a march along the river. When he deposited the seed, he could not know that it was pierced, support for a night when thrown from the horse. The gymnast, abruptly shifting the tiny rubber ball with a steel center from his hand of remembered smoke to his other hand of bitten gold, opens his eyes and linearity in his weariness, exhausting himself to attain the height, duration and weight of a saurian. It's not strange that whenever he throws the instruments with which he strengthened the steadiness of his hands, he should stumble over a flower because of his fatigue, and that each monstrous fatigue should be paralyzed with the earthborn attached burning sensation of the seed pierced by the man thrown from the horse.

Ecstasy of the Destroyed Substance

AND you, Promachus, close the double chain of ants. Did you count the cattle? Destroy the body and the sign of its hollowness so as to attain the reminiscence of its transparency. Destroy the inverse relationship of unity and substance, of number and perceptible thing, resolved in the figure detached by the ecstasy of participation in the homogenous. But first, the sphere is encompassed by the boy's hand. The violent substitution followed by a hollow gust prepares the void, the whale, and the bottle, where there is coming and going as by a principal originator, covered with smoke and extremely hurried. Now, blind am I. I encompass and understand myself, blackened in the bottle that contains the dead armillary sphere suspended by boreal magnets. Blind am I, my home is the whale. Alongside the void, I emit my yawn or give away plaster hats, and an immense funerary ceramic takes from the temple those who have been decapitated in order to establish with their simultaneous fury a dense hum of memories. Thus, in a marshy grotto, with a waltzed floor squeezed from tortoise eggs, the master watchmaker trembles at the frightful coincidences and the fleur-de-lys-covered farmer receives, as he sows the only false document, the shameless blessings of the law. The substitution of metaphor and act, pulverizing the thing in itself, illuminating it like a stained-glass window distributing the light of day. The ecstasy of what is beautiful in itself breathes a participating breath into the thing in itself, because of the transparency of man and the reading of the rocks. Linear development of instant, erotics, being (unity), existing (act), metaphor (substitution of being), participation (substitution of existing), Paradise (ecstasy of participation in the homogeneous, intemporality). Linearity broken or swollen by the three circular moments of germ, entity, eternity, necessary for taking over their refuge, leaving at the door Doctor Faust's flaming dog. The destruction of substance, illuminating its variants or metamorphoses, because of the dryness of its suspension or withdrawals. The Son of Man destroyed, transformed into the lasting substance of the body of God, because all transfigurations are followed by a suspension and the exercise on the Mount of Skulls was only an apprenticeship for being plunged into a violent and superhuman negative capacity. Frantic self-destruction which makes all metamorphosis ridiculous, in order to reach the constant germ within the entity. The power of the scorpion—Revelation 9:5—which does not attack any green thing but instead attacks only the men who have no seal on their foreheads. The power of the scorpion in alliance with the *splendor formae*. Natural substance does not change. The rational soul receives the intelligible light by means of the illuminated figure or plenitude. When the witness exclaims: *only thus does a god die*, he has been broken and has fallen in battle against the mute or incessant waking spirit.

Resistance

RESISTANCE always has to destroy the act and the potency which demand the antithesis of the corresponding dimension. In the world of *poiesis*, opposed in so many things to the world of physics, which is the world we have had since the Renaissance, resistance has to proceed by rapid inundations, by total trials that do not want to adjust, clean, or define the crystal, but instead to surround, to open a breach through which water may fall tangent to the turning wheel. Potency is, like hail, everywhere, but resistance recovers itself in the danger of not being in the earth or in hail. The demon of resistance is nowhere, and therefore it presses like the mortar and the broth, and keeps leaving its mark like the fire in the golden glitter of visions. Resistance assures that all the wheels are turning, that the eye sees us, that potency is a delegated power dropped upon us, that it is the non-self, things, coinciding with the darkest self, with the stones left in our waters. Hence the eyes of potency do not count, and in resistance what crosses our path, springing either from ourselves or from a mirror, is re-organized into eyes with currents passing through them that perhaps may never belong to us at all. Compared with resistance, morphology is completely ridiculous. What morphology allows, the realization of an epoch in a style, is very scant in comparison to the eternal resistance of what is not permissible. Potency is merely the permission granted. Method: not even intuition, not even what Duns Scotus called confused abstract knowledge, reason in disarray. Method: not even creative vision, since total resistance prevents the organizations of the subject. When resistance has overcome the quantitative, the ancestral recollections of the steward and the last sterile figurations of the qualitative, then the man they have repented making begins to boil, the man made and set loose, but with a daily repentance for having made him by the one who made him. Then…. *On this night, at the beginning of it, they saw fall from the sky a marvelous branch of fire into the sea, at a distance from them of four or five leagues* (Journal of Voyage, 15 September 1492). Let us not fall into the idea of paradise regained, we come from a resistance: the men who came packed into a ship moving within a resistance could see a branch of fire fall into the sea because they felt the history of many in a single vision. Those are the times of salvation and their sign is a fiery resistance.

Thoughts in Havana[1]

Because I dwell in a whisper like a set of sails,
a land where ice is a reminiscence,
fire cannot hoist a bird
and burn it in a conversation calm in style.
Though that style doesn't dictate to me a sob
and a tenuous fright lets me live in bad humor,
I will not recognize the useless movement
of a mask floating where I cannot,
where I cannot transport the stonecutter or the door
    latch
to the museums where murders are papered
while the visitors point out the squirrel
that straightens its stockings with its tail.
If a previous style shakes the tree,
it decides the sob of two hairs and exclaims:
mi alma no está en un cenicero.

Any memory that is transported,
received like a galantine from the obese ambassadors
    of old,
will not make us live like the broken chair
of the lonesome existence that notes the tide
and sneezes in autumn.
And the size of a loud laugh,

broken off by saying that its memories are remembered,
and its styles the fragments of a serpent
that we want to solder together
without worrying about the intensity of its eyes.
If someone reminds us that our styles
are already remembered;
that through our nostrils no subtle air thinks forth
but rather the Aeolus of the sources elaborated
by those who decided that being
should dwell in man,
without any of us
drooling a danceable decision,
though we presume like other men
that our nostrils expel a subtle air.
Since they dream of humiliating us,
repeating day and night with the rhythm of the tortoise
that conceals time on its back:
you didn't decide that being should dwell in man;
your God is the moon
watching like a balustrade
the entrance of being into man.
Since they want to humiliate us we say to them:
el jefe de la tribu descendió la escalinata.

They have some show windows and wear some shoes.
In those show windows they alternate the mannequin
    with the stuffed ossifrage,
and everything that has gone through the forehead of
    the lonesome buffalo's tedium.

If we don't look at the show window, they chat
about our insufficient nakedness that isn't worth a
     figurine from Naples.
If we pass through it and don't break the glass,
they don't stress gracefully that our tedium can break
     the fire
and they talk to us about the living model and the
     parable of the ossifrage.
They who take their mannequins to all the ports
and push down into their trunks a screeching
of stuffed vultures.
They don't want to know that we climb up along the
     damp roots of the fern
—where there are two men in front of a table; to the
     right, the jug
and the bread that has been caressed—
and that though we may chew their style,
no escogemos nuestros zapatos en una vitrina.

The horse neighs when there's a shape
that comes in between like a plush ox,
that keeps the river from hitting it in the side
and kissing the spurs that were a present
from a rosy-cheeked adulteress from New York.
The horse doesn't neigh at night;
the crystals it exhales through its nose,
a warm frost, of paper;
the digestion of the spurs
after traversing its muscles now glassy

with the sweat of a frying pan.
The plush ox and the horse
hear the violin, but the fruit doesn't fall
squashed on their backs that are rubbed
with a syrup that is never tar.
The horse slides over the moss
where there is a table exhibiting the spurs,
but the perked-up ear of the beast doesn't decipher.

The calm with stumble music
and drunken circus horses in a tangle,
where the needle bites because there's no leopard
and the surge of the accordion
elaborates some tights of worn taffeta.
Though the man doesn't leap, there's a sound
of divided shapes in each indivisible season,
because the violin leaps like an eye.
The motionless jugs stir up a cartilaginous echo;
the shepherd's blue belly
is displayed on a tray of oysters.
In that echo of bone and flesh, some snorts
come out covered with a spiderweb disguise,
for the delight to which a mouth is opened,
like the bamboo flute elaborated
by the boys always asking for something.
They ask for a concave darkness
to sleep in, splitting open, with no sensitivity,
the style of their mothers' bellies.
But while they sharpen a spiderweb sigh,

inside a jug passed from hand to hand,
the scratch on the lute doesn't decipher.

He was indicating some moldings
that my flesh prefers to almonds.
Some delicious moldings riddled with holes
by the hand that wraps them
and sprinkles them with the insects that will accompany
    them.
And that waiting, awaited in the wood
by its absorption that doesn't stop the horseman,
while not some masks, the ax cuts
that do not reach the moldings,
that do not wait like an ax or a mask,
but instead like the man who waits in a house of leaves.
But in tracing the cracks in the molding
and glorifying the parsley and the canary,
l'étranger nous demande le garçon maudit.

The same muskox knew the entrance,
the thread of three secrets
continued till it reached the terrace
without seeing the burning of the grotesque palace.
Does a door collapse because the drunken man
with no boots on abandons his dream to it?
A muddy sweat fell from the shafts
and the columns collapsed in a sigh
that sent their stones tumbling down to the brook.
The flat roofs and the barges

safeguard the calm liquid and the chosen air;
the flat roofs so friendly to the toy tops
and the barges that anchor on a truncated hill,
tumble down confused by a stuffed gallantry that
    catches unawares
the weaving and the obverse of the eye shivering
    together in masks.

To think that some crossbowmen
shoot at a funeral urn
and that from that urn leap
some pale people singing,
because our memories are already remembered
and we ruminate with a very bewildered dignity
some moldings that came out of the hunter's pecked
    siesta.
To know whether the song is ours or the night's,
they want to give us an ax elaborated in the sources of
    Aeolus.
They want us to leap from that urn
and they also want to see us naked.
They want that death they have given us as a gift
to be the source of our birth,
and our obscure weaving and undoing
to be remembered by the thread of the woman beset by
    suitors.
We know that the canary and the parsley make a glory
and that the first flute was made from a stolen branch.

Thoughts in Havana

We traverse ourselves
and having stopped point out the urn and the doves
engraved in the chosen air.
We traverse ourselves
and the new surprise gives us our friends
and the birth of a dialectic;
while two dihedrals spin and nibble each other,
the water strolling through the channels of our bones
carries our bodies toward the calm flow
of the unnavigated land,
where a wakeful alga tirelessly digests a sleeping bird.
It gives us friends that a light rediscovers
and the town square where they converse without being
    awakened.
From that urn maliciously donated,
there came leaping couples, contrasts and the fever
grafted onto the magnet bodies
of the crazy page boy making a slick torture even more
    subtle.
My shame, the magnet horns smeared with a cold moon,
but the scorn gave birth to a cipher
and now unconsciously swung on a branch.
But after offering his respects,
when two-headed people, crafty, correct,
strike with algal hammers the tenorino android,
the chief of the tribe descended the staircase.

The beads they have given us as gifts
have strengthened our own poverty,

but since we know we are naked
being will alight upon our crossed steps.
And while they were daubing us in wild colors
so we would leap out of the funeral urn,
we knew that as always the wind was rippling the
    waters
and some steps were following with fruition our own
    poverty.
The steps fled with the first questions of sleep.
But the dog bitten by light and by shadow,
by tail and head;
of dark light that cannot engrave it
and of stinking shadow; the light doesn't refine it
nor does the shadow nourish it; and so it bites
the light and the fruit, the wood and the shadow,
the mansion and the son, breaking off the hum
when the steps go away and he knocks at the portico.
Poor silly river that finds no way out
nor the doors and leaves swelling their music.
It chose, double against single, the cursed clods,
but I don't choose my shoes in a show-window.

As it lost its contour on the leaf
the worm sniffed and inspected its old home;
as it bit the waters that had come to the defined river,
the hummingbird touched the old moldings.
The violin of ice shrouded in reminiscence.
The bee hummingbird unbraids a music and ties a
    music.

Our forests don't oblige man to become lost,
the forest is for us a seraphine in reminiscence.
Every naked man that comes along the river,
in the current or in the glassy egg,
swims in the air if he holds his breath
and stretches out indefinitely his legs.
The mouth of the flesh of our wood
burns the rippled drops.
The chosen air is like an ax
for the flesh of our wood,
and the hummingbird pierces it.

My back is irritated and furrowed by the caterpillars
that chew some wicker changed into a centurion fish,
but I go on working the wood,
like a wakeful fingernail,
like a seraphine that ties and unbraids in reminiscence.
The forest, breathed upon,
releases the hummingbird of the instant
and the old moldings.
Our wood is a plush ox;
the city state is today the state and a small forest.
The guest breathes upon the horse and the rains, too.
The horse rubs its lips and its tail over the seraphine of
        the forest;
the naked man intones his own poverty,
the bee hummingbird stains and pierces him.
My soul is not in an ashtray.

The Dance of Jargon[1]

Remix black, greenish yellow and at the end blue.
                                        LEONARDO

Being creates its snail
and the earth goes quickly to its song,
naked over the snail's back
it shows itself undulant over the water and its branches.
Being is born and its birth fulfills the look, its vapors
dissolve into water, its hardness closes with its dawn,
pity for us in its change erases its former state.
Of the knife the butterfly had been it traces the circle
and the motionless one returns skewed by the night
and distracts the butterfly with its disguises.
A stable construction of the object doesn't matter
nor does a gaze that eternally reviews its pair of plurals.
The snail also distracts its lair
with different earthly juices and surprise
never surrenders in an academy of ripe flowers.
Why did the Greeks, such sensible strollers,
leave us the legacy of being? Another lair up ahead,
another lair licks its night like a wolf.
The spark was stolen, why is there being in us?
And in their flight the gods left being to us.
Thus their void has flowers with eyes, a void which

> unquestioningly
accompanies the errant population of what has been lost.
And being is not a slow construction of an object,
it doesn't separate from an adulterous Venetian flesh.
The five prisoners can't be heard,
they are the five wines following one another in the
> bottle.
To eternity. May eternity be repeated.
One, which is a fetus in a niche wielding a greasy
> serpent,
plumply feeds on lamb roses.
Another swims in its cell, proclaims itself a sylph,
intends to depart like smoke.
Third organ, also captive, is surrounded
on the floor by dishes it doesn't eat.
Tetra puffs out its cheeks for a name,
the serenaders will hear it buzz its emphatically repeated
Riosotis de Miraflores,
between one and the other I see or spin.
It throws, sweetens accursed pills
For tenorinos or premature growths
Only about him does his wooden gullet insolently ask.
Five the fingers caress along the wall
or five depart on the neck of a guitar.
Being a butterfly it evidences its knife
and the knife returns blue and orange.
It exchanges the beach houses for besieged tortoises,
the ox blue and orange in the night.
The night blows in the night

and leaves blue stains on the ox,
and the Neapolitan butterfly runs along the knife.
Fix the line of the horizon and you, Horeb, expand the
    borders.
The convergence of the prisoners in the instant of the
    wall
illuminates their friendly faces and a specially fine
    manner
from the very beginning of beginning the new somber
    flaccidity.
After the wall the subtle line of the horizon.
The outside between being and song. Its landscape
cared for by the eye held captive
keeps the man burnished in the midnight silence of the
    Rialto bridge.
His madness, his does anyone hear my song?
makes of being a lair and suspects the outside.
Does anyone hear my song? Does anyone hear my
    song?
What is the outside in man?
Why, why is being born in us?
When we reach the line of the horizon the woman
returns and we touch.
The five prisoners avid for that woman who returns
from the labial line of mute virgins.
The old madnesses asked about,
which threw over the carapace or the burner
the old titular disguises
return upon us like being, the outside and the song.

Contrasted with the line of the horizon is the other
silent ship where the woman dreams the dream
of the five prisoners who offer her their energy.
She strolls in the shade of the sycamore and thus frees
    her eyelashes.
What is the outside in man?
One, goes to the outside wagging its dialogued tail,
if the pith of the conversation catches you, you're mine.
Another, infinitely surrounds the contours, its voyage
returns to the flesh like an ocean, this salted one
slightly sprinkles what comes like a dolphin to the flask.
Third organ, isolates a meaning, the sycamore's lesson
makes it tremble like a clock abandoned in an old house.
Tetra, seeks the velvet secret of the lady that returns
from Monferrato to Varadero, that returns to her secret
that has two smiles, that covers the bush it sinks into.
Titus Androgynus, the indifferent door lets the secret
    pass through,
not the form of the outside, trembling and not diverse.
Five, halts the method where the seed ascends
to the spirit given back after a dangerous interruption.
Tetra, once again shows its portrait, its distinction—the
    ring where it keeps cynical maxims—, with nasty
    whims.
The copy of the Dioscuri plunges toward the final flow,
the swimmer is protected by the grotto of kingfishers
    and anemones
from the current surrounding him, his limits
harden in proportion to the coral facing Cronos.

The five prisoners
wander over the body protected within the line of the
    horizon.
The shell of natural dew expands the frontiers.
Now what is outside in woman departs to its shadow.
It walks along the aloof shore coincided with the avidity
of the five prisoners that, after they leaped over the wall,
a lightning flash was taking to the road to the beaches.
The incessant caress of the serpent with a thousand
    hands
closed the ball of yarn Puck leaps out of, his quickness
finds no way out and dances on the flowers.
I'm barefoot and carefully lock the living room. The
    bolts
keep the flame on the promontory from penetrating into
    my dream.
That fire heats the sheet of copper at the corner
of the living room where, barefoot, I secure the bolts.
At night, Puck at the piano and Euphorion plunges
over the cliff with the pigs.
The glass of cane brandy poured over the copper
    sweeps away
the smoke coming densely from the molehill.
The recommendation is to pour two half liters of brandy
    over the copper.
Another, with a strip of burning paper penetrates the
    bolts.
The germ gains a space between the bonfire and the
    jaguar's steps.

It waits and someone receives it with determination
The bark of the Sabaean tree repeats again in a
    concealed manner
the escape of the cortege, with its hands in the wave.
Oh you roguish user of styles, beyond the grasshopper
    and the paperweight.
You would like to escape in the broken pieces of the
    Dioscurus in the small town square,
the pompous confounder made more precise your
    inopportune racing, the destructive one.
Oh roguish user of enterprises, the light concealed him
    and the mask
on the face of the motionless person watches over the
    besieged tortoise.
Oh breezes from the east, walk gracefully, like a worm
    through the desert,
and fill the dress that played only while an outside
    whirlwind took shape.
Primal, decides not to play the dance that has appeared
for the body and the flute, hesitating
between the challenge of the body and the slow story of
    a development
with its flute prelude.
Another, irascibly throws his transferred boar,
thirsty for transparencies the water darkens him.
Third organ, recognizes what no one was sending him,
without its being the basket of serpents on the stained
    glass windows traversed by the ray of light.
Tetra, makes more precise what is detached, blowing it

    toward an unnamed adventure,
returns like an Etruscan and slowly they recognize each
    other;
the voice penetrated until it was engraved on the sheet
    of copper:
In the protections of a stiff winter,
when clothes again cling or exceed
and it strikes us that someone out there may fit,
like a small animal of cradled gentleness
or like an excessive monster blowing a cornet.
When we relax and remember the record player
and its needle is left to fall onto scratchy shellac.
And its cordage of vinegary hair becomes a needle
that tunes its tiny snouted voice,
that weighs like a knitting needle that won't pass
    through again.
They're coming to fondle the new record player.
Don't begin yet, we have to put the ring away in the
    handkerchief.
Now you can, it's been three days since the Prokofiev
    record
arrived on the Queen Elizabeth. Now you can
begin, the record player looks cold
and the needle throws out a spark that is a cold drop.
The cold drop is on my face at the beginning.
Someone stares at me and I feel ashamed.
I look again, he's looking at me, I despair.
Everyone, I think, is looking at me, I dissolve.
My cold needle has touched them on shellac.

It squeaks because it's slow and cold in raspy sand
and again releases the cold drop.
Needles are scarce. Just one will last all night.
Five the fingers interpret over the body the pretense of
     surrender,
its captivity in ecstasy only expresses its secular rescue.
Does one have to disguise oneself as a barber to dance
     one's own dances?
The dense mask will join the density of the night.
I need to move in the dance made for others,
my memory makes the dances of my birth more precise.
In disguise I was able to attend the dance after the
     taking of the fortress,
the barber strolls through the ashes and no one is
     astonished if he says do you want to give me your
     hair?
And this way he proposes and clears the sad day for the
     crowds who broke down
the gates and saw the wax centurion and the syrup from
     Pompeii.
It was the other people's dance and now I dance my
     own dances,
they have eliminated one of my rhythms, they have
     ruined one of my pair of plurals.
I came in when I didn't hear the adulterated note and
     that's how I could enter the other people's
dance without being startled. At night, disguised as a
     barber, no one recognized me.
If I touch my being will my metamorphosis be slower?

Disguised as a barber, can I penetrate into the external
      whirlwind? If I'm in front of the mirror, stick out
      my tongue, does anyone hear?
Can I take to the line of the horizon the conclusion of
      the five wines that follow one another in the jug?
      Does it belong to me?
Do I have to penetrate the other people's dance in an
      adulterated rhythm?
One, I went in and I come out like a lizard through the
      eyes of a mask.
Primal, can no longer break the millenary lizard.
Another, is bored by being the sheet of copper and the
      cane brandy
can't pass through the bolts. I'm barefoot.
Another, chills the drop of bronze that was going to
      engender the night
of the besieged tortoise. There no one recognized me
and I could slowly forget the rhythm.
The duration in the song forgets the hostility
between tortoise shell powder in being and Lusitanian
      grapes in what's outside.
Disguised as barbers we can dance our own dances,
but from song to song, "does anyone hear?" sings again.

III.

ESSAYS ON POETS: LEZAMA AS A READER
OF MALLARMÉ, GÓNGORA AND VALÉRY

New Mallarmé[1]

THE name of Stéphane Mallarmé has begun to distill its marvels as it attains to new figures, new entities in time. Twenty years after his death his name was associated with exquisiteness or refinement, with insinuations, with the subtle variants of distillation, with the labyrinths traced in order to attain an ultimate drop or diamond. Half a century after his death, the feast of delights, the *liqueur framboisé*, the *jus de cerises*,[2] have been overcome in order to penetrate into the man deeply absorbed by the provocations and mockeries of words, the exorbitant price these exact when, once exhaled, they regain their suspension and dissolve into an alien labyrinth. Pursuing in total reverence and compliance the dictates of his calling or his vision. He's no longer the man concerned with precision, unity or simple irreducibility in distilling a drop, the man urgently seeking that the corpuscles of words, turned into a substance, should preserve their incandescence. In that dimension the name of Stéphane Mallarmé extends his shadow as an enigma, which, upon dissolving, reappears as a new, pure and permanent enigma in time, alongside the Pléiades or Cassiopeia. Now he is like Empedocles, Pythagoras, Hamlet, Pascal or King

Sebastian,[3] whose permanence in posterity does not depend solely on their works, but rather on their gestures as reconstructed by their images, on the counterpoint they were able to establish, or on the enormous novel in which after death their Egyptian scribe-like fingers, as in a dream, keep turning out new chapters. He is then a quality, a pure vocation, an unknown variant in the history of ceremonial. In that sense, Thierry Maulnier, when referring to a poet contemporary though antithetical to Ronsard, spoke of an *intensité mallarméenne de pensée*.[4] That is the current and most lasting presence of Mallarmé: there is a Mallarméan intensity, just as there is a moan in Pascal, a voluptuousness à la Montaigne, a dignity in Racine, a lucidity à la Baudelaire. A name transformed into the splendor of a quality, of an essence that acts and reacts like the person himself, his testimony and the resistance of his contour.

The splendor, the irradiant force of that essence was such that it could react upon the past, in a hyperbolical paradox, as a cause. In the same way that the rediscovery of Ronsard, even within the difficulties the 19th century opposed to it, and accompanied at the same time by the necessities imposed in that encounter regarding certain unavoidable laws of French verse, is due, more than to the surprising scrutiny of Sainte Beuve, to the slow serpentine movement in Baudelaire's verse. In that sense, the *école lyonnaise*, in its two ramifications of Maurice Scève and Louise Labé,[5] cannot be considered as an antecedent for the skill and prodigious discoveries of Mallarmé's verse, but rather, on the contrary, when Mallarmé achieved the incomparable results of his alchemy and of the irradiation of his words, that area of the 17th century became illuminated, as if Mallarmé's glow had been the spark for the historical evaporation of the Square of Lyon, when musicians and poets began their strict and circumspect visits, their amiable conversations for recitation and dance, and Maurice Scève himself enlivened his words by having them accompanied by the proud demands of a delicate instrument rigorously played.

The course followed by French verse throughout the 19th century had strengthened the position of peril, the risk of discovery, the arrogance of an adventure that had arisen with the enormous demands of a separate self. That acceptance, without reservations and in the full pleasure of sympathy, of novelty, of challenge, of presumption of the infinite, which made us weaken and as it were force ourselves to give in to indolence, had reached a dangerous prestige whose gleam still fascinates the linkage of generations. Hugo had already achieved those evaporations by means of which the verse gave forth the reflection of nocturnal harangues in submerged cities or the pleasant provocations of magical potions. To which Nerval had added a hieratic force as of an officiant who began by taking poetry to the implacable, nocturnal stones of sacrifice. Baudelaire had played in a heartrending way at slowly, voluptuously leading poetry from *areteia*, a destiny, a spirit in the blood, to *aristia*, which is the protection of Pallas Athena in combat. But it was for

Mallarmé that the secret of the enormous accumulations demanded by the movement of the verse or by the penetrations of the stanzas was reserved. The tremor which follows upon his powerful verbal resources, when he has to achieve his transmutations in his verse, came to pursue him to the limit of apathy or rejection, since the very act of creation seemed to extend its waves to the scribe or listener ready to give himself over to the same investigations or identical ecstasies or torments.

We have wanted to group together the most significant moments of Mallarmé's development into four seasons that comprise the fashioning of his work or the secret containments of his designs. The day at Tournon, the night of Idumea, what was sensed at Valvins, the intelligence of the Rue de Rome, clarify in their polarization the various groupings of his works.[6]

Those four moments indicated are not meant as a yielding to banal causality, to mere chronological succession. Not stages, but integration of being into being, identity of a substance turned back upon itself. Groupings in time for a writer correspond to the moments when such groupings attain to the status of signs. Thus, for example, *Igitur* corresponds chronologically to Mallarmé's beginnings, and yet it was in the last stage of his life that those pages take on their full meaning and destiny. Mallarmé revised those pages, put them away with specific indications, and it's there, in the coronation of their form and their destiny in the Rue de Rome, that they should be assigned. *Les loisirs de la poste*, his circumstantial verses, were written, with incomparable gracefulness, throughout his life, and yet we prefer to include them in the Night of Idumea, in other words in his moments of apathy, of inability to work, where, in their gracious calls to intelligent friendship, they acquire their meaning, not as games, but rather as a need to stay afloat, to renew himself in the pleasure of evanescence.

Mallarmé's Hamlet-like life in pursuit of the distillation of words begins, once he has married, with his trip to London. Then he appears to us as a kind of Julien Sorel plus voluptuousness, precisely at that moment when Julien Sorel also goes to London, in the same way that Thibaudet claims Baudelaire is Sainte-Beuve plus poetry. Of course our Mallarmé is dominated by the ascents of Hugo and Baudelaire, as Stendhal was by those of Napoleon. In his urge to restore to words a tribal meaning, Mallarmé studies English words, at that moment when the British and Norman coasts are covered with fires.[7] His book *Les mots anglais*, as Paul Valéry claims, is perhaps the most revealing document we have concerning Mallarmé's most personal way of working.[8] "Sometimes it seemed to me," Valéry adds, "that he had examined, weighed, held up to the light all the words of the language as a lapidary his precious stones: the sound, the brilliance, the color, the limpidity, the meaning of each of them, I would almost say its *orient* luster…."[9] From the first chapter in which he establishes a distinction between families of words and solitary words, what philologists now call parataxis or linkage of words placed at the same level, he seems to be offering a prelude to that conversationalist on the Rue de Rome, endowed with a knowledge of those incredible details that shape the culture of a poet, studying the nuances of abstract words, according to whether they end in *-té*, like *verité*, in *-tion*, like *transition*, or in *-ment*, like *entendement*,[10] mixing, as don Miguel puts it, Salamanca witchcraft with pedantic gentleness.[11] But the delight of an education, while those studies about the birth of words are disentangled, also needs the adventures, the metamorphoses, the disparities or nominal disguises, among Hellenic or Roman gods. All that, as Mallarmé himself said, is aimed at demonstrating to us how the gallant personages of fable have been transformed into natural phenomena. "To extract divinities from their natural appearance, and take them vaporized as it were by an intellectual chemistry back to their primitive state as natural phenomena, such as sunrises or sunsets, this is the objective of natural mythology."[12] In this way we see in his disturbing apprenticeship in Tournon how his attempt to restore to words their tribal meaning is accompanied by that calculated, subtle tapestry in which men and gods again bathe in their magical sovereignties. *Our friend the sun has died*, Mallarmé slightly emphasizes as one of the pleasures accompanying the words of that primitive man, *he will return again*.[13] And then he feels the immortality of that irradiation, the feast of the seasons, the repetition of the primordial, following it in the ceremony of his daily tasks or in the mysterious pauses of his blood. Three centuries later, it seems as if Mallarmé had written the mythology that should serve as a portico for don Luis de Góngora. In the last portions of air where one's breath is extinguished, how can one rediscover those words, along with the hesitations of tribal man when faced with the flight of his friend the sun, and fix them like the evanescence of nymphs caught in the uncertain, momentary mirror of a wave?

February 26, 1956

II.

In order to answer in his work those bold questions, Mallarmé sought to combine simultaneously or in rapid succession the emptiness, the terrible void, that hounded him, with the skill of the senses for spreading over the body that provoked them. The obstinate urge to escape that appears in *Brise marine*, suggested perhaps by Andromeda, Cellini's ivory figure in the Louvre, where the enchained body intensifies its tension to flee;[14] to hear like Baudelaire the song of the mariners;[15] to redeem his sense of "the desert clarity of the lamp on the empty paper defended by its whiteness"[16]—all this contrasts with the aridity of the night in Idumea. Obviously, as Villiers told him in a letter, a temptation of the devil in which there seems to have been eliminated from the very basis of the poem any creative possibility of dialogue, leaving instead something like an all-devouring, superhuman, monstrous menace.[17] This need of Mallarmé's to join together the non-existent articulations of the void with a sensation of bodies and objects takes on its most grandiose and tragic form, in the succession of his poetic works, in the *Hérodiade* followed by *L'Après-Midi d'un Faune*. *Hérodiade* is the poem of sterility, of the virgin dancing before the diabolical riches of the mirror, of the nurse who awakens with each of her questions about her mistress' perfumes a dance of complementary pores. In the vapors of summer, where the accumulation of sexual fervor is resolved, with the solar parabola coinciding with the rise of the stars and the fall of Saint John's head after his decapitation.

> ... *a distant shadow,*
> *but also attentive in your severe springs.*
> *What horror! I have contemplated my great*
>   *nakedness*[18]

Faced with those twisted gods of winter, the fauns begin to stick their horns into the syrupy bark of the trees. We have gone from the contemplation of sterility, from the emptiness of the body when turned into an absolute, to the frenzied dances of Nijinsky reaching for the fruit on high.[19] Benign spring, with the flame of its violence, has removed us from the yawns of the mirror. It also seems as if the poet were removing from his own sterility, with a rhythm greater than that of free verse, as he demanded, the drama of the faun in its efforts to pre-

serve the temperature of its energy. It's there we find, as
Paul Valéry said, the most beautiful verses in the world:

> *Tu sais, ma passion, que, pourpre et déjà mure,*
> *Chaque grenade éclate et d'abeilles murmure...*

and where we might point to the origin of Valéry's own
splendid sonnets about pomegranates and bees.[20]

Is it possible that Mallarmé used Boucher's painting
of Pan and Syringa[21] as a basis for his poem? We don't
think so, in the same way that years later he thought Debussy's work was unnecessary with regard to his poem.
He thought that the poem contained its own musical accompaniment and that any other gloss or variant tended
to divert the poem's direction.

From what we have related about that first stage
of Mallarmé's, which we've called the day at Tournon,
it can be appreciated that Mallarmé underwent an extremely urgent apprenticeship, close to the desert of his
lamp, as he said, for many nights in order to shape each
word. If Valéry has said of Mallarmé that, in order to
read him, one must learn how to read all over again,[22] it's
undeniable that he began in just that way, by learning to
reread all the astonishing diversity of poetic knowledge
and activity.

His apprenticeship remained unchanged in his more
efficient moments or when, concealed in apparent apathy, he sought refuge in accumulative virtuality. Here we
have his other great moment, the night of Idumea, when

Monsieur Latente ("the latent lord"), as he said, the anti-becomer, the Hamlet adverse to placing an event as an impurity in time, couldn't arrive at a poem, at a promised land for words.[23] As he later confessed, he would then feel, whenever he went over the viaduct at Batignolles, a desire to leap to his death. It wasn't just the mediocrity of his duties at the *lycée* that drove him to such madness. His sick little boy, with his splendid blond hair and heart disproportionately large for his age, always in bed, beside the bright colors of their parrot Semiramis, a blazing rainbow. Then, shaped in his first approaches to the poetry of Lamartine, in Hugo and even in Béranger by the abundance that he would very soon chasten with Poe and his exacerbated lucidity in the making of a poetic clock. Furthermore, certain projects of a bewildering vastness, such as a history of certain expressions, a history of certain modes of thought, efforts that have remote antecedents in Lull and in Leibniz. By now we know that an expression like "the smile dances" is only possible by the 4th century AD, *subrisio onis*,[24] when it is used for the first time by the Church Fathers. The inexorable way in which he had become impregnated by Baudelaire, to the extent that a large number of his own verses, lingering as he did in his insect-like obsession with detail, in his pursuit of syllables in his adolescence, are variants of Baudelaire's verses. His readings of the more mature Hegel, especially of the *Philosophy of Spirit*, where he traces a conception of the absolute, with antecedents in Spinoza's *causa sui*, proceeding from virtuality to the idea, and of Schopenhauer, whose ideas about intuition and generative powers, from which Bergson so often drew support, would allow him, when he drew closer to music, to deepen his own microcosm. At Valvins, in his *hameau* or cabin, the little sonnets, the *Prose pour des Esseintes*, perhaps the poem of his most charged with accumulative gifts, with ambivalent references to idea and meaning, which Thibaudet has studied brilliantly in his book on Mallarmé.[25] The senses at Valvins, as we've called that stage of his life, is perhaps the moment when Mallarmé accomplishes the most, when that living vestment that Goethe spoke of attains its form. He ascends to the level of sacred services and liturgy, extracts from his poverty a bas relief like that of an Assyrian king, of a semi god of the time of Amphion or Orpheus, as he was seen by his principal disciple,[26] and he attends the Concerts Lamoureux. A Wagnerian cascade descends upon his notebooks in infinite tiny scrawls, in pinpoints to avoid syrtes. What was sensed at Valvins goes riding upon his incessant cigarettes. How could any *criollo* of ours, in voluptuous alarm, in the best of our 19th century, in Tristán de Jesús Medina, in the Zambranas, in Julián del Casal, in Ricardo del Monte or in José Martí, fail to decipher those scratches at the end of his sonnet to tobacco:

> *Le sens trop précis rature*
> *Ta vague littérature.*[27]

Those criticisms so often made of Mallarmé, among the vulgar of course, about preciosity, obscurity, sterility, failure in communication: what is a correct attitude toward them? Almost all poetic language since the Renaissance is imbued with preciosity. In Shakespeare, in the *Sonnets to Sundry Notes of Music* or the sonnets for that enigmatic personage, there is a decisive influence of Petrarchism, which is given to preciosity. The opposite of the precious is not the great and human, but rather the base and insignificant, since Shakespeare, Johann Sebastian, Lope and Calderón were also precious, by which observation we can soothe a certain kind of maliciously quick and superficial response so fashionable among us, or at least say that in their works there are elements of preciosity. The opposite of the obscure is not the solar or stellar, but rather what is born with no enveloping placenta. As for communication, he possessed it to such a high degree, by virtue of his work's power of irradiation, of magical accumulations, that he is, along with Rimbaud, one of the great centers of poetic polarization, situated at the beginning of the contemporary era, and one of the most enigmatic and powerful attitudes there have ever been in the history of images.

Mallarmé dies while trying to take the possibilities of a poem beyond those of an orchestra, by combining word and gesture and the organization of color. He attempts in his *Coup de dés* a movement back and forth of timbres and a spatial placement of the poem in a hierarchy of constellations.[28] An individual word is emphasized, like a martial *andantino* in gracious subdivisions of the flute, or these are prolonged and closed to the infinite extent of their serpent-like form, their opening and reception becoming the same as their farewell, as in the impulses of the brasses. The transparency of the paper, its margins participating like an accusation or a joy, its irrefutable combinations of black and white, take on a chiaroscuro, an unknown dimension. I think at times, as at the end of a Greek chorus or in a new epiphany, that his pages and the murmur of his timbres will one day be lifted up, as on a polyhedral lectern, to be read by the gods.

March 4, 1956

Compliment for Mallarmé[1]

SYMBOLISM? It had been turning into a banquet with no guests from which there emerged only the final chill of the tablecloths and the initial gleam of the candelabra. A murmur, a reflection arose, but we disdainfully took our distance in order to inhabit a substance distributed— instantaneous unity of the continuous and the subtle—to the degree of somnolence in the serpent's muscles. Symbol was mixed with cymbal, just as the serpent coils itself around the almond branch (mobile, nourished with autumn, semimobile). The same music did not accompany, in its original peasant situation as an equal to words, as taking advantage of an imperturbable condition, but rather, in the intoxication of not being there, it attempted to feed the residues of each poem, of each abandoned experience, with organ pipes in their most difficult midnight situations.

The music did detain the words, did give them a new impulse, infinitely now, until it made them turn over and over, in such a way that that impulse thought to be powerful ended up as a polyhedron of rock crystal that one's fingertips take pleasure in turning over and over. Mallarmé found in that what he called *the joy of an inequality in motion*.[2] He thought that that mobile instrument put words at the same level, making of them only a special kind of swimming, only a special tunnel of clouds. In that now displayed snail shell, the letters became the corpuscle, the thread and the very labyrinth for finding again the one who had not been lost, the words thus remaining in their condition of uneven evenness, transformed into their own royal cortege, their own uneven hour of the faun, or monotony of a glassy fish within a larger liquid that is also crystalline.

Mallarmé believed he could feed his resources upon what he considered to be *inverse reflections* (see his *Crise de vers*). That final light that one word throws upon another obstructed the banal presumption that there might be a single word, distinct, distinguished, different, if not a word that turns in its own foam and in that of its musical scale. If words feed upon their reflections—evenness of their movement—there will be ennui: the case of Valéry. That *reciprocal reflection*, feeding upon equal primary sound, upon the same distributed light, ends up with the statue or allegory of a destiny all too invariable, all too indivisible.

The reciprocal reflection deserves to be decapitated by the inverse reflection, while the verbal reciprocal was lost in the indestructible homogeneity of the motion of the impulse; in the verbal inversion, what was being obliterated as an equal to the progression itself was a different, accompanying world, but which was to remain as a tragic knowledge of non-being, existence of non-existence. In the inverse reflection if I say: *forest of Germania* or *branch of fire in the ocean* or simply *cortege*, I am forming a pertinence that is different but dilates and extends. What has become detached is a word detached from a mute person, from someone ineffective and forlorn. Since, doubtless, no one can savor words as well as a mute or as someone who is allowed to speak only once after the choral song.

Mallarmé wanted to achieve what he called a *replacement of perceptible breathing*. He was attempting to efface all indications, all traits, in order to obtain just a living thing in which the external or gross signs of the life of the poem couldn't surprise anyone with their non-interposed cavern. He could be disturbed on occasions by the perverse presence of the reminiscent or by certain objects already given in advance as precious. When that breathing as an external sign was removed, the poem had to feed upon its own survival but felt it was going to fade away as soon as some confirmation came, so that it had to shape and dissolve itself with an array of corpuscles as numerous as they were invisible. What then remained was a rhythmic trail, a tiny void that might encompass the ocean's flux. All that has come after Mallarmé has ruthlessly clarified, distorted and appropriated him. Two of his most frequented words, mirror and half-opened, subtly distinguish him from what has come later. The mirror

> *Ô miroir!*
> *Eau froide par l'ennui dans ton cadre gelée*
> *Que de fois et pendant des heures...*[3]

is not the mirror of Valéry, *eau froidement présente*,[4] a frozen extension that surrounds us, a present moment that displays its reflections like the serpent displays its metal. When Mallarmé uses the word *entr'ouverte* he applies it to lace,[5] but when Valéry calls upon it he transfers it to the pomegranate.[6] In that play of air and lace, blasphemy is interwoven with the ultimate purity of its sustenance, but when the pomegranate half-opens, the wind imparts a sacred lightness to its grains. Thus, by this excess of distance, the poetry engendered by Mallarmé seems to inhabit delights corresponding to the earliest monarchies, when, with the most enduring refinement, tunics were sewn with fishbones.

May, 1942

Circumstantial Prose for Mallarmé[1]

Invited by the Pen Club to speak on the fiftieth anniversary of the death of Mallarmé, I said the following words:

I am lifted and ventured, traversed and enhanced, assisted and fortified by the fact that the Pen Club has fixed its arrow upon me with such a gaze. Having always had since adolescence a sweet tooth for those distillations of don Luis and Stéphane,[2] I've been enamored of those labyrinths, those painful proliferations reduced to a point to which men are led in order to obtain a few resistant products, like proverbs, cognac, gold and perfumes.

In some treatise on working precious metals, there is mention of the two procedures for making casts: lost mold and *grosseria*. If we transpose such treatments to matters of poetic endeavor, the first of them, despite its exceedingly extended rhythmic measure and its non-causal quantitative fever, decides to strike or be resolved at a single point, where it remains as a germ or birth. Emptying out over and over, in a slow, Hindustanic nourishment, in which gods and desires, twilight and hunger, are all part of an enormous, irresistible participation in the homogeneous. And like that age-old nourishment, it culminates in an ecstasy of sudden expression. And like that rhythm, which had expanded until it reached the most perverse forms of invocation or magic spell, it closes in order to offer a single word. Hasn't the history of the word *aboli*, "abolished," ever been traced from Hugo to Nerval, until in Mallarmé it takes on a gleam all its own, irreplaceable and cabalistic? Even in those poets who had refused to work with molds, and in whom the possibilities of an enormous pride centered man upon the sovereignty of his gifts, ending in a Lucifer-like renunciation, so as to turn to the other form of casting, *grosseria*, which consists in taking the mold to be buried under ground in order to await its return, its mysterious reappearance—even those poets have been unable to keep from contemplating themselves in the mirror of an identity, of a questioning solitude. Doesn't Whitman himself, located at the other hostile extreme from Mallarmé, shoot at us like a dart this question: What does it mean to exist in a form?[3]

In going back over the identity of its instrument and forgetting the orphic conditions of song, poetry had to attain to a second nature, in which its reductions and abductions might display their bases, the possible reproductions of a presence that in its original force might be unattainable and unprecedented. Poetry was thus placed in the proximities, in the impossible closeness to a mystery, of which the poem was like the fixed reflection of an unattainable spiral, and if it weren't for the influence of Stoicism in Valéry, his verse *I inhabit my own mystery* would lack poetic meaning. A blank canvas seems to gather poetic statements and then dissolve them in its expanse of snow. *Le blanc souci de notre toile*, as Mallarmé said.[4] He seems fearfully to allude in that white concern to his hesitations and withdrawals even before arriving at the whiteness of the canvas. He leads us in his flatteries and courtesies to what will always be the undulating other side of the most fixed poetic calligraphy: the mystery of the linkages and the secret of the pauses. With such a polite firmness, recalling those gestures of his which according to Manet revealed his descent from high prelates and ballet dancers, he proceeds to interweave that *splendid and obscure India* in a verse of his with some verbal associations where dream and suggestion develop in exquisite missteps and extend to the final verse, *the pale Vasco's smile*, in which the pauses seem prolonged until they attain the quality of a mysterious marine succession.[5]

Obtaining a word like an irradiant substance had to attain conditions of perverse magic. A word that would take total possession of the object, replacing it, amounted to tracing the same attempts of absolute idealism, where thought and the thing thought and the wave of taking possession of the external world would always want to offer the verifications of a naive animism. When he confesses to us, alas, with a moan, that he has lost the sense and reason of even the most familiar words, in order to find them again in their tribal sense.[6] With his fingernail, in a dictionary, he had underlined *comme*, "like" or "as," in order to avoid all comparative references and approach only his identity as tribal chieftain. "I affirm, Mallarmé says, that between the old procedures of magic and charms there is a hidden similarity. To the circle that perpetually opens and closes a rhyme we shall devote a similarity to rounds on the grass or to fire and magic."[7] That wasn't the moment when Mallarmé attained his most willful decision and the most complete organization of his material. In his terrible crises of sterility, as by an all-devouring Pascalian paradox, he would reappear and show us an *Hériodiade* or an *Après-Midi d'un Faune*. He needed thus that there should show forth in him, and inhabit him totally, an all-devouring indolence, an unending emptiness, the snow of all snows, an infinite absence, the futile mold of an incessant nirvana, so that his accumulative energy might be discharged, might glow at a point of permanence or dispersion. That energy would arise from a titanic purity that has made his poetic statement one of those most saturated with a precise meaning like an exercise and as incomplete as the progressions of music. That vicious Hindustanic nourishment, that indolence and that irradiant accumulative energy, have made of him one of the most enigmatic, polished and French of elaborations. Let us briefly contemplate his portrait. "He has," tells us one of his contemporaries, "a benign and tender grace, an *ancien régime* elegance of gesture. He resembles a Frenchman of the 18th century. He is perhaps the most courteous man of his time."

It's a delight we find in poetry after Baudelaire to pursue in each of the traces left behind by a stanza a meaning for remaking the first intangible obscurities. What subtle derivations we find in a stanza from "Prose pour des Esseintes"!

> *Car j'installe, par la science,*
> *L'hymne des coeurs spirituels*
> *En l'oeuvre de ma patience,*
> *Atlas, herbiers et rituels.*[8]

Those hymns hidden behind his patience, behind his Work. And names of cities brought to a nascent brilliance (the fruit of a night in Idumea[9]). And the herbals (a delicious allusion in a stanza to the family of iridaceas). And the charms and rituals so that words may leap from the fire like salamanders or golden lemons.

The night in Idumea, the land of sexless kings, of Edom, of Esau. Vegetative reproduction, each man putting forth ramifications like a tree. The family of the iridaceas, saffron, gladiolus, ananas, tiger lily.

> *Tout en moi s'exaltait de voir*
> *La famille des iridées*
> *Surgir à ce nouveau devoir,*
>
> *Mais cette soeur sensée et tendre*
> *Ne porta son regard plus loin*
> *Que sourire et, comme à l'entendre*
> *J'occupe mon antique soin.*[10]

And so at times it's a nominative precision that unbraids something like a suggestion under the ocean. And at other times it's like a desire that doesn't manage to touch the word or the contours of the gestures. Dance seems to him to simulate *an impatience of plumes toward the idea.*[11] As if as it approaches a body or an idea, an artificial disturbance of plumes, were to proceed, the idea itself, to reconstruct itself in its resistance which dissolves, a white combat of the garland, turned back upon itself like a fire.[12]

Criticisms against Mallarmé, almost always made from outside his orbit, are born of a lack of sympathy from the first approach. He sought, some people say, synthetic gold, a criticism momentarily attractive if one doesn't think that behind the quest for synthetic gold lay the Rhine gold, and that Mallarmé, like the hero of the tetralogy, had seen Brünnhilde's ring fall into the pool, leaving him with a corrosive melancholy for something never to be found again.[13] Synthetic gold combined with the Rhine gold, incomplete in the waves of its obscure becoming, which advances like horses in the foam of something that has no name. He just added together, others say, little beads of colored glass, but his work didn't start off from discontinuous fragments joined by the progressions of the music, but rather from the tradition of Maurice Scève, from an *essence replete with a living eternity*. The only criticisms that can be made of him, like those of any enduring creator, are those that he himself noted as impediments or bastions in his development. Empty spaces or perplexities of his own as necessary for his self-realization as the parabola of his integration. No great master in the acuteness of literary perception can free himself, when he stresses his disagreements with a work, from emphasizing the empty spaces of no interest to his spectators or to the producer himself, if he doesn't proceed on the basis of the absences, of the impossibilities that the artist touched as his own and found to be as fundamental as his moments of splendor. When Mallarmé points out to us one of his own barriers by telling us he possessed the impossibility of being unable to pass into action, of remaining negative in virtual richness, he is also pointing out to us the contrasts, the shadowy distances where his formal splendor showed forth. His heart-rending crises of sterility, the absent atmosphere that his errant stars needed, had led him to the Nothingness of Pascal and Heidegger. Remaining negative in virtual richness reminds us of Heidegger's statement that "in nothingness questions and answers are a contradiction in terms."[14]

Contradiction, a mystery; sense, a secret, or perhaps a poetic reason, a sense derived from momentary associations. Questions and answers that negate and destroy one another by that pursuit of an incessant contradiction that nothingness lends it. Mystery and secret split apart, irreconcilably. A poetic statement so flooded with sense that it becomes elusive, the way a trout in an oily hand takes on its mystery. It becomes so external, so detached, that it constitutes a monstrous, incalculable source of sustenance. Made into something incessant for man, that mystery penetrates him, in a penetration as successive as it is infinite, as expected as it blows where it will. For a mystery will always be a sustenance so boundless in us that the measure of it we attain will be full of an unknown presence that we manage to make our own by the pursuit of that unknown that penetrates into our equation like a sleeping dancer in the grips of a nightmare. But, alas, poetry moved away from a mystery in order to break open a secret, and far from seeking a paradoxical, almost monstrous sustenance, turned back identically, shimmeringly upon itself. Valéry's arrogance when he tells us in a verse *the slightest movements consult my pride*,[15] presupposes the Stoic dignity of a body active in the face of nothingness, of a secret of total empowerment and exact communication. What incredible mad geometry will be capable of engendering that poetic reason which operates on a word made into a secret, leaving behind its mystery. What a worthy artifice it would be to demonstrate in an impossible geometry that, as in another verse of Valéry's, *each atom of silence bears the shadow of a dead fruit...*[16]

What Mallarmé leaves us, beyond the exquisite invitations that like a fury of matinal bees awaken in the presence of each of his verses, is the pleasure, the lasting joy of a great tradition: for only the energy accumulated in the care and calligraphy of the whiteness of his canvas resists the corruptions of time and the succession of autumns. And even the very raptures of inspiration remain as bounteous concentrations of energy in ecstasy.

I leaf through Anne of Brittany's *Book of Hours* and the golden borders with which the master illuminators of 15th century France, the Fouqués, the Limbourgs, embellished those prints that intersected with meditations during canonical hours.[17] They are works that have battled against time's devouring squadrons, leaving behind on that monster the genial clarity of a golden border that resists five centuries. Those friars would for months smooth with a boar's fang the parchments that were to receive the golden touches. They would spend years wandering through localities and herbariums in quest of pure colors, to satisfy the finest longings of those parchments. Time is entangled in those snail shells that resist it as they extend, like natural hypogea, the whiteness of their canvas.

October, 1948

About Paul Valéry[1]

I

IN the Alexandrian-apocalyptic period, which we can situate in the intellectual circumstances of a contemporary of Proclus, the human eye is not content with its status as a *pastiche* of blazing Helios. Ancient theogonies liked to claim that knowledge became integrated by following the curve of the eye's development: from the eye of the insect, faceted for the spectrum, to the eye as pure radiation. The insect's eye, which has to struggle against senseless impulse and muscular suspension, tends to decompose into infinite gyrations, into landscapes that proliferate and clash with one another, that which its own impulse will finally assimilate in a destructive linearity. That impulse will serve it in order to start seeing, penetrating into its own eye. In order to struggle with the air and its incessant refraction it will show the multiplication of its corneas and crystalline lenses. The eye of the octopus needs to feed upon that animal's verifications by touch and its eyes that struggle with an opaque resistance are obliged to leave its tentacles in suspension, like an excessive assurance in the fleshy darkness that circumscribes it. Since the octopus's eye develops slowly, its tentacles are obliged, with a fascinating rapidity, to fon-

183

dle the object it has acquired. Touch and sight reinforce one another in a form that corroborates the atrophy of certain senses, and that collaboration leads one to think that none of those senses alone would be capable of arriving at its destiny. Thus a poet, referring to the period which in knowledge represents the eye of the insect and of the octopus, tells us:

> *I am all mouth from the waist up,*
> *And I bite more without my teeth than with them.*
> *I have in opposite places two warriors,*
> *My eyes in my feet and in my eyes my fingers.*

The flow of rival temptations, their multiplication and intersection, their breaking up of the independence of the senses, in order to provide us with a new sensorial nebula, provoked the faceted eye of the insect. Its nerve fibers prevent it from attaining a fixed representation. The incessant refraction of the eye struggling with its demoniacal impulse and the acute resistance of the air allow it a certain quantitative pleasure. The appearance of the critical state is the result of that proliferation of the eye, which thus acts as a stable contraction of the nerve fibers. The ancient paradise of a sensation for each sense is destroyed, due to an absence of visual demands for representation, and in that amusing duel the memory of the amoeba dares to weigh upon the angel's wing.

Our present day Alexandrian-apocalyptic period is located between the eye of the insect and the eye of the

octopus. Hasn't Valéry shown a preference in his sim-
iles for the insect? Doesn't he use it like a pin *at the
edge of the siesta*? *When the future is indolence*, as in
that stanza in *Le Cimetière marin*, the insect scratches
the liquid dryness of the summer.[2] Hasn't he placed, in
his sonnet *Baignée*, at that moment of quick delight, the
woman's wet hair capturing the simple gold of the intoxicated flight of an insect?[3] A siesta, some rival temptations which, if they tolerate the arrival of the insect, it's
because of the gyrating penetration of its eye, a product
of the light driven by its crude inquiries. Another amusing duel between the insect's buzzing and the eyes of the
Minervan owl.

Valéry made use of those contributions and temptations, which in his intellectual development had fanned
out in easy and opportune arrivals and form a type of
apocalyptic-Alexandrine writer, equidistant from an un-
timely penetration of substance and a timely habitabil-
ity of essences. He had enjoyed the experiences derived
from surrounding and seeing from inside and close up
the patience of Stéphane Mallarmé, his relationship with
whom would endure for him in the *magnets of a myth,
avoiding a closeness all too compromising* for both. *An
expected recourse of words*, he heard Mallarmé say in
his adolescence, *under the comprehension of our eyes,
places itself in definitive traits, in silence*.[4] Valéry never
forgets that struggle between idea and gaze as posed by
Mallarmé. *Under our eyes*, Valéry tells us in his mature days, *idea becomes sensation*.[5] By the end of the

19th century, that century's scientific thought was already available in comfortable summaries for a poet's sensual curiosity. He had heard in frequent days the work and theory of a visual artist who thus communicated to a poet a carnal and passionate geometry. *A drawing*, he heard Degas say in his adolescence, *isn't a form, it's a way of seeing a form*.[6] And about all the powerful resources derived from watching the materials that poetry is going to use from some prior prose writers, which Symbolism enjoyed with regard to the prose of Flaubert, in which, in the words of one acute critic, prose had attained in *Un coeur simple*, adding a page to the page, an intensity comparable to that of Villon's *Heaulmière*.[7] As the romantics communicated to us their external personal concerns, the substance of poetry had begun to expire, in such a way that a prose writer like Flaubert had attempted to rescue that poetic substance in order to transfer it in a diluted and degraded form to prose. If we recall the opening of *Salammbô*, *it was at Megara, a suburb of Carthage*, we realize how this honorary tetrarch, as Thibaudet has called him,[8] made use of a brilliant but corruptible substance; metallic, but which had to turn to developments that distanced his prose from poetry, without being able to transfer to it those inverse reflections, due to the special condition of French prose.

He had also found, by that magic of encounters a poet employs to eliminate certain visible influences, a skill provided by the *lirici medicei* and a certain courtly poetry which, by studying Voltaire, was going to act in an unexpected and even opposite direction. Voltaire had appeared with regard to Corneille like an epic dust to remove poetry from the violent Corneillian shock, in order to bring us a poetry as dry and dusty as a 18th century clock. That dry but extremely neat substance, which had served in support of supreme guarantees, was going to become, as it entered in contact with *fin-de-siècle* Symbolism—we're speaking here of minor, almost invisible influences—, a form of circumspect development that retained a reminiscence of that bite into knowledge and into the breast of the woman despised. The assurance of Voltaire's art, which fluctuated between Corneille and Latin epigrams for the Marquise de Pompadour, was also going to merge—we still speak here of minor, almost invisible influences—with another poetry, lesser but courtly and with correct liquid volutes like that of the *lirici medicei*. May we not situate as expected predecessors of that line of Valéry's, one of the most fascinating in all French literature, *Comme le fruit se fond en jouissance*,[9] these lines from Lorenzo the Magnificent's *Ambra*?

> *Como le membre verginale entrorno*
> *nell'acque brune e gelide, sentio,*
> *e mosso del leggiadro corpo adorno…*[10]

He had also rubbed up against the significant content of voluptuousness in Baudelaire. The latter had derived from his prolonged sensual excursions a kind of natural voluptuousness that was like a long and constructive hope created by the impossibility of forging a new destiny for himself. That natural voluptuousness benefitted from a controlled joy, since it moved amid objects which it attempted to seize not by possession but by atmosphere and condition. Here Valéry would also act by reduction: in the face of that natural voluptuousness of Baudelaire's, he would derive and oppose his own concept of a particular voluptuousness. In that voluptuousness he sought for himself an identity in which he could dispense with tentacles for taking possession of an object or for lingering over each of its pores or cells. Proceeding on that basis he would manage to express his attempt from a position very much opposed to that of poetry. He came to desire for poetry, in his "L'amateur de poèmes," a singularly finished kind of thought.[11] The voluptuous identity or particular voluptuousness seemed especially definite when confronted by the substance of poetry. He had no longing for the singularly felt thought of a Pascal, or for the gentle craftsmanship of a feeling rigorously shaped, but rather, in a dualism unnecessary for poetry, he preferred to elaborate with artifice, perhaps with each of the senses, a conceptual cosmos. With those prior acts of taking possession, with those subtle summations which poetry clothed in invisibility, there appeared a quantity governed by an act of will, there was revealed then as a first characteristic of the Alexandrian-apocalyptic period: the faceted eye.

II.

For a mediocre and diligent journeyman like Joseph Marie de Hérédia, Valéry's silence had to seem incomprehensible. Hérédia had forgotten that laziness weaves its golden treasure over a slow fire in the shade of the tree of knowledge. Silence as a form, but at bottom the senseless, maddening impulse of the desire to understand. Silence as a motionless hero, and knowledge within the contours of a body's skin, a Stoic theme that in those years Valéry longed to endure. The numerous references to the body appearing in his works inspire a Pascalian pity: the body, its limits and knowledge, the void like a halo surrounding the body's contours. Laziness joins us to the serpent, the serpent to knowledge. A terrible laziness. In those years Valéry couldn't listen to music, because either the succession of its measures was weakened by its later thrusts or the emergence of that same suggestion alone, prompted to a strange vigilance, prevented the continuity of later suggestions.[12] Nor could he read in those years, because the conditions of reading were incompatible with his excessive precision of language.[13] Why in those years did Hérédia think Valéry was lazy?

That acute, senseless precision of knowledge stops. For the time being it becomes a non-existent assault, an ardor. Hérédia believed in the rigor of certain transmissions, and therefore attributed the metallic slowness of Valéry's voice to shameless adolescent concerns. Hérédia didn't know that the circumstances were fates, hostile divinities or an invisible ocean thread. He didn't know that after Mallarmé and Valéry all prose had to be *commanded*, in other words, directed, and all poems *demanded*, in other words, summoned from the shadows, fatally and punctually, just as a person strolling through some hanging gardens comes to a halt to justify with his instantaneous death the importunate pretensions of a gymnast longing to be an archer. *Only exhaustion exalts me*, Valéry said,[14] abandoning the voluptuous tradition of *bien-être*.

That conception of poetry as an external impulse makes Valéry, when obliged to offer us an album of old verses, have photographs made of the verses of his first symbolist period, rather than copying them out again, which would have meant creating them anew by passing them through that swift blood that remains faithful to its initial changing impulse. Valéry countered Hérédia's accusation of laziness by considering this the *external consequence of a profound modification*. He was faced with what we might call the erotic stage of poetic knowledge: the themes of necessary obscurity and necessary incoherence. Obscurity as a visual theme that we might call Apollo emerging from the foam, the theme of birth; and incoherence, symbolized by the snail and the loyalties to himself that do not permit betrayals, relinquishments, uninhabited fragments.

Valéry was struggling with *durée*, by favoring it. He was seeking to intensify resistance in order to attain an alert tension, exasperating his will. A diligent will, an unrewarding counterpart to those diligent dreams of the surrealists. The mixture of dream and reality, and at an extreme, the will activating a body that is understood. Why do I need more questions if I dominate my body and dominate my dreams?

These were not yet the years when Valéry, between the eye and the night, as in his poem,[15] would anchor himself in the body. Those were the years of his adolescence when he lingered over *conventions*. These conventions have always accompanied him, since his first attempts in *Monsieur Teste*, when he was attempting to define poetry or those who had defined it in the 18th century. He was then grounding his viewpoints in conventions, a courtesy of culture, and in the esthetics of the arbitrary, pure control, libertinism of will. If we add to the concept of convention, of established arbitrariness, the concept of the properties of language and their sole necessary reduction, we witness Valéry's move to the great and exclusive theme of Stoicism: the body in the face of nothingness.

Nothing more opposed to a convention than a conviction. The former makes use of a web born of its communications, makes us think that a lack of courtesy is answered by the falling of a lamp, an inopportune frown by the breaking of candelabra. Those conventions lead Valéry to reject what he calls monster ideas. Here we have Monsieur Teste offering a toast with the first glass on his tray: reason should only ask what truth can answer. Those monster ideas are those of a primitive or of someone asking at the wrong moment, they constitute *an inopportune exercise of our questioning faculties*. But now he places those conventions within the possibilities of an activity in space. But Valéry places some impossible things, like Monsieur Teste and poetry itself, inside the demon of impossibility and of infinite appetite.

Teste is a germ that has to live a quarter of an hour at a time.[16] Valéry likes to contemplate the germ independently, through a glass, instant by instant. Can the germ and the instant be seen through a glass? In other words, birth but without the ascending path of passion. The rising sun, a metaphor for the intellectual moment of creation, consciousness of the unconscious, but considering night and morning as monsters or impure abstractions?[17]

Valéry fondles his little monster Teste, a germ with no development, replete with problems and *durée*, a chimera, a hippogryph.[18] Teste doesn't manage to become a monster like Euphorion, he has no reason to cast himself into an abyss, because he doesn't attempt to live. Euphorion, who asks himself: are the melody and the rhythm now what they should be? But he constantly receives his parents' invitation to be the ornament of the plain. Euphorion cultivates violence and abduction and sets out swiftly to pursue the ascent of the flame rising from the rocks. Not so Teste, who isn't even interested in testing his instruments, since he considers these as given to him by the goddess of fortune at the very instant when she weaves his nest.[19]

A point followed by a point, a line; a cell or germ multiplied, a body. Creation is by rupture, like Satan; or by detachments, like 19th century scientists, "detachment of rings into fragments, following the impulse given them by a center." Or we are, and this is the case of Valéry, at the creation of the germ, an instant-point, of the absolute purity of the flow of time that finally is inserted into the geometrical figure, into the human body, into the nascent word. What is that moment?

Valéry remains uncertain as to the ends and derivations of that germ. How to achieve the integration of that germ into an organ, totally dispensing with its derivation into an instrument? In other words, how to resolve whether poetry initially is a germ and in its development an instrument due to craftsmanship. And then, if poetry is a germ or creation, how not to isolate the image, considering it as a unit distinct from its absolute and see that image solely as a pre-figure, seeing it only as an incomplete fragment. The capacity of the germ to create a body stands in inverse relation to its capacity to produce instruments.

And if poetry also tends toward figure, how is it that it doesn't manage to consider a body as an instrument and considers it as *the measure of the world*?[20] Here we see a momentary solution, we now have a split between being and body, which is Valéry's shifting ground, since the germ, at the splendid moment when it is creation, is resolved as total poetry. The transfer of that fire by means of devices and machines puts it in the category of an abandoned residue, as an instrument at the service of Stoic discipline. But the germ delivers to us poetry, body and being as totally indistinct, resolved, but in applying them it establishes a tragic distinction between service and destiny.

Here is the root of the definition of poetry which Valéry has delivered to our time in order to confuse by clarification. Enclosed within his adjustments, within his infinite verifications, he sees that the influence of movement or even of a tiny whirlwind provokes the contractions or extremely rapid wrinklings of his own surface. This perfect germ accumulates in the succession of its instants the certainty of the presence of its own body, and its potentialities that do not arrive at an act preserve its equestrian gift, enduring verifications with scorn, but with a somber joy.

Just as Valéry advises preserving language as an accusation,[21] extension endures movement or, if you wish, endures the arrival of God with no need for any Annunciation. The arrival of movement would provoke the dispersion of meaning or the distribution of its atoms, which thus find themselves driven by their blindness to gather at a point, where we have to endure a secret assault. That tension toward the very center of the body provokes the rupture of the homogeneous body by its perfections, which thus finds itself obliged to repeat the perfect like a reflecting dihedral. This creation that multiplies perfection feeds upon its ennui. Mallarmé's insistence on the mirror is as attractive as is Valéry's on ennui. The attraction of the mirror goes on insisting after it is no longer touched by presence, then a tension is created in which the symbol has to be recovered, to maintain its halo. But that creation by splitting, by successive central contractions and slow detachments from the outer limits, which impel an expected causation, provoking a sort of law for the inheritance of ideas or sensibility. What we find now is a valuable controlled suicide and the ennui of meeting again. But, before Monsieur Teste spreads out his blanket and dusts off the ashes of his ennui, let's select some of his most valuable quarters of an hour.

As they leave the opera, Monsieur Teste's disciples think he would make a great dramatist. He would place his theater at the extreme limit of all sciences and at the beginning of all negations. These adulations by his disciples are promptly cut off by a curt: *Personne ne medite*.[22] There is talk of incoherencies, but the listener's loyalty obliges him to maintain a suspicion of coherence in the face of incoherence. The mind is constructed in such a way that it cannot be incoherent to itself.[23] The disciples continue their procession, seeking a miserable solution: *abstract sensations, delicious figures of all that is loved.*[24] The senses that had turned their backs on archetypes, wind up nourishing them, and nourishing themselves. And in a completed *mélange*, a pathos finely calibrated in mercurial stages ready to hand. Here is a trap which the disciples are offering and which some amused passers-by recommend, clarify, distribute and begin again. Everything that one conceives of is easy, he clarifies.[25] The learned man doesn't know what he's saying and the self is irreducible.[26] In the development of his ideas, Valéry has spoken at times like Teste, at times like his disciples. Let's not see this as a dualism: every man lives at the edge of his self and listens to his disciple, but it can be grotesque when the greater and the lesser figures go along, either pointing out a comet or holding hands, and this turns into an anguishing contemplation as soon as, within us, inseparably they turn against one another in accusation. One at the edge of our self, at the limit of our skin, leaping into the void; the other, the disciple, who was able to disguise himself as a devil and counsel extraordinary things, but who essentially sleeps and forgets. Teste knows he has to reduce himself to his self, in the same way that the germ reduces itself to a point in order to bring forth the perfect new body. Here Valéry showed himself to be rather un-Cartesian, since that philosopher had distanced himself from Elizabeth of the Palatinate, deciding to take to the road to attend the coronation of the Emperor of Germany. Turning to the landscape and to a study of the world, leaving his own country and closing his books, and all this, as Descartes confessed, with splendid results. This anti-Cartesianism of Descartes is usually delightful.

Leaving the theater at midnight and then his walk have weighed heavily on Monsieur Teste's eyelids. Now he enters into sleep savoring with his fingers the falling sands. Let's enter into the sleep of someone always interested in being awake. The candle goes out and his body is invaded, surrounded. His disciple will also use the candle to go down. His disciple comes to know Teste's body when he discovers it, Monsieur Teste recognizes it from memory. We take, says Valéry, our right foot in our right hand, and put that cold foot in our warm palm.[27] Sleep yields, disappears or approaches by pressing us clumsily, but our body, surrounded by sand, offers it a limit. Confronted with that current of sleep, we momentarily offer it a thought which, in turning into an object, also goes down. In death the soul feels incomplete and longs for the prison left behind, but in sleep the soul walks around, continues, becomes attached to a thought difficult to trace that rules us with invisible despotism. Dispossessed in this way, the body must continue an idea, but which? This is a harsh and inflexible sleep: to go on without knowing, answering precisely that which we don't dare to ask, which we cannot unanchor from ourselves and which sleep evaporates into a bright dew. Sleep for Valéry is only an enormous movement. Suddenly we feel that *that* is coming, we cast a spell and take possession of an unfinished idea or of a twisted problem. A shout that is expected like a clock. It now envelops us, the idea having become an object, still carrying its candle, goes down to our inner life.

Then the enemy goes away, and the object that has gone down returns itself in clear response to an idea we don't recognize, invisible, that cannot be our friend.

III.

For the Stoics the body was a spectacle, it existed as an object, belonging to the outer world. For them adjusting sensations was the artist's goal. *Pour tenter les démons ajustant bien leurs bas*, says a verse of clearly Stoic adjustment.[28] However, Valéry seems to incline toward the unitary solution of Thomist Catholics. In certain pages on Leonardo he confesses as much. There is not, nor can there be, the slightest analogy between the spirit of men and the body of angels. But that's why it's strange and irregular to maintain like Valéry, from the point of view of sensations, a Stoic attitude, and maintain about the body a Thomist Catholic criterion. I now observe that Valéry doesn't hold to the classic use of *logos spermatikos*, which is the fundamental basis for Stoicism, but rather to that of *germ*. If we add to this his use of the word *durée* the same as Bergson, whose influence he always has refused to accept, we then have Valéry within Bergsonism more than within Stoicism. Another distinction: the Stoics took pleasure in the use of *forma substantialis*, which could even include the inert, yet the Thomist Catholic uses *esse substantialis*,[29] a being which is always substance, which is substantial. Therefore, in the Stoic the will can be at the service of that *forma substantialis*. The will in the Stoic is directed up against his skin as a limit. To that impulse, we have to add the regressive force of the inert on us, the radiations of the external world, to which we seek to adjust ourselves. To be sure, that im-

pulse and that adjustment offer a universe totally inhabited by a substance and which feels like an error or a yawn
the fear of an empty pause. Stoicism in art has given the
idea of limit a possible sense of dignity. When Goethe
said proudly, we the patricians of Frankfurt, when he believed that what distinguishes a master is the fact that he
works within limits, he's surely inhabiting the world of
the Stoics, the world of their *forma substantialis*.

IV.

Just as the body endures the surrounding nothingness,
figures find themselves obliged to counteract the flow of
images. Valéry has not wanted to arrive at an essential
distinction between image and figure, as two different
means. He has seen the image in its movement, he thinks
the finality of images is to arrive at figures. Images, he
tells us, are pre-figures. He couldn't endure the fact that,
while images cloud his mirror, figures also have to endure the negation of movement. He had to trace a violent
separation, like the one Thomism had arrived at, in considering form as an ultimate stage of matter. The image
contained an awkward presence, whose finality seemed
to flee until it was lost or could not be halted. In this
Valéry seemed to depart from Mallarmé for whom verbal
progression was driven by a murmur, in such a way that
the sum of images produced a tonal result, but without
Mallarmé's desperate patience ever believing in the vir-
tuosity of figures.

That had been the Aristotelian possibility of figures, in other words, possibility stripped of form, in this case images, which would give us as a consequence the empty space of the Platonists. But that is an inadmissible position for poetry, which, by mistrusting the fixity of perception, mistrusts all categories. Both in Lucretius and in Valéry, that struggle between movement and void wants to be resolved in the symbol of a fish in movement which, as it proceeds at the dictate of its instantaneous impulses, vacates a void. Can a void be tolerated as a trace of movement? Pascal doubted the relevance of this because he believed that nature did not strongly abhor a vacuum. But the movement of a fish provokes an impulse in the wave in order to allow itself the freedom of its infinite movement. Thus in Lucretius:

> ...to the gleaming fish
> the water opens liquid paths,
> and then the space abandoned
> is occupied by the wave withdrawn.[30]

In Lucretius the existence of a void seems momentarily to be accepted, but in order to counteract it with the body: all we have left is body and void. Thus movement seems like the unfolding of a body in a void. Valéry reproduces the problem of the fish's movement just as Lucretius had posed it, "for himself he felt, he tells us, how the favorable form of these fish in the quickest manner carried from head to tail the waters they met in their path and in order to advance had to push backward."[31] If the Stoics exemplify the struggle of body and void by the movement of a fish, for Christians the problem appears in the form of a violent combat. The struggle against the fish is necessary, and cannot be delayed. Its simplistic and elegant vertebral consciousness destroys free choice. Its instantaneousness passes coldly between our hands like a memory of the impossibility of stopping time. At the same time that the fish doesn't feel the presence of the void as an anguish or an understanding, it totally achieves with the passage of its scales a Nietzschean joy in terror and comes to feel like silk the instantaneous pressure of the infinite dead points, like Satan's long solitude amid the rocks, while waiting for the rupture.

The figure is sought not as an elegant selection, as a weaving and unweaving, with an assured resumption: it doesn't free itself, doesn't break with our body, doesn't dare to fall before our eyes. It is sought for, longed for, by a finger that touches, by a kind of penetration, by circular potency, because it assures us against becoming, since, otherwise, expression, art, existence, would be a stage in a progressive well, a ridiculous point in the well, a cat's eyes at the center of the well.[32] Otherwise, if the figure isn't accepted, what remains would be our mouth wide open, the gesture with which we die, a becoming, the earth taken away from under our feet; a long breath of air that passes and doesn't find the earth. The figure that doesn't struggle with the a priori, the spatial figure is futile or a Cartesian tool. But the figure struggles against becoming, because that which struggles with time is sterility, the disguise of the sterile, the chorus of rocks, the *insensible abstract*, phosphorus or plaster on a blackboard, foot at the water's edge, name at the water's edge. That's why Pascal, Cézanne and Valéry are inside the figure. The most dissimilar sensibilities within that anguished detention and those certainties of figures.

Ah, but in Pascal let's separate figure from symbol. In Cézanne, figure finality from figure secretion. In Valéry, figure from pure act.

For Pascal there is no cessation of figures: there are demonstrative ones, but there are also indubitable and apocalyptic ones. Would an apocalyptic figure be inadmissible for Valéry? They pass and insist, they diverge or diversify: bright and serene or they may tear out their hair, sound like comets. Figures are a sting of the furies, a smoke of the blood. If one goes to them it's in order not to have the pride of creating a new order, beyond the heroic and the supernatural. Figure of the cause, in other words, grace; symbol, figure without end. Let's emphasize the antithesis between the Pascalian symbol, figure without end, and Valéry's phrase: images are pre-figures. In Pascal, beyond the figure, begins the symbol; beyond the law, the new law; beyond the sign, the rupture of servitude and the new alliance. The justification for the figure is not a different order, it is the gaze that receives and the eye that impels, it is the visitation, the visibility of grace. The figure, like the Thomists' form, struggles with grace because it can't contain it entirely. The figure cannot encompass grace, doesn't capture the instant point; it's between the murmur of the existence of the symbol and its expiration; between the image that begins and the image that is lost. It doesn't foresee successive images or the image that is summed up in the image, in other words, the poematic body. It emerges and is maintained by the struggle between two appearances or two essences, and between them it traces the meaning of its designs. Two natures in Christ, two advents, two states or natures in man: recognitions of creatures and impossibility to approach them. Then the figure emerges in the face of contradictions. It goes beyond and moans. But, in the other aspect, in their struggle against becoming, figures please and displease God, who always sees in them a place of temptation and vigilance. On the contrary, in Pascal, the place lent to the figure is traced upon a painful and moaning sand.

That all artists feel the vacillation and attraction of the figure is what Cézanne reveals when he tells us: *L'aboutissement de l'art c'est la figure.*[33] We now cite Cézanne because his natural contrast with Valéry is extremely significant in order to attain points of reference. That *aboutissement* which may mean finality, may also mean suppuration. The suppuration form in Cézanne opposed to the object form of Valéry. Of course, Valéry attempts to isolate the figure from its abstract process. He allows a mirror into figures of the nascent act, since when figures become detached from us they attempt to reproduce that act. Of course, Valéry's prior distinction isn't satisfactory, he opposes inspiration to mechanism, and the phrase comparative analysis of mechanisms is, properly speaking, a figure, as he tells us.[34] We come to the conclusion that the figure is realized as a convention that may prolong the nascent act, but after evaporating from us it persists in the atmosphere of an analytical mechanics of language.

In Stoicism an appetite for figures is due to a concept of the tension of the skin, a consequence of the proportion of substance and its total occupation, but not to an artisan-like insistence on matter, since a medieval artisan sees in matter the joyful probability of a combat with the enemy who repeats, whom we can't keep away. The figure presupposes the pure branch, the pure fruit. But the tree only shows us its image: its shade. The shade is the vegetative image of the figure, but the image receives the pure tree, the necessary pure shade, breath of air, dampness, breeze, invisible growth and visible clouds of smoke. That's why the artisan created habit in confrontation with matter, continual vigilance and exercise, since otherwise the challenging decision of matter could find the creator asleep. Finding himself, for lack of habit, confronted with matter, obliged to turn to violence and sudden recuperation. Abduction and rupture presuppose a circumstance walled in by habit in order to keep away the sleep that approaches when we find ourselves under a prolonged siege.

In itself, form may exist, but what we have of a tree or a friend is their image: their insistence is, as already

Saint Thomas Aquinas saw, the transmission of the form of one being to another. The first born of all creatures, when patristics considers that only the Son could be an image, frees us from the danger of an intellectual truce. Thus the Father enjoys figuration; the Son is image, and the Holy Spirit is expressed by way of the Son, image of images. And the Son, who is the image, is expressed by the Word. In all words we always contemplate the breath of the second birth, the contour of the shadow on the wall. The eye creates the figure; the night is expressed, falls upon us, by image. The eye feels a passive pride when it is extended in the figure. Our body feels a possessive pride when it penetrates into the image of the night. Here then is our study, as a gloss on those already alluded verses of Valéry's:

> *And breaking a serene tomb,*
> *I reduce myself restlessly and remain sovereign,*
> *since my visions between eye and night,*
> *the slightest movements consult my pride.*[35]

1945

Conversation about Paul Valéry[1]

I detest public speaking, so I'll just briefly state my points of view concerning the phenomenon of Paul Valéry, in accordance with the Chinese proverb that tells us: "if you're not an orator, try to make your harangue as short as if spoken by a dwarf."

a) One of the last representatives of a style that transformed the poet into the commanding center of a system of enormous coordinates. He cultivates the most severe forms of hermeticism and closure, and in his venerably mature years is heard with absolute reverence in Geneva and Locarno, at the Collège de France and the Sorbonne.

b) In Parmenides, in Lucretius, in Goethe, the creative function of poetry appears as a consequence of learning, not of the sovereignty of sensibility or of the precision of intellect.

c) The substance of unanimity has been lost. Nations don't evidence freely their acceptances or rejections, but instead are coerced by the implausible forms taken on in our time by agencies of propaganda. Nations penetrating into the obscure led by the hero or the learned man. Chesterton speaks with delight and profundity of the joy that spread over all Europe when Don John of Austria assumed his greatest responsibility. Or Bossuet preaching at Lent and being heard by Louis XIV and the people of God. In other words, the belief that a nation is a substance that projects itself in Time.

d) This criterion of unanimity is the one that has shaped our tradition that the learned man or the hero is the interpreter, the reader of the forward movement of the people of God. If the people no longer believe in the learned man, this is because stock markets and agencies of propaganda have imposed foolish peacocks.[2] That's why Valéry, after many years of silence and accumulation, was heard when he spoke and his success was omni-comprehensive. And so we let him tell us about Marie Monnier's embroideries,[3] about reason by recurrence in his polemic with Poincaré, or indirectly refute Proust concerning his concept of the novel and what he called sacred coincidence. We have to go back to Goethe to find a similar case of veneration and total reverence. And so, in a few days, we see him [Goethe] slip into Eckermann's ears ideas about the beauty of the young counselor von Spiegel, receive some lithographs from Stuttgart, study the violet vapors given off by burnt iodine, the discovery of the latest salt springs, or admire, surrounded by friends in their delight in learning, a medal he's been sent from Bohemia.[4]

e) Why does the veneration for learning arise in a nation? The ancient ideal of the learned man as an interpreter of life, which culminates in the Greece of Pericles, has found refuge, perhaps as a Spenglerian homology, in the culture of the poet, in what the poet should know.

f) The great French tradition: La Fontaine called himself a *Polyphile*, a lover of all things, and Valéry [says] that the artist is the Condottiere of the nine Muses.[5]

g) In these conditions, when in our adolescence we wondered what a poet should know, in what form learning should appear in the poet, we came upon "Le Cimetière marin,"[6] which worked its dazzling influence on all of us.

h) Studying that poem put an end to the following things: To poetry as a copy of pictures traced by dreams. Proust's nightmare. To facile pastiches of folklore in the Spanish style. To all that *verde que te quiero verde*,[7] and all that *verde, verderol, endulza la puesta del sol*.[8] To the superficial accumulations of surrealism.

   To the mandarin forms of certain masters of symbolism who offered as the basis of their work the impulses of music, in a kind of symphonic impressionism that indefinitely prolonged the phrases of the English horn into a ferment of the harp and not into a world view, into a penetration, into a battle between becoming and duration.

i) Glossers. Their excesses. "La Jeune Parque" is the change of a consciousness throughout a single night. The "Narcisse" is being taking possession of the body. "Les grenades," creation, and "Le Cimetière marin," in Cohen's interpretation, poses the problems of being, non-being, aporetic moments, logical jokes of the Megarians, Pascalian moments of a Cartesian and the progressive murmurs of the dead as they break upon the pines of a country cemetery.[9]

These glossers appeared in this way, in the form of disciples for whom Monsieur Teste showed a constant scorn, since they only sought abstract sensations, delightful figures for all they loved.[10]

What engendered this error? Great French poets sought complementary values. They moved away from *faire le contraire*, *faire autre chose*. Such was the case in Hugo and Baudelaire, Baudelaire and Mallarmé, Mallarmé and Valéry.[11]

Hugo lost himself in infinite apostrophes, bowed down to common sense, the partiality of his flashes moved in tune with overall banality, flirted with the masses and dialogued with God. Baudelaire and a particular voluptuousness: A phrase of Thibaudet's: "Baudelaire is Sainte-Beuve plus inspiration."[12] His prosaisms. Mallarmé and *chinoiserie facile*, his crystal enigmas. Hugo and the orchestra. Hugo's most beautiful, most resonant poem felt itself swoon over the possibilities of the orchestra, the power of its resources and the sumptuous form in which it offered its lies.

Mallarmé and the orchestra. He sets up relations with the orchestra not by way of the dressing room, like Baudelaire and Nerval, but instead attends the Concerts Lamoureux. The same year that Baudelaire witnesses imperturbably the jeers at the Paris première of *Tannhäuser*, he becomes a candidate for admission to the French Academy. "If the orchestra were to cease in its influence, the gesture would turn into a statue."[13]

Valéry accepts the murmur, the echo of Mallarmé: "Between emptiness and dream I await the echo of my inner grandeur."[14]

Pure poetry is hyperbolic, just as Descartes termed hyperbolic the first doubt. In other words, the Monster that cannot come into being.

Criticisms made against Mallarmé: he was seeking synthetic gold.

He accumulated multicolored and extremely tense but dissimilar crystals.

To seek a basis in the theme of the echo and locate his poetry at an impossible distance. Valéry's lesson:

The poet's intuitive rigor depends upon his accumulations, upon the pressure, Eliot tells us somewhat grossly, under which he has made his mixture.[15]

His concept of duration, in a Stoic rather than a Bergsonian sense (Valéry always denied any influence from Bergson). This serves him to define form in poetry and in knowledge.

Thus form is a difficulty ("A hundred divine instants, he says, do not constitute a poem, which is a duration of growth and like a figure in time"[16]).

He situates *knowledge* between becoming and duration. When they are equal to one another the *absolute zero* of recognition is engendered.

The intense study of Valéry began to plunge us into doubts.

a) Teste is a germ who lives for a quarter of an hour. How is it possible for poetry in its beginning to be a germ and in its development an artisan's tool, a work of my patience, as Mallarmé said?[17]

b) Monster ideas: the inopportune exercise of our questioning faculties. "Reason should ask only what truth can reply." A somewhat lighthearted struggle between conventions and arbitrariness.

c) To know in order to construct. The ideal of the architect, which leads us to the android, to Leonardo's or La Mettrie's automaton, to Monsieur Teste.

d) How is it possible that the work of the mind only exists

in act, poetry is pure act, and then speak of machines that transport fire.

Thus Valéry was becoming for all our generation a doubly venerable master. In our adolescence he had filled us with concerns, [but] the passage of time was leading us to render him the greatest of homages: that of our disagreement with his work.

a) Poetry is a hypertelic manifestation of the mind. It leaps beyond its finality and destroys it. Like some insects it destroys the male after copulation. (The white-faced decticus.[18])
b) Poetry is a protoplasmatic manifestation of man, it seeks primary, pure bodies.
c) The tradition of Maurice Scève, apparently continued, basically was interrupted.

These verses by Maurice Scève:

Essence full in itself of latent infinity,
which only enjoys itself and is content with itself.

remind one of another stanza of Valéry's:

Midi là-haut, Midi sans mouvement
En soi se pense et convient à soi-même...[19]

But what an exemplary difference. In Maurice Scève, that essence was God; in Valéry, perfection. In accordance with his demoniacal verse: "*Les moindres mouve-ments consultent mon orgueil.*"

Now that he strolls in the company of Phaedrus and Eupalinos, of Socrates and Stephanos,[20] he will know how in the myth of Amphion architecture is born of the progressions of music—the singing temple[21]—, and how the bee, now homeless, now bodiless, flies away to transmit to him, as in our adolescence, the dawn of an immortal desire.

The Poetic Act and Valéry[1]

THE mischievous Pound and the careful Valéry seem to have been coinciding for some time now in a repeated assertion: *poetry is an inspired kind of mathematics.*[2] But what is that mathematics inspired by? And since we are approaching a moment of reassessment and synthesis, more than of facile orphic solutions, it's well for us to situate ourselves in that introduction to poetry, where a bit of fire leaps out and the cryptic cunning of Eratosthenes's sieve shows forth.[3] Behind number and proportion, we discover not only the simple play of favorable combinations, but also the *daimon* of music and the unexpected grace of Harmony. We find, then, that this momentary coincidence of two dissimilar spirits in a phrase, far from granting us repose, prods us again to position ourselves at an unexpected equidistance from the gift and the calibration of the quantities or groupings of metrics. Let's recall that Pythagoras found no better name to designate the Most High, the Unique Name, than that of *quaternary*. The pyramid, the octahedron and the icosahedron, engendered by fire, air and water, according to the Pythagoreans. Careful then with numbers. Out there, too, are the ungraspable, the inexpressible, the unfindable. Inspired mathematics leaves us with another, ineffable side, where others converge who did not conceal themselves in order to confess to us, like Walter Pater: *all arts approach the condition of music*.[4] And between mathematics and music, nominalism, the act of language, with all of which Valéry now grapples in his latest work, *Introduction to Poetics*.[5]

What does Valéry tell us and what does he now see behind words? And when will he provide us with a definitive separation of established language from nascent language, thus detaching the joy of the act, of the poetic act?

Valéry, the old symbolist who maintains his preferences, approaches poetry as the highest realization of language, but the distinction whose clarity he has so long pursued, between the action that accomplishes and the work accomplished,[6] would be so subtle that we could only seize it as a simplistic causal act. The secret development of a work, prior to its appearance and justification, remains a closed realm of conduct: how can it be incorporated into the work of art? That mechanism perhaps cannot be transmitted, since in order for it to gain its ethical profit, it would always have to be begun all over again, and we would then see that mechanical effort as an achieved work, but whose generative process would always be unnoticeable as soon as effected. To the filial possibilities of language Valéry adds the consideration of language in the act. Animistic language offers us its body of doctrine in a history of the mind obtained by decanting the acquired from the given, in other words, the "consideration of language as the masterpiece of all masterpieces of literature."[7] That well defined part of works of art: the mechanism of the act of the writer—the use of *figures*—as traced by the old Aristotelian rhetorics. Whoever multiplies figures gives us the pure birth of words.[8] Other less well defined conditions: inspiration, sensibility, are always ready to elude the control of a monarchical omniscience, but it would be illusory to consider that a command of the mechanical part does away with the risks of inspired fragments, of whims or of demonic friendships, in the same way that in philosophy defining, distinguishing, naming with efficient grace are of no use to us in another kind of knowledge, that of communion, of religation.[9] Perhaps in a poetic-Catholic solution—for no one can be sure of his salvation—the consequences of keeping away from those internal secrets, which remain hidden until their total release, would give us an absolutely loyal knowledge, paradisal sign or key. "Delicate reasonings in which the conclusions take on the appearance of a divination."[10] Divination after a long excuse, courtesy that may one day provide the Easter of a fulfilled prophecy.

Can we some day arrive at an exact definition of words that so far have been extremely dangerous, such as form, rhythm, influences, inspiration, composition? Isn't perhaps the word "infinite" also a sign entering into mathematical formulas? It's a pity that Valéry, in his urge to attain that clarity of definition in words used in poetry, should have proposed to replace "author" with "producer," "reader" with "consumer," and "historical grace" with "production of the value of a work of art." Shall we arrive at specifying artistic evaluation to the extreme of exact meaning that in economy the word value has, with its accompanying spiritual and historical motivations? Would it be convenient to replace the grace of matter with that which should be worked by the instrument that allows us to operate? Perhaps we may ask ourselves again as in ancient theology whether presence is verified by the grace of words or by the virtue of he who operates, of he who prepares the Ascension.

Careful then with numbers. If they are used as defense and contentment, the hare may leap forth and deprive us of our joyful surprise. As we know, William Blake placed the Analytic Angel between Saturn and the fixed stars.[11] Between self-destruction and the monotony of constant opera, of a secure diamond.

June, 1938

Lezama's Diary Entries on
Descartes and Valéry[1]

NOV. 12, 1939.—Valéry's often cited phrase, in which he alludes to his being situated *between void and pure event*,[2] is inspired by the following phrases in Descartes' *Meditation on First Philosophy*: "and I see myself as halfway between God and nothingness, that is, placed in that fashion between the Supreme Being and non being."[3]

A result of which is a difference in nuance in Valéry's favor. Of course it's a bit harsh and dissonant to call God pure event. Especially after Thomist Aristotelian philosophy had coined for such purposes the expression "pure act." The latter has a certain imperial lineage whereas pure event seems to have been made to be swallowed up by time, like some ordinary journalistic event.

Whereas substituting nothingness for void casts not only a difference of delicacy in Valéry's favor, but also one of very Christian piety.

However, Valéry and Pascal, who according to hasty judgments would seem to be enemies, always use the same word: void.

NOV. 12, 1939.—"…Since error is not pure negation,"[4]

says Descartes. Here we have a phrase that can help us establish an initial difference between void and nothingness. Nothingness would remain as pure negation. Whereas void would be a manifest error, or rather an error of our own, because of our failure to accord with that void or rather a momentary error in the outside world.

See void as error but not as enemy of all creation. Nothingness is impossible, whereas void can be overcome, penetrated someday by light, by some "let there be."

Nothingness only passes in front of a mirror that reproduces nothingness. Void, on the contrary, is the abyss of the opening pages of the Bible. There is even a ray of light in the abyss, that is, a void defined, grabbed by the throat.

Nothingness would be an irredeemable punishment; whereas void seems to refer to the fact that knowledge is not yet infinite, but it can be touched by grace, and then.

NOV. 12, 1939.—When Descartes refers to things relating to truth and error, he thinks that the latter is due "to my weakness in not being able continually to adhere to a single thought,"[5] he seems to agree with the surrealists, who think it's possible to achieve a quantitative-extensive reconstruction of memory, a grasp of what each of us is at each of our similar and different instants.

NOV. 12, 1939.—Descartes also seems to refer to the surrealists and their aims when he tells us about a *continuous quantity or extension of longitude, latitude and depth.*

NOV. 13, 1939.—"So it is that this way of thinking differs from pure intellection in that the spirit, when it conceives, enters in a certain fashion into itself and considers one of the ideas it has in itself; but, when it imagines, it turns back to the body to consider something in conformity with the idea that it itself has formed or received by way of the senses."[6] Descartes, *Meditation on First Philosophy*.

Now we understand why there is a line of intimist poets, from Lucretius to Valéry, who have wanted to establish the metaphor of the body:

> J'aime... J'aime... Et qui donc peut aimer autre
>   chose
> Que soi-même?
> Toi seul, ô mon corps
> Je t'aime, unique objet qui me défend des morts.[7]

says Valéry in one of the stanzas of his Narcissus.

What appears in the paragraph cited from Descartes is not a charge against the imagination. There's a certain nostalgia in it. When every day we hear it claimed that Valéry is a Cartesian, we must see with pleasure the surprise with which Valéry discovers in Descartes those passages a superficial eye would judge to be anti-Christian. Discovering what we might call the afterworld of clear and distinct ideas.

Serpent of Don Luis de Góngora[1]

STERN browed king of lances, he covers changeable incitements with such a transparent shield that, as in a hunt on an Assyrian bas-relief, he makes disappear more than he detains, intoning more the consecration of the weapons than the action upon the prey. Everything proceeds from that disappearance, by the protection of the light and the shielding of its sparkle, whose invention makes it all reappear at the other poetic limit. In the *Soledad primera*, with the tedium of an invasive fatigue, which prepares the beginning of sleep inducing metamorphoses, the hunters hang on a pine tree the head of a recently killed bear. The light returns to set the bear's head at a distance, but it reappears, turning the clouds of lances into shafts of firs. A slight breeze brings the bear's head closer to the feigned lances, assuring, by that inverse process, the reappearance of the hunt. Again the bear kisses a single lance, happy to be free of that consecration of weapons which had transported it, causing it to disappear into concealment.[2]

Not only do his kills as hunter disappear, his luck angers him, transforming him into a white frenzy with nowhere to turn. He admires El Greco, but knows him only through Paravicino. He is painted by Velázquez, and not by El Greco, almost as a favor to Olivares. The

Count-Duke deals with him through the intermediary of the Count of Villamediana, but the Count's turbulent life obliges him to keep a guarded distance. He constructs *La gloria de Niquea*, but in accounts of the celebrations he is hardly named, the Count carrying off the poetic embers and the major prize. Pride tightens his lips and his terrible gaze hardens the basilisk, finding himself obliged to write, when the Count of Villamediana sends him his carriage and furs so he can negotiate a winter in Madrid: "please note that I must eat while letters go back and forth and for fifty days I've had to make do with four hundred reales" ... "and fasting while they all belch from stuffing themselves" ... "I'm tired of tiring and being tired."[3] His imagination requires the display of a particular genealogy and has to be content with a position as archdeacon of Córdoba and being watched to see whether he remains silent as he sits between a deaf person and an indiscreet cantor in the back choir of the cathedral, while the Count of Villamediana, "master of the posts of Aragón," heads the entry of the king and queen into Naples and Sicily. During the decline of Felipe III, he remains like a flash of resentment, like the mordant determination of a punishment never applied.[4]

Góngora is the proclaimer of glory. Urged on by the passage of time at every instant, his cry awakens us to contemplation, and Góngora appears as a somber Tobias holding in his hands glorious bodies so the light will define them for our eyes.[5] Proclaimer and relator of glory, he lifts up in his hands forms of splendor so that God

and his creatures will find them and contemplate them
again. He proclaims them so they will be contemplated
in the light, the branches with rabbits hanging on them,
the pines with the bear's head, the subtleties in the variations of fish, and then he relates the time of their permanence in splendor. Succentor seated close to the beam of
light falling through the stained glass window, he intones
before God the concentrated glory of the relator. In the
midst of that banquet formed by the succession of cries
and relations, he appears with the swiftness of an antelope in its awareness of being pursued, for he knows that
those bodies completed by the light will have to be lifted
up as an offering.

Góngora's light is a lifting up of objects and a time
in which their incitement is seized. In that sense we may
speak of the Gothic quality of his light as it lifts up. A
light that absorbs the object and then produces an irradiation. A light that is heard, appearing in company with
angels, a light accompanied by their transparence and the
transparent songs made by their wings rubbing together.
Objects in Góngora are lifted up in proportion to the light
of seizure they receive. It's just that that light and lifting
up are subjected to Renaissance vicissitudes. The frenzy
and elevation of that metaphorical beam are driven by a
Gothic impulse and then subdued by a recognition according to Greco-Roman fables and usages. Leonardo's
light, in its most typical Renaissance aspect, must be
valued not as a body and a creature, but as a question
addressed to the distance, to the landscape. "Make the

shadow with your finger on the illuminated part," Leonardo recommends.[6] From the rebirth or decline of the light in the distance, deceive and conceal oneself in the depths that that light crosses in order to keep it in relation to the matter one wants to darken with shadows. Here now the light liberated from that voraciousness and rage for lifting up objects is followed by the finger in the mutations of a flame.

Approaches to don Luis have always been after the manner of sages of Zalamea.[7] They aim to oppose critical suspicion to his successions of words and cosmetic seriousness to his sly tricks. They aim to read him critically and miss his wild stampedes, his whirls and his parades. Deciphered or blinding in their zenithal evidence, his smiling hyperboles possess the joy of poetry as a secret gloss on the seven languages in the prism of a visionary glimpse. For the first time among us poetry has been transformed into the seven languages that intone and proclaim, constituting themselves as a different and reorganized organ. But that robust intonation within the light, shaped with words as much deciphered as unintelligible, and which impress us as the simultaneous translation of various unknown languages, evinces that sententious and solemn burst of laughter that clarifies and surrounds everything, since it shapes a greater amount of breath, of current penetrating into that newly invented meaning. When Góngora says:

Ministro, no grifaño, duro sí,

que en Líparis Stéropes forjó,
piedra digo bezahar de otro Pirú,

las ojas infamó de un alhelí,
y los Acroceraunios montes no;
Oh Júpiter, oh, tú, mil veces tú.[8]

the oracular source of poetry doesn't keep it from being revealed by a minstrel. An unusual visit to a castle becomes reversible when the undeciphered visitors display an unusual communicativeness in the minstrel's presence, he who is going to display, as he displays himself, that he is a mystery that has been provoked: that he has arrived as mysteriously as the pilgrims. That's why there was such a thing as *trobar clus*,[9] a hermetic or esoteric minstrel. All those who cling to the calm infancy of a poetic scission must find the presence of this hermetic minstrel as irritating as the discharge of an urticant vesicle, this minstrel who follows the customs of Delphos, neither saying nor concealing, but instead making signs.[10] Those ejaculatory prayers and signs, that manner of showing himself as entertainingly mysterious so that the pilgrim may momentarily take possession or penetrate, those devices thrown forth by either the intoning or the hermetic minstrel, must lurk in all poetry. In Góngora, that hermetic minstrel-like basis has a vast hidden tradition, it's just that sometimes the lightning bolt hurled like a comet by the minstrel is devoured in its own parabola, without reaching that obscure oracular body, since the signs of the lord of Delphos emerge on a nocturnal blackboard that busily tends to erase them.

Góngora conceals his counter meaning, evaporates it so radically, that he adheres to the singular meaning. The flow of becoming, as it passes over the surface of his verses, neither enriches nor punishes them with the variants that each historical period may provide. Neither the excess of suggestion nor the mutations of epochs manage to split apart the crystal flash of their origin. He becomes distant, it's into that singular meaning that he survives, that he submerges. His light, which is not even light but rather luminosity, which is a faculty or a derivative in nature, strikes its other side; the numerous quantity seeks to show forth, gathering at the surface, where it establishes its evidence. (In this Renaissance baroque, the compass needle disappears and a thousand windows are ajar.) Those who despaired because his carbuncle beast wasn't to be found in Pliny the Younger, will have to recognize that that animal, a friend of darkness invented by Góngora, shows its carbuncle aspect on the other face of the substituted metaphor or gesture.[11] Adjustment of meaning in its unity, gaudily colored diversity that gathers with no loss at the surface, and that carbuncle beast that gathers on the face of every metaphor to produce the sparking arc that will join it to the greater luminosity of the offering. Sacrifice after sacrifice, in which the carbuncle's head delivers its quick and total stroke in the side.[12] That stroke of light is the one that obliges us to turn our face, and then we are the ones who in confusion

225

believe in adding a centipede of interpretation. On the contrary, that stroke of light delivers the singular meaning, the plenitude to spear momentarily a single prey of taste or invisibly unhook a fish, and our confusion, now turned into an enigma, is as great as before.

We realize that he demands of us that tension in the presence of the luminous harshness of his poetry's meaning, which no longer spares us. Making us forget that our enduring position with regard to that meaning should not be a violent occupation of it, but rather a steady gaze into its face.

He has created in poetry what we might call the time of objects or beings in the light. His New World turkey or his viscous eel, wrapped and sustained in an allusive quickness of mythology, don't want to impose upon us their exoteric nature or the proportional rank they hold in succession. Before they are offered up, they receive their time in the light; the duration and resistance of the light while it surrounds and defines a body.

Góngora, without intending it, prepares the splendor of meaning, the annunciation of what now has to be sacrificed. The fixity or time that objects resist under the light. One of his marvels and of the marvels of his time consists in the fact that near him there is someone who destroys meaning. He is proud of his scaly skin under the light, but very close to him is the humble one who personifies no meaning. The light glitters upon the Cordovan's skin but, after the offering, all that remains are what San Juan de la Cruz calls "little children's exercises."[13] Meaning gathers under the principal light, bathes in the delight of its time of luminosity, but then devours itself and fades. Peerless mark of appetite in the light, but, very close to him, San Juan warns us: "for if it is spirit, it has no more to do with sense; and if sense can comprehend it, it is no longer pure spirit."[14]

Góngora seeks the singular meaning no matter how hard the light it maintains, but is poetry a meaning that dissolves or is it a breath that extends and occupies, not in the space of meaning, but rather in a hardened, resistant movement, as an entity of temporality, with a body to occupy that breath?

The circumstance of the Counter Reformation makes of Góngora's work a Counter Renaissance. It removes the landscape whose center his luminosity might occupy. The Jesuit baroque, cold and ethical, willful and entwiningly ornamental, emerges and spreads in the decadence of its poetic word, but it had already surrounded him with a cold circle and a landscape in plaster, opposing cardboard hands to his lances. His hunts filigreed by the half moon of the target,[15] fade before the lack of meaning and the distancing breath of San Juan de la Cruz's imaginary discourse. And so, his luminosity broken, converted into offering, he furthermore has to contemplate how the Counter Reformation, if earlier it was already chilling his zenithal light and glory, is going to put curtains around his landscapes. His exercises with an incessant flowering of the senses, the banquet where the light presents the fish and the turkeys, the metamor-

phoses of the trees and the teeth of the boar, have, beside him, the apparent accompaniment of "and the other
things on the face of the earth are created for man that
they may help him in prosecuting [the end for which he
is created]."[16] And so, that luminosity has to remain silent in the presence of divine sacrifice.

The mountains of Córdoba do not limit his flash.
The dryness or deficiency of their landscape lead him
always to place on a hill the goat Amaltheia,[17] whose
horns, by Jupiter's willful design, proliferate in ceaseless flowers and fruits, and her phosphoric bristles feel
the stars ascend until they are dissolved into the zodiac.
A goat held captive between ocean waves and wind, she
halts in order wisely to reconnoiter a certain distance and
mark the places for trees and satyrs.

In the *Soledades*, in the jubilance of syrinxes and
hornpipes, the goat Amaltheia can always be seen ascending, as the sign of an unattainable height of wisdom,
in order to preside over the procession, above the hidden
pilgrim or the old leader of the fishermen.[18] Her wisdom,
which has received from Jupiter the gifts of ceaseless
creation, releases from her horns a surrounding space or
receptive concavity for the light.

But the goat, Jupiter's nurse, unbraids such a multi-
ple and bewildering number of fish, gerfalcons and constellations that the landscape is halted by the narrowness
of its own mountains' terror, or by the disproportion between the opulence and the insufficient hands and trays.

In this way two animals useful to him are singled

out: the carbuncle beast and the goat. By means of the carbuncle beast, which very soon becomes for him an organ, he discovers and befriends and bestows the time of luminosity corresponding to them. The goat ascends, seems to become metamorphosed and wield an enormous staff; also turned into an organ, the goat directs the festivities, preventing confusion and drowsiness.

But at times the carbuncle extracts things in order to touch or appropriate them, and the surroundings then are transformed and shrunken as within a flask. The goat enlarges her horns to such a degree in her ceaseless bestowal that everything around her is compressed so as to prevent an overflowing. Góngora has to change his setting, as the carbuncle drowses; the goat fixes upon her horns the announcement of the setting and then raises the curtains upon the Nile.[19] His metamorphoses had remained within allusions to Greco-Roman fables. After the wedding, after the awakened procession of colors participating in the music of the seashell, the Cordovan feels an inopportune and overwhelming need: to extend the confines of the landscape. To lead his flocks of carbuncles and goats to pasture in other surroundings. From the possible mountains of Córdoba the scene is to be transported to the Nile. The trees, hung with arrows and bears' heads, hiding places for the pilgrim, disappear and give way to a new background (whose setting, unfortunately, is the Nile and not the discontinuous forests of America):

Pobre entonces y estéril, si perdida,
la mejor tierra que Pisuerga baña;
la corte les infunde, que del Nilo
siguió inundante el fluctuoso estilo.[20]

An opulent mountain wedding turns into an Egyptian wrestling match (in order to avoid the vulgarity of a Roman match, don Luis prefers to transfer his setting to the Nile, instead of displaying it gaudily on atlases of sargasso). Previously he had the goat's horn in order to speak of fruit and fish, of somniferous metamorphoses, but now he needs the portrayal of the body in the wrestling match. The goatherds leap from the mountains of Córdoba to the banks of the Nile. The new Egyptian Hercules finds it difficult to award the prizes. The new procession requires that they all besmear and mask themselves; the mountain women have turned into nymphs and the goatherds into satyrs. And from that whole play and struggle of clouds and foam, what is released is like a transparent weight of feathers. Feathers of dense sleep that fly quickly from the peacock into sleep, wandering through the air of their absolute zenithal transparence, with no weight to contradict them nor gravitation to submerge them into the earthly ocean.

Amid the stern browed goat, the metamorphoses of the goatherd, the nymphs of charcoal[21] and the trees, the way is prepared by an initial allusion to the American turkey, to be sure as if desiring it and embellishing it, "since when angry it changes the nacre of its face into a pouch," in order to begin the banquet.[22] There, in the discourse of the imagination, the banquet doesn't appear as a sculpture but rather in order to favor the procession. The banquet is like the center from which to contemplate the procession, the sequence. The somniferous vapors, spreading over the countryside, reach the mountain women and the goatherds, who, upon awakening, stretch their limbs within the same landscape. The turkey from America has served only for the beginning of the banquet.

That feast is interwoven with the descents of sleep. But dense sleep and an *amateur* of scholasticism form, in Sor Juana's *Primero sueño*, a landscape.[23] In Góngora, however, the landscape is an amazement suspended between a prior situation and a surprise that has just arrived. The hidden pilgrim appears after sleep has fallen over the mountain women and the feast. Sleep comes to obliterate the pursuit and insistence of the feast, preparing, by a decrease in ardor of what had previously been contemplated, the arrival of the pilgrim, in other words, someone whose identity is unknown. A fear that the presence and movement of the pilgrim will diminish if he penetrates into the identical landscape. In Sor Juana dream is an identical nature, a homogeneous night, with no acuity for any penetration or demoniacal gravitation, and it does not bring forth for us any new forms or trees. *Cuerpo finge formado—de todas dimensiones adornado—cuando aun ser superficie no merece.*[24] It is not born of the Leonardesque shadow on the wall[25] of the evaporations of her dream, which might awaken a new and penetrating friendship in the landscape. With Góngora's arrows diminished in her hands, the flow of her dream nature does not return as the fixity of a landscape reencountered.

In Góngora there are frequent allusions to the compass, "the compass of sleep,"[26] and to numerous limits, thus the old mountain man is disturbed because during the wedding more than five candles have been lit, which is the number specified for nuptials.[27] With the compass now lost, there is a descent into sleep, into the night or the underworld. Then Ascalaphus emerges, the tattletale with topaz eyes.[28] He who prevents Proserpina from returning to the light, who tells Jupiter that Proserpina now contains in her body food from the underworld. But always in his descent, not descending like the night upon the body or the trees, his eyes get ahead of him, Ascalaphus's eyes of topaz, because this descent, like water seeping down to the center of the earth, has to prepare Pluto's copulation with Proserpina.

From that sleep Góngora sends not only the topaz eyes of Ascalaphus the tattletale, but also the deadly lightning bolts of birds of falconry. From those moderate, slow and penetrating descents, such birds leap forth. Lightning bolts that from their darkness plunge down as zenithal points in motion. Let's fix upon the osprey, an American bird of falconry, which makes don Luis suspicious, "fraude vulgar, no industria generosa, / del águila les dio a la mariposa."[29] How can he accuse the American osprey of contradictory faults, such as that of not having been studied, not being tempered, in its transmutational point of fire, and, at the same time, of exhibiting deceit? America, then, is a nature that has fallen into original sin, into a paradoxical unresolvable illness between nature and spirit.[30] The osprey hunts with hunters who use nets, in which it brings down indiscriminately the eagle and the butterfly, but who should be disturbed by those exercises of hand and sight, by that indistinction of sleep and original night, by that spirit which has not yet attained absolute consciousness of the forest?

At times Góngora's treatment of verse recalls the practices and rules for handling birds of falconry. The heads of such birds are covered with hoods that create for their senses a false night. Once released from their artificial nocturnal coverings, they still retain the memory of their adjustment to night vision, so as to see in the distance the incitement of a crane or partridge. Their lightning bolt of seizure surges from the night, but then, once overcome by the light, the incitement disappears into its voracious whiteness. The luminosity is released from the verse onto a surface or shield, the ray of light on arriving there is refracted and sparkles, in that momentary incandescence acquired by the object, that singular meaning of which we were speaking is captured. But, since those objects are not extracted from their night or sleep, the succession of those luminous points, uninterrupted and cruel, is refracted without contrast and thus blinded. As in the Greek myth, in order to descend to the depths, it was necessary to do so clad in black wool and remain there three times nine days. Góngora, on the contrary, attempts to descend armed with his ray, frightening the nocturnal dampness with the lightning bolts of his lances of falconry.

We were speaking of that scandal of the light, recalling one of the birds of falconry, the gerfalcon, called by don Luis "escándalo bizarro / del aire,"[31] and also later by Calderón, and we did so to differentiate Gongóra's concentrated and incandescent baroque from Calderón's curved, relaxed and languidly successive one in which the discharge of a pistol also produces a "gran escándalo del aire."[32] "Estimar los contrabajos / de todos tus contratiempos"[33] say Calderón's verses. What a distance between the Cordovan's arrogant ray which releases the lightning of its seizure, tragically seeking the coincidence of the time of objects in the light, and that Calderonian facileness which releases a damp and deadly ray as if to move forward in a bog of stagnant water!

Góngora is not touched by the poetic sensualization of late scholasticism, which appears in the joyful didacticism of Maurice Scève, or in that breath of an older poetic subtlety, in which the linkage of stanzas reminds one of the design of a poetic syllogism, as in Jean de Sponde or in John Donne. "This bed thy centre is, these walls thy sphere," a verse by Donne[34] that glides in a delight that spins out the verse like a voluptuous occupation of thinking substance, and not of a sensation that penetrates, extracts and then slowly reviews and redis-

covers it. Góngora experiences more a baroque that remains like the incandescent ash of the Gothic, than that
moribund Calderonian spark, vulgarization of grace,
diminution of the grandeur of the Tridentine mysteries or of the conception, diminished valorization of the
Tridentine justification. Luminosity without contrast or
surge appears as touched by a world in which medieval
syllogisms may crystallize or sparkle, in which professors feel something like the feast, animation and swirl of
their programs of Aristotelian *prima philosophia*, in the
sense that a contemporary feels that certain stanzas of
"Le Cimetière marin" are the sensualization and opera
of Victor Brochard's studies on the Eleatic paradoxes.[35]
As an epigraph for one of his books, Paul Valéry incor-
rectly cites a verse from Góngora; his error is important
for the interpretation of our claims.[36] "On crystal rocks,"
Valéry quotes, "brief serpent." His preferences lead him
to think that those serpents must advance by forming and
destroying their letters upon a fixed contrasting material.
He seeks a background of immobility, "crystal rocks,"
where those serpents' dark games may advance. This is
the first verse of "La toma de Larache," "in crystal coils
brief serpent." The difference between this verse and the
quotation indicates the desire, the prior vision that destroys the reality of the verse. Valéry sought a material
to support the emergence of those serpents along clear
rocks, turning the serpents into the sparkles of a diaman-
tine material. In Góngora it's a question of an impulse,
of a constant allusion to a movement that is integrated

metallically, of a metaphor that advances like a hunt and then self-destructs in the light of a relief more than that of a meaning. The impression we receive from the word "roca" continues and fuses with that of the serpents, as the crystal is being reduced to a brief sequence. The incessant nature of light in don Luis doesn't seek dark areas in which to sparkle, it unfolds in an extension where the sparkling and the lights slowly open the succession of their flashes, their lanterns in the excessive extension of a darkness that begins by causing the object targeted, the impulse of falconry's lightning bolt, to disappear.

The luminosity of his poetic knowledge becomes equidistant, hovering on the balancing point of a total isolation from any landscape. His ray will not leap over the ruins of scholasticism or over those of the knowledge of the supreme essence, of the *esse substantialis*, nor will it leap into a penetration of the city of God or into an unknown land. He had taken principally from the Arabs that secret desire in their poetry to move a spice, a living irradiation, over to another element of structure, in order to sensualize the verse, turning it into a corpuscle. "Beauty shines in the ray from his forehead / and from it comes a waft of musk and camphor," says an Arab poet.[37] A stanza which releases the union of the ray with the breeze, one of the reveries of that caliphate.

But the Roman tradition in its glow of decadence, his ardent and irritated solitude, his haughtiness that seeks and disdains, and the operative magic or condensation of the Caliphate will create in him a deep consciousness of how to seize the poetic impulse. His inner substance, more disposed by a glimpse of that impulse than by an accumulation of will, releases the unconscious overcoming of the distance that poetry covers when in a parabola it hurls itself upon the silences of the partridge or the enigmas of the fish.

In the *Soledad primera*, desires also for new dwelling places spring forth in a quadruple refrain. "¡Oh bienaventurado / albergue a cualquier hora!"[38] is repeated like a hammering cuckoo, glimpsing behind his fabled Greco-Latin desires a few threads of superior union. After the coronation of Vulcan, the flirtatious whistles, the symbol of the shepherd's staff, the sun's rays in the foam of wax, he starts to manifest his hunger for new shelters and ascents.[39] Fatigued at times by that ray, gruff transfer of the air's phosphorus, he no longer seeks momentary decipherments but now ciphers of sustained shelter and unitive state. Why does he have to come and be frayed into that fragment of metaphor, of glimpse and of sound accompanying a body in its parabola?

At each new metamorphosis it seems as if the pilgrim, with his fixed measured steps and his errant sound, were completely concealing himself behind a tree. If he takes a few steps, a transitional shower encloses him like a permanent state: it spreads its hypnotic and odoriferous spices over the battalion of mountain women and goatherds: it again places the hollow tree as a vantage point for him to hide inside of and indicate the intersections of sleep amid the figures and songs, intonings of the Lilybaeum experiencing its transports to Cambay.[40] Always a hiding place and a brief pre-established distance, troubled by the lance stroke, by the calculated curve of the ray of seizure. What was lacking here that was being dissolved? What was he concealing as he ran from tree to tree? Everything has required its pin of attachment. After establishing, by a reading of the moon's subtleties on liquids, the best moment to catch the variations of fish, the old man sends his two sons out to fish.[41] If everything was pre-established and well marked for success, what impediment was there for penetrating into the city, surrounded in advance as it was by a hundred bonfires of metaphors, before a hundred gates of incessant metamorphosis?

What that penetration by luminosity lacked was San Juan's dark night, since that ray of poetic knowledge without an accompanying dark night could only display a lightning bolt of falconry upon a plaster cast. Perhaps no nation has ever had its poetry posited in such a concentrated way as at that Spanish moment when Góngora's metaphorical ray, evidencing its painful incompletion, needs and calls out for that amicably enveloping dark night. His incapacity for that other landscape covered by sleep which the discontinuous forests of America had come to occupy; for the integration of the new waters extending far beyond the Greco-Latin metamorphoses of rivers and trees, joined to that absence of dark night, that damp shell denied to the Gongorine ray—all this drove don Luis in his irritation and resentment over the mountains of Córdoba. What an impossible image if, on some night of friendly Cordovan solitudes, don Luis had been invited to dismount his decoratively harnessed mule by the delicate hand of San Juan!

The mystics also did what we might call the vigil of their arms, but as was necessary for the *via unitiva*. Thus the metal of the arms did not become pure by virtue of its own pride, but rather by reason of that higher unity, of superior scope... "[because] in order to attain the said union to which this dark night is disposing and leading, the soul must be filled and endowed with a certain glorious magnificence in its communion with God."[42] Then the metal, as it becomes more constricted, will undergo the fine concentration of the energy which is set aside and abjured until the thread of supreme luminosity is attained, "...the spirit must be constricted and inured to hardships as regards its common and natural experience...."[43] In that constriction of luminosity, with the singular meaning set aside and the penetration of the spirit like a lynx in its consciousness of being pursued, a poetry of God-given unity returns to its culminating point of delight in wonder, in a new birth of seeing and hearing... "and it goes about marveling at the things that it sees and hears, which seem to it very strange and rare, though they are the same that it was accustomed to experience aforetime...."[44] That threaded sense made evident by its time of luminosity undergoes at night *the inflammation of its appetite*.[45] A new sense seems to require the gravity of a new flavor. But before they reach the point of testing that flavor, leaves, which here serve as an example of porous appetite calmed by the subtlety of dew, have to become dilated and distended for penetration. This is the *sentire cum plantibus*, which indicates the greatest amount of night that silently plunges down into us. In the ecstasy of Bernini's Saint Teresa, the greater loosening of the folds doesn't succeed in concealing the inflammation of appetite. Supported by that inflammation, prepared by the health that channels them toward the naturalness of appetite, the inflamed senses also begin to make customary what otherwise would be the astonishment of a destructive surprise. The dark night bestows upon us a certainty of meaning and not a summation of ineffable culminations. Night-wandering certainty that prefers to go secretly, on secret stairs (…"Thou shalt hide them in the hiding-place of Thy face from the disturbance of men; thou shalt protect them in Thy tabernacle from the contradiction of tongues…").[46] Because the night which falls upon us with its homogeneous tegument commands a decisively individual excavation, a rescue that each of us must understand, arriving on stairs of personal and intransferable measurement. In this way the night contradicts and unsettles us, because an ocean appears between the particular nature of each sleep, between the momentary glimpses gathered by the new night-wandering senses.

Concealed, its nature goes out unnoticed, with an indication now of disguise and second composure. A going out to the metals and to vegetative distention, smeared

with a lunar mask. But that very distention seems to prepare a new disguise, which now in the voracity of the
inflammation of night-wandering senses begins its combination and play of numbers. As it goes out in disguise
one might say it fears the consciousness of its pursuit,
like an antelope casting a backward glance at its own
traces and stages. It appears unnoticed, but its fear of the
fracture of recognition leads it to wear masks. In place
of those aqueous metamorphoses of Góngora's, of his
plain of somniferous goatherds or the precise measures
of the hidden pilgrim's rhythms, San Juan provides a
new disguise with which to leap through the night and
innermost substances: tunic, green shield and red coat.
In the play of those colors, figure is transfigured, form
is transformed, for it seems that with that nocturnal disguise, the distention of sense seeks the transfiguration of
metaphor in imaginary discourse, in an incessant transmutation of images. The scandal of the air, produced by
don Luis's luminous objects, angrily releases the bird of
falconry upon the very parabola of its own identification,
while the disguise provided by San Juan[47] fills the senses
with nocturnal towns and squares. We discern the tunic's
penetration into the red coat, brightened by the eyes of
the dew; the transfiguration begins when the penetration
disappears under cover of the green shield. Then the majordomo in his red coat, fencing with the green shield, as
in a Viennese Enlightenment ballet, disappears, dazzled
by the tunic. The tunic can produce the twists and turns
of the green shield, when the majordomo in his red coat

blows out the candelabra and hides. A graceful disguise of San Juan's, which comes to establish the midnight choreography and leave the Gongorine ray within its singular meaning, with no landscape in dark night or hiding place for preparatory darkness.

All life in the realm of poetry *in extremis* provides the configuration of a paradoxical, hyperbolic life of salvation in that realm. Thus don Luis, static, idle, indolent, distant and liturgical, was the creator of a life of appetite or impulse for metamorphosis. To acquire that form one had to live apart from all quests, adventures or configured instants, in other words, statically. Destiny here prepares a person's own development, seeks the subject of growth expandable in the sense of an innate metaphysics of space. "In sleep the soul has the eyes of a lynx," "all those who sleep are co-workers," sayings from a culture in which leisure and the manner of wearing one's cloak distinguished the man of wisdom. Actually, the idle man is always busy. Indolence is an entry into a culture of refined animal grazing. Visible in sacred animals or in those that display an ancestral return, those of large size. All bulls have wings, all lynxes are fat, all eagles have two heads. Culture or, if you wish, this dimension of poeticizable poetry, leads to innocence, according to the Arcadian idealism of Nordic criticism, as much as or more than what is primordial or savage. If poetry leads us to innocence—according to German ideologists of rupture, so distant from the Greek tradition of the *daimon* as true opinion between good and evil—and only in this innocence do we find a liberation from work as a vulgar form of homogeneous transport, it is precisely in poetry where leisure shows itself most concurrent within the diversity of the simultaneous. A European who exacerbated that great tradition could write: *I shall wind up on the sands like the Rhine.*[48] A tradition that is no longer there, that cannot be touched, that cannot be visualized as writing, since all the great poets of our time, from Paul Valéry to Antonin Artaud, seem to have attained the most acute and sacred forms of animal magnetism, which has to attain a pause and reduction in its vision, and becomes liturgical.

To that appetite for metamorphosis San Juan adds what has been called the affirmation of the nocturnal world,[49] or, if you wish, the yes of no. San Juan prepares that going out unnoticed, when the dark night surrounds that mount of approval until it reaches the ocean as *res extensa* or the waterfall as incessant flow. This is, as it has been called, the yes of no. An absence of total Neptunian occupation, which is fulfilled as a presence before the supreme form. A no of withdrawal and aqueous simplicity which ends as a gently placental occupation of the yes. Those two great styles of life or, if you wish to put it in a more dangerous manner, of unpoeticizable poetry, have prevented the existence in Spain of great poetry. When Spain abandoned its theocratic world or, to put it differently, when the *criollo* of America was the only surviving Spaniard, though with a hobbled laxity in his shaky legs, and in the Spaniard all connection was lost between his life and a clear mysterious sense of life, and he began to live in tragic frivolity, losing the sense of great poetry, and perhaps forever within the crepuscular perspective of the time, since one cannot predict a deposing of the old gods or an emergence of new ones—in opposing by his senselessness a theocratic life; with a dualism becoming evident, to be sure in one of the most grandiose forms attained by Western culture, between the Gongorine ray of reencounter and recognition and the blessed placental waters of San Juan. Whenever that dualism is overcome and there is again a submersion in that sparkling God-given infusion, in which one's own sense of life takes on a more sacramental form, a mystery known by touching man's flesh, poetic necessity will again appear as a nourishment that goes beyond voracity for knowledge and gratuitousness in the body.

We must find in Spanish poetry a tradition of aqueous, Neptunian metamorphoses. The nymphs in Garcilaso play in the aquarium at the tops of the trees or cover themselves with the foam of the shores. "Todas juntas se arrojan por el vado," a verse by Garcilaso, brief frolic in well defined foam.[50] The Renaissance establishes an equivalence between the Plutonian and the Neptunian dimensions. The Greeks projected their unlimitedness-limitedness toward the center of the earth (descents, food of the underworld, cries of the dead in their longing to escape through a crevice that the Greeks in their fear covered with a stone, Erinnyes, "hermanas negras mal peinadas").[51] The center of the earth was the underworld,

the unlimited realm, and one's eyes traced a naive separation of heaven. In the Renaissance, in order to overcome the metamorphosis of nymph into tree, of tree into
stream, there is an equivalence between water and earth
and, ultimately, a new dimension in the predominance
of the Neptunian. For the ancients, seeping water would
reach the center of the earth, for which reason they considered the ocean a "sterile plain."[52] The ocean in the
Renaissance leads us to the incunabula, to the *inconnu*.
The survival of baroque Spanish poetry will consist in
the ever contemporary possibilities of Góngora's metaphorical ray enclosed within San Juan's dark night. The
Spanish baroque opened up the unknown of those aqueous metamorphoses, beyond the curtains of sleep or rain
used by Greek mutations.

In the extension or risk of those transmutations
we can pinpoint the moments at which those aqueous
metamorphoses are either approached or forgotten. The
first vision, "y ésta la fuente hermosa y cristal frío," in
don Luis Carrillo,[53] stays close to a fountain in a Roman plaza or to an Arab spout. The rising water like the
backbone of a *manjuarí* structures and convokes in that
form the deities and finally makes them cling to its vertical fatality.[54] Dying in that prison, where isolation is
imposed by a single line of water, cuts off the possibility
of a new submersion in order to attain another form. But
in the *Polifemo*, the feet of the trees pass into the veins,
according to the final stanza.[55] Here the metamorphoses
of the deities are as operative and ready as the metaphors

245

themselves. "A Doris llega que, con llanto pío, / yerno lo saludó, lo aclamó río."[56] The God that arrives can be greeted equally well as a relative and as a river. Here we find the culmination of that Neptunian baroque, typical of the Renaissance. A bit later the first metamorphosis stops at its own limit. The youthful Mnemosyne for returning the deity to its initial figure or to what it follows is erased. Already in Pedro Espinosa, "porque la ninfa, viendo el caso feo, / y su virginidad así oprimida, / quedó, llorando, en agua convertida."[57] The conversion is abrupt and radical, like an imposed causality; the nymph, doubtless confronted with a youthful vegetative awakening, decides to show herself as a reflection, thus destroying herself in order to evade.

The feather that in the *Soledad primera* receded in the pride of its levitation remains in the rest of the poem as the theme of the feather fish, the feather submerged in a hostile element. Those who linger over the mistakes concerning animals the Cordovan liked to allude to and who detach them from poetic needs and requirements, thinking he took them from Pliny the Younger, such as when he speaks of the scales of seals, forget that he included these for the submerged metallic reflections and transitions he needed.[58] Because if a seal doesn't sparkle, it gleams, protects itself in a flurry of scales. How could he seat himself in another circus of metaphor? Because the reflections he needed couldn't be slight sensations fitted inside one another, but rather the derivations or turnings of a body or shape we touch in that momentary dialogue of luminosity.

In order to leap over and fulfill that Neptunian test, Góngora will save in his Ark of Commandments his symbols and preferred animals to touch and caress: the horns of the murex, the half moon, the sunbeams in Taurus, the competition between Pallas and Arachne.[59] But even on those high palisades where the laws of the ray of his metaphor preferred to blind themselves to the *thanatos* of their sparkle; where his metamorphoses of goatherds have been limited to the Orphic ritual of the opium poppy, without their dreams ever extending over the discontinuous forests of America, or their marine mutations going *au-delà de* the Nereus of the Odyssey.[60] But, alas, even though Pallas claims to be the daughter of the warlike Anchialus, "lord of the Taphian men who love their oars," her decisions were between Temese and Rithron, and the sea of Góngora's nymphs never went beyond columns and sargassos.[61] After that Renaissance growth of the aqueous, the objects and animals kept by Góngora in his ark return to savor sparkling effects, to make hard mouths with carbuncles and pincers from the curls of wrought-iron gates. All houses in Córdoba have a vat of lime that old women keep in order to paint over any graffiti on their walls. At noon in Córdoba, houses gleam like the cloaks of Arab cavalry. Thus objects saved by Góngora, which had been momentarily blinded by the ark's vinous dampness, receive a lance thrust of pious light, need that thread that the zenithal ray exudes to justify the pride of its offering.

Liberated from the nocturnal growth and surfeit of the waters, those objects that were saved return to their irresolution, since what remained had recovered new amplitude for being intoned, taking on with its symbols an efficacy of reference. Pomegranates, wreaths, tendrils, flames, hands, voice, cellar, had become keys and ciphers for decoding poetic unanimity. The goatherds fled before the learned apparition of the goat of Amaltheia, since, even emerging on the hills after the mutations worked in them by sleep, they sensed her as a hostile vigilant deity, indifferent and irreconcilable. Now the pomegranate lights up with its innumerable secret corpuscles, the instant of its vehemence doesn't corrupt the growth of its fragmented temperaments, it culminates in a flame that takes a fruit-like form, traces the mansions of the instant, which it perceives as ample and extensive. Wreaths and tendrils trace and conceal the acute refinement of the branches for the maiden who is preparing herself in the feast of consecration. Refinement of the branches that envelop the woman like a tree and give her a vegetative flesh with its language of desirous evaporation. Flames that also propagate their language and a center for conversation, since they are like the first gateway to a protection invented by man. Hands that come forward to see, groping vision that slowly reconstructs the statue, when vision recoils in the face of the diverse proliferation of threads. Voice that marks the breath, shaping itself in meaning and dissolving itself in extension. And the fragment of chosen enclosure: the cellar.

There one descends to find the darkness that surrounds and preserves. It's the zone where the poetic ray is perceived as hostile and dispersive. One descends to equate the seasons with the essences of must. Going down into the cellar is as much of a test as descending to Hades. One seeks in the darkness as it were workers for subterranean labors. There in the cellar is the feast and descent into substances that have fled the light, the preparation for the *via unitiva*.

In the *Soledad primera* there is the zenithal evidence, the heliotropic test, objects burn and are reconstituted; in the *Soledad segunda*, objects tend to dissolve, since the Icarian wind fades and refracts.[62] The arrival of the pilgrim, to the astonishment of the mountain men and women, is accompanied by an allusion to the metamorphosis of Clytie into a heliotrope. In this way a circumscribed field of poetic bipolarity is created between the heliotrope, viceroy of Helios, and the lodestone, subordinate in the service of the polestar.[63] After the pilgrim has slept, when the wind has swept away the numbers and rhythms of his feet, Góngora alludes to the lodestone. His poetry acquires its field of bipolarity and refraction, between the heliotrope, its blinding clarity, and the lodestone, which gathers the swirl toward one direction, the polestar. His objects, cordages and manes of hair, his fish and birds of falconry, seem to attain the sum of their index of refraction, since the zenithal ray of his metaphor tends to be refracted on that heliotropic shield. His harrier or his eel, presented in direct light, attain their maximum of luminosity and then in memory seem sustained by that heliotropic support. After that extreme of luminosity, Góngora's objects seem to be swept away by a throng of hunters, by the sudden agglomerations of a magnet. The goatherd appears on the hill, highlighted in relief by that heliotropic test, receiving the arrival of the throng of hunters, who like magnets have been gathering the most detached and haughty levitations. The warrior shepherd's torso stands erect,[64] like a coinciding of the astonishment of luminosity with the pull of the magnets, of the diversities set in motion in order to lead the swirl to the impulse of the hunt, the throng to a stern browed ongoing procession.

In that bipolarity between heliotrope and magnet, don Luis creates and clarifies in our language a meridional cunning in a vision reduced to what is seen. If he specifies a tree (a tree that releases a woman like a chip from its bark) he then lets loose the incessant rabbits, the bees.[65] He compresses, like the squeaking strings of a musical instrument, those rabbits and those bees between the tree of metamorphosis and the learned goat Amaltheia. In that circumscribed poetic field, intensified by the lance thrust of zenithal light and by the impulsive agglomerations of the magnet, the contrasts and their circular limitations create, as it were, submerged and projected ciphers of an animistic counterpoint, its luminosity vibrating as if it had been constituted as a corpuscle. He contrasts the tree with the rabbit, the goat with the bee, which come to be situated as points in that poetic field governed by the diffuse light of the poplars, and then the enormous banquet of offerings and the refined counsels of the moon, indicating the best kinds of mesh for nets to catch the cunning mutations of each kind of fish. In the *Soledad primera*, before the maiden gets up to dance, she has been reshaping herself through a succession of maidens, previous figures which prepare for a gracefulness in the time of the dance. The maiden who dances would not begin her sculpture if previously it had not been broken down and reconstructed by the figures of other maidens in procession. The first maiden appears as she looks into the lake, seeks her own image and advances and recedes as in jests at the seashore. Then a maiden with flowers in her hair and, finally, a maiden with black slate between her white fingers. In the shifting outlines of these three maidens, in the irradiation of their reflections, the firm flanks of the girl dancing are formed, an image hardened against time.[66]

Góngora possibly culminates in all Romance languages the triumph of the heliotropic test. His index of luminosity fixes the center penetrated by the metaphorical ray and its time of permanence within the luminous beam. Thanks to that lucifugous time he acquires the singular meaning, the hardening of the poetic logos, by which he offers not a play of interpretive mutations but rather the singular meaning that isn't attained. An anemonic test as opposed to a heliotropic test, in which it is hoped that the breeze welcomed by vegetative flesh will display in its totality an opening for the image. Anemonic test which Góngora's irritated and swift verse doesn't like to endure, since it throws itself upon objects rather than taking refuge in their distention. But neither will it display the cunning of the amellus, that veined aquatic leaf, a favorite of Goethe's, which under the water's surface turns the light projected by the stars into a roof. Its meridional cunning can't attain to that invention commanded by the stars.[67]

A shape governed by a zenithal will seems to accompany that heliotropic test, but if some darkness doesn't enclose it, it is lost due to the homogeneity of the light, to the non-differentiation of the ray operating in the evidence of the light. Under that discharge, the object sulks, seeks shelter and withdraws. That heliotropic test is of a heroic willful order, just as the anemonic test is infused, nocturnal and dependent upon the capricious wanderings of the breeze. Those two tests oblige poetry to live in a vigil of arms and impose a slow distribution of pockets of air through our limbs or through the flesh of plants. The amellic test, a reductio ad absurdum of inverse starry skies, which retards even more Góngora's verse in its fragments, with no insertion possible in an *apeiron*, in a sphere of totality, which releases metaphor as a character in the poem, a fragmentary narrative within a larger narrative.

Toward the Renaissance Neptunian incitement and its nymphs along the shore, Góngora evidences the same hesitation he shows toward the novelty of America, which he sees as akin to the tribe of the Laestrygonian

Antiphates. He considers the men of the incunabula to be the same as senseless devouring Laestrygonians.[68] At moments, the presence of the eleventh book of the *Odyssey* is also perceptible in the *Soledad segunda* of shores and currents. It's the liquid of honey, wine, water and blood of black lamb that trickles down to Hades, in convocation of the dead. That pernicious night seems to be symbolized by Ascalaphus, the owl who flies up to Jupiter's ears and returns. Ascalaphus, melancholy murmuring philosopher, suffers for having precisely pointed out when the moon is in the underworld. Soaked in boiling water from the underworld, he is changed into an accusing and gossiping owl. Letting Jupiter know when Persephone, as in an unhappy marriage, spends half the year in the underworld with Pluto, and the other half, when the moon escapes from the underworld, with her mother Ceres. But Góngora's incitements are halted by the same terrors that Odysseus son of Laertes felt toward the head of Gorgon, the monster vomited up from Hades. His monsters and his descents remain anchored in Greco-Roman imagination. At moments it irritates us that his powerful ray of poetic recognition should be put to use in the familiar home of Laestrygonian monsters. If that ray had destroyed itself upon the new calendars and masks, upon the new vegetative somnolences, Góngora might have overcome that irritable lassitude that seems to encumber the fate and final risk of the *Soledades*. His fierce sense of belonging, which seems to fuse in his verse the hardness of Roman quartz with the magic of the light of Córdoba-Baghdad, is torn and ridden with clashes, is subdivided into the slow metaphorical towers of his harsh nervous ennui, when he has to recognize familiar Laestrygonians. His ray was made for plunging down and taking possession of new monsters. His luminosity, the most concentrated luminous beam that ever operated in any Romance language, falters at the end of its sparkling, because, having been made for new glimpses, it fixes and holds the old masks and the expected second birth after his arboreal metamorphoses.

Great perplexities and a plague of astonishment come together in wanting to cast don Luis, so fond of dancing, into euphemisms or in supposing he creeps along with Renaissance metamorphoses. Hidden behind a tree, the pilgrim follows the course of rounds and returns, their advances and extinctions, remaining in his disguise, since the medieval vulturism of the light prevents the mutations that found refuge in the intervals imposed by the opium poppy. In Nordic countries, imagination traces its Dulle Griet, its Mad Meg, but in Hispanic disguises, those of the Princess Micomicona, Altisidora or Goya's Sardine, it's always an intercommunication between reality and the equally real gravitation of that other nature created by the disguise. Compare Pieter Bruegel's "Fight Between Carnival and Lent" with Goya's "Burial of the Sardine." Whereas in the former imagination creates its new couplings, since in the momentary changes of disguise, the central figure wields a hook to seek *the other*'s partner in unreality, in Goya it seems that the same body inverted—in his unreality they all laugh in mutual wonder—attains by the contortion of the dry grape vine of its entrails another possible and quickly glimpsed figure, which is its disguise, but we never find in Hispanic disguises an imaginative levitation, a breaking away toward another momentary nature. The violence of that Gongorine light avoided the leafy hypnotic intervals favorable to Greco-Latin metamorphoses, since the light, as it voraciously pursued these metamorphoses, avoided the suspensions, withdrawals and reappearances in that foreign land. The carbuncle beast, given prominence by Góngora, and whose place humanists diligently sought in Pliny the Younger without ever finding it, we can locate in medieval symbolism. The carbuncle used in heraldry as a mineral and as a gratuity that tries to begin to break a magic spell, in a slow fear of the adversary, we find in *La Chanson de Roland*, when it speaks of Climorin, "who never was a man of honor" and who, receiving the oath of the traitor Ganelon, kissed him on the mouth and gave him his helmet and his carbuncle.[69] The light, the surfeits of the light and its reflections, in the carbuncle located on the shield conspired so as to penetrate into the other's *entourage* of darkness. It was, then, impossible to find the carbuncle animal in Pliny the Younger, since Góngora saw it as dwelling like a pyrophoric insect on the shield that would unravel the light and devour it.

Today the enigma of don Luis de Góngora has become entirely closed; similar to the enlivening of the valves of certain Chinese gastronomers' moluscs, to the obtaining of colloidal gold or to the theory of Etruscan splendor, it is defined in the distention of vision, but disappears if an attempt is made to situate it within the optic field of poetry. The relationship between our solicitations and its offerings settles into a darkly ironic relationship, since, like de Quincey's Malaysian cook, it appears in a storm, at the kitchen door, speaking classical Greek, normalizing the implausible, since the person hearing him was a Hellenist.[70] The key to many of his verses has for us turned into a *badinage*, like the discovery of a new vertebra by Johann Wolfgang Goethe or Marat's electric frog. The vicissitudes of the spirit of corn as it changes into one of its roosters are unknown to us, but we are glad when we find that certain Nordic tribes called fire a red rooster. His writing and his singular meaning have for us turned into a sign, closer to lived experience than to his hermeneutics, and in the face of that incessant fear we prefer to rest in the lukewarm quality of his non-existent euphemism and suppose that it's found among the banal and Renaissance-like reappearances of gay science. On a Persian tapestry, a lion roars at a crayfish shielded by the watery surface of an artificial pond. What is our reading of that paradoxical combination? Do we perhaps think about how the lion would shiver if his whiskers were to touch that surface? Our reading is ironic and of an invasive sensorial delight, in the face of that combination, whose expression must originally have been perceived as symbolic and theocentric, and which comes to demonstrate to us the relativism or pessimism of any reading of a cultural cycle. And it is acute and heartrending that that impossible reading should begin with poetry.

Somber Tobias, without knowing that his companion is an angel, comes to be constituted—his splendor is now for us as distant and enclosed as the theory of Etruscan splendor—as the priest who again makes an offering for the fourth day of creation.[71] The rabbits, fish and birds of falconry are displayed in the theory of that splendor, disappearing in the offering when his angel makes himself known. Far from coming closer to us, he has taken on such a distance that he seems to represent what we might call with no malicious excess the Etruscan moment of our poetry. It is in the light of that dark splendor that he says to us:

> *¿Quién oyó?*
> *¿Quién oyó?*
> *¿Quién ha visto lo que yo?*[72]

No, no one has seen him nor remained so long in the beam of luminosity. But what is it that he saw? Did he see only the rustic minuets of the mountain women and hypnotic stumblings of the goatherds, the idle moments of Polyphemus contemplating the dolphin's mistakes when it copies the deer's steps,[73] or the belated hunts of the ghost of the Count of Niebla?[74] He saw, we too see him—the sharpness of the arch of his nose, sign of mineral voluptuousness, just as the fleshy reduction of his lips shows his unrestrained pride—, how his face slowly closed down to a point of crouching in readiness to seize his prey, like an ill humored lynx. He saw how with the passage of the autumns his work kept slipping away from him without his ever having written it, since the *Soledades* seem more like the product of the scorn of an officious dismissal than the contentment of his being at their center. He saw how people attributed to the Count of Villamediana, his most fascinating and labyrinthine friend, sonnets against Córdoba[75] containing jokes about him, and how jokes and epigrams against the Count were charged to him when the crossbow eviscerated his friend, thus assuring in the rabble's certain malice an enduring and hooded hatred for the poets who weave the great resistance against the disgusting and progeric, porcine and retarded protectors of letters.

> *¿Quién oyó?*
> *¿Quién oyó?*
> *¿Quién ha visto lo que yo?*

No, no one has seen him, but they have seen how his light of seizure, disappearing before the derived light, slowly hardened and became a substance, changing him, as today we see him in his Etruscan distance, into a stony venomous animal.

June 1951

Ode to Julián del Casal[1]

Allow him, greening, to return;
permit him to leave the party
and come out to the terrace where they sleep.
The sleepers he will watch over and complain,
noticing how the chill morning gathers.
The errant spark of his errant green
will trace circles in front of the sleepers
on the terrace, the silk of his lapel
sheds the water gone over by the triton
and another triton on his back in dust.
Let him return, half plum tree
and half pineapple lacquered in front.

Allow him to accompany without speaking,
permit him, softly, to turn
toward the fruit bowl where the bears are
with the plate of snow, or the reindeer
on the writing stand, with the amber backscratcher
in back. His happy cough
sprinkles the Japanese warrior mask.
Inside a dragon of golden threads,
he walks quickly with the rain's requests
all the way to the Golden Shell at the Teatro Tacón,
where rigidly the chorus girl will place

his flowers on the swan's beak,
like the *mulata* of the three shouts in the vaudeville
and the neo-classical breasts hammered out by
    Clésinger's
pedantry. It all passed
when it had already passed, but the dawn also passed
at its exact snow point.

If they touch him, his sands squeak;
if they move him, the rainbow breaks his ashes.
Motionless in the breeze, held fast
by the gleam of the green chandeliers.
He's a mist that thickens on the windows.

He brings the funeral card with the opal.
He brings the handkerchief with the opoponax
and complaining water to the visit
without hardly sitting down, with many
please stay, please stay,
that come closer to weep in his sound
like the wicker armchairs from the ruins of the
    plantation,
in whose ruins remained forever the anchor
from the sailor jacket of his childhood.

He asks and doesn't wait for a reply,
they pull his sleeve with trefoils of ashes.
Cold are the ornate little flowers.
Cold are his hands that never end,

he squeezes hands with his cold hands.
His hands are not cold, cold is the sweat
that halts him in his visit to the chorus girl.
He gives her the flowers and the mannikin
breaks on the broken tiles of the cliff.
His cold hands enliven the drunken chandeliers
that are going to swallow the beach mannikin.
Be careful, his hands can enliven
the cold chandelier and the chorus girls' mannikin.
Be careful, he goes on hearing how
his own maternal earth evaporates,
keeping time with the coral space.
His happy cough goes on structuring the rhythm
of our vegetal growth,
as it extends in sleep.

The forms in which you used your disguises
could have managed to influence Baudelaire.
The mirror that connected the Countess of Fernandina
with Napoleon III didn't extract from you
the same flowers you took to the chorus girl,
because there you saw the black aleph at the top of the
        fountain.
Chronicler of the wedding of the Moon of Cups
to the Page of Wands, you had to offer a toast
with *champagne gelé* because of the cold sweats
of your midnights as a dying man.
The sleepers on the terrace,
whom you only touched as you complained,

spat on the breakfast bowl you were taking to the swans.

They didn't respect the fact that you had glazed the
    terrace
and taken the waning of the hare to the mirror.
Your disguises, like the samurai admiral
who blotted out the enemy squadron with a fan,
or the monk who doesn't know what he expects in the
    Escorial,
could have produced another chill in Baudelaire.
Those somber scratches, Chinese hexagrams in your
    blood,
equaled the influence your life
could have left on Baudelaire,
just as you managed to astonish Silenus
with his toad-like eyes and frontal diamond.
The resinous ghosts, the cats
who slept in the pocket of your star-studded vest,
were intoxicated with your green eyes.
Since then, the biggest cat of all, the dangerous
    kneeling one,
hasn't been caressed anymore.
When it finishes the skein,
the cat will like to play with your bangs,
just as the creases on the tortoise
give us the exact page of our end.
Your caressable quality,
which put a wicker sofa in a Japanese print,
the sofa floating, like the backdrops

in hagiographic tales,
that came to help you die.
The mail coach with trumpets,
arriving to wake the sleepers on the terrace,
interrupted your scant early morning hours of sleep,
for between midnight and waking
your grafting of azaleas onto cold chandeliers
engendered the sobs of the Venus Anadyomene
and the bracelet stolen by the kingfisher's beak.

May anyone be damned who blunders and tries
to offend you, laughing at your disguises
or at what you wrote in *La Caricatura*,
so successfully that no one has been able
to find what you wrote for fun
so you could buy the Japanese mask.
How the angels must have laughed
when in astonishment you greeted
the Marquise of Polavieja, who came forward
to pat you on the back in front of the mirror.
How awful, you must have let loose
a lizard on the trefoil of a teacup.
You make after your death
the same initials, now
on the wet copper shield of the night,
that had been evidenced by touch
by that dark-haired twelve-year-old girl
and her crazed father hanging from a tree.
You go on tracing circles

around the people strolling on the terrace,
the errant spark of your errant green.
We all know now that none of these were yours:
the fake velvet of green magic,
the steps counted out over carpets,
the dagger diving the decks of cards,
so as to join them again with swan soot.
Nor was yours the separation
that the evil tribe attributes to you,
between the mirror and the lake.
You are the glass egg
where the yellow is replaced
by the errant green of your green eyes.
You invented a solemn color,
we keep that green between two leaves.
The green of death.

No stanza of Baudelaire's
can equal the sound of your happy cough.
We can retouch,
but in the last analysis what remains
is the form in which we've been retouched.
By whom?
Let the answer come from the errant green of your
      green eyes
and the sound of your happy cough.
The vials of perfume you began to open
now make you rise up from them like a homunculus,
an image-entity created by evaporation,

bark of the tree where Adonai
fled from the boar to attain
the resurrection of the seasons.
The cold of your hands
is our fringe of death,
it has the same frayed edge
as the green-gold sleeve on the death disguise,
it is the cold of all our hands.
Despite the cold of our initial timidity
and the cold suddenly found in our final fear,
you took our green firefly down to the valley of
        Proserpina.

The mission entrusted to you,
to go down to the depths with our green spark,
you chose to carry out right away and that's why you
        wrote:
longings for annihilation are all I feel.
For all poets hasten unknowingly
to carry out the indecipherable orders of Adonai.
Now we know the splendor of that statement of yours,
you wanted to take the green of your green eyes
to the terrace of the invisible sleepers.
That's why, here and there,
with the excavators of identity,
among the reviewers and the shady ones,
you open the parasol of an immense Eros.
Our scandalous love pursues you
and that's why you smile among the dead.

Baudelaire's death, muttering
over and over: Sacré nom, Sacré nom,
has the same quality as your death,
since, having lived like a dolphin dead tired
you managed in the end to die laughing.
Your death could have influenced Baudelaire.
The one who among us said:
longings for annihilation are all I feel,
was covered by laughter like a layer of lava.
In those ruins, concealed by death,
now reappears the cigarette that was burning between
    your fingers,
the spark with which you went down
to the slow darkness of the chill terrace.
Allow him to return, he sees us now,
what great company the errant spark of his errant green,
half plum tree and half pineapple lacquered in front.

Notes

Introduction

1   The reader reception that the novel had in the English-speaking world was varied and not always enthusiastic. One of these emblematic readings because of its emphatic rejection of the novel is Michael Wood's review that appeared in *The New York Review of Books*, April 18, 1974 under the ironic title of "Purgatory." Lezama, who was always very attentive to reader responses to his work outside of Cuba made the following comment to his sister Eloísa in a letter dated October 1974: "I read the somber critique written by Wood in *The New York Review*. It is a dogmatic critique that we know where it comes from. The antipathy that he claims to have for words such as unreal, invisible reveal his compromised limited sensibility. And the eternal, idiotic comparisons with Proust, Joyce, and Mann demonstrate the closed and negative willingness with which he read the work. I am tired of these ridiculous simplifications. Because there is asthma, grandmother, mother there has to be Proust, as if I were not as asthmatic as Marcelo."

2   For further reading about this issue see the chapter "Paradiso en el Boom" in Rafael Rojas' book *La Polis Literaria. El boom, la revolución y otras polémicas de la guerra fría.*

3   I have taken this quotation from José Prats Sariol's article "Paradiso: Recepciones" that is included in the critical edition of *Paradiso* that appeared in the collection Archivos

de la Unesco.

4   Heberto Padilla was jailed for his book of poems and forced to make a public confession in which he accused José Lezama Lima of being a counter-revolutionary.

5   Worthy of highlighting is Volume 74 of the journal *Review* dedicated to *Paradiso*. The volume contains a translation of the essay "Confluences" by Andrée Conrad, we also include our own translation of this essay in this anthology. Included in volume 74 are various essays about the novel among them texts by Mercedes Cortázar, Julio Cortázar, Mario Vargas Llosa, Emir Rodríguez Monegal, Julio Ortega, Severo Sarduy, J. M. Alonso and the previously mentioned Andrée Conrad.

6   In 2002 *The New Centennial Review* published a dossier dedicated to the Cuban journal *Orígenes* where a few of Lezama's essays appeared: "De Orígenes a Julián Orbón," "Orígenes," "Las imágenes posibles," "La secularidad de José Martí," "La otra desintegración, "Después de lo raro, la extrañeza."

7   "Literature is fundamentally a syntactic event. It is accidental, linear, sporadic, and otherwise common" ("Elementos de Preceptiva," 1933).

8   Despite the importance that these poets have to understand Lezama's poetics, little has been written about this topic. Rubén Ríos Ávila's article "The Origin and the Island: Lezama and Mallarmé" and Pablo Lupi's book *Reading Anew: José Lezama Lima's Rhetorical Investigations* as well as his essay "Espectros de Mallarmé: apuntes sobre la crítica imaginaria de Lezama" included in the anthology *Asedios a lo increado. Nuevas perspectivas sobre Lezama Lima* are important reflections about the relationship between Lezama and Mallarmé. Of what has been

written about the relationship between Lezama Lima and Góngora, the most important articles are "Apetitos de Góngora y Lezama" and "Lezama, Góngora y la poética del mal gusto" by Roberto González Echevarría; "Exclusión y afirmación en Góngora" by Arnaldo Cruz Malavé who approaches Góngora through a study of the baroque that Lezama and Severo Sarduy traced in their essays and "Soledades habitadas por Lezama" by Remedio Mataix. About the relationship Lezama-Valéry I only know *Paul Valéry y el mundo hispánico* by Monique Allain-Castrillo. To study Lezama's reading of Julián del Casal, see Arnaldo Cruz Malavé's book *El primitivo implorante* and his introduction and his annotations of the essay "Julián del Casal" that appeared in the online journal *La Habana Elegante* in 2013. The book *From Modernismo to Neobaroque: Joyce and Lezama Lima* is one of the most important to learn about the relationship that Lezama had with other writers.

9   The only known letter where Góngora defends himself from his critics states that "the confusion of those from Babel was not because God confused them with many languages. It was they who in their own language got confused 'taking rock for water and water for rock.'" The obscurity and confusion for which his poetry gets attacked arises from a language that has lost its capacity to refer to things such as they are. Gerardo Diego in a text entitled "Góngora y la poesía moderna" comments the following about this letter: "It was a warning that he, Góngora, wants to be interpreted at face value, even though the language from *Soledades* because of the delicate nature of the allusions and the supposed previous learned could result obscure for the non initiated, but after clarifying it it should remain unambiguous."

10 We can hear echos of Damaso Alonso's "Claridad y belleza de las *Soledades*" in Lezama's essay. Alonso tried to separate two of the topics that had accompanied every reading of Góngora's Soledades: obscurity and difficulty. In order to dissolve this association between obscurity and difficulty, Alonso returns to the classic topos of *perspicuitas* where the clear and the difficult are not always considered antonyms and can counter the obscure. Lezama says that there is clarity in Góngora, too much of it; so much that things disappear and are hidden by a light that blinds. The light is so intense that it has a similar effect on things as darkness. Instead of speaking of light, it would be more accurate to speak of a sparkling to describe the disintegration of objects in light.

11 For Aby Warburg see *Atlas Mnemosyne* and also Giorgio Agamben's article "Aby Warburg and the Nameless Science" included in his book *Potentialities*.

Translators' Note: In Praise of Fidelity and Hospitality

1 Roberto González Echevarría in his text "Lezama y Góngora, la poética del mal gusto" defines this trait that he considers defining of Lezama as well as Góngora's poetics in the following terms: "Fundamental element of this poetics is poor taste, or the rejection of explicit and implicit rules of poetic decorum, of beauty pursued through aesthetic norms, that have their social corrections" (428-29).

2 Many of them: "Pensamientos en la Habana," "Diez poemas en prosa y "Danza de la jerigonza" are included in this anthology.

Notes: Confluences

I. AN AUTOBIOGRAPHICAL ESSAY
AND AN INTERVIEW

Confluences

1   Text taken from *La Cantidad hechizada*. Habana: UNEAC, 1970, pp. 435-457.

2   The references to the old military camp Columbia where Lezama Lima spent part of his childhood are common in his work. The camp is now a school and its name is Ciudad Libertad. The first chapter of his novel *Paradiso* is perhaps the best-known passage that recreates this environment. As will be evident during your reading of these notes, there are many affinities between this essay and *Paradiso*.

3   Lezama is referring to the passage that we quote below from *Die Aufzeichnungen des Malte Laurids Brigge* by Rilke (1910). Stephen Mitchell translates it like this: "On one occasion, when it had grown almost dark during her recitation, I was about to tell Maman the story of 'the hand': at that moment I could have done it. I had taken a long breath before beginning; but then it occurred to me how well I had understood the servant's hesitation at approaching their faces. And, in spite of the growing darkness, I was afraid of what Maman's face would look like when it saw what I had seen. Quickly I took another breath, to make it look like that was all I meant to do[...]" (*The Notebooks of Malte Laurids Brigge*. New York: Random House, 1983, p. 90). In the translation that we consulted the fragment dedicated to this episode of the hand is found from pages 90-95. The hand and the night are also protagonists in one of Lezama's poems entitled "Catedral (Noche y gritería)."

4   There are many mentions in Lezama's work of "that realm

the Taoists called the silent sky": "Cortázar y el comienzo de la novela," "La biblioteca como dragón," etc.… In "La biblioteca como dragón" Lezama includes the following fragment that sheds light on the reference that we are trying to clarify: "Now tao, the operating understanding of the word tao, is transformed into two new words, ki and li. Tao is no longer the one without a name, it has transformed into the wu wei, the emptiness, where the tai ki or the condensation of the nebulous supports the concept of li, the laws of nature that direct the creator of condensation. We are no longer in the paradisiacal period, where brothers succeed each other, after thousands of years of governing, where Lao-tse, contemplating the silent sky felt the coming of the being like a silent fruit fallen from a motionless tree. But tao is not a tree, it is not the fruit, it is the creator space that encompasses the polarization of the embryo and the image (Lezama, "La biblioteca" 223). We have not found in the *Tao Te Ching* an exact equivalent to the silent sky of the Taoists, the only entity that is "silent and void."

5 The expression "Le Moi Est Haïssable" by Pascal appears in his *Pensées*. In his English translation, Honor Levi translates this phrase this way: "The self is hateful" (*Pensées and Other Writings*. Oxford: Oxford University Press, 1995, XXXVI, 494, 118).

6 In an interview with Fernando Martínez de Laínez, Lezama states: "I owe my knowledge to the Mediterranean and its opening to the Atlantic. The Greco-Roman tradition weighs heavily on me and after that the Alexandrine tradition. Some Alexandrines like Hamlico and Plotinus have had great influence on my work." Lezama must be referring to Plotinus' theory of the soul as a unique entity but that it contains three psychic levels or powers: intellectual, ratio-

nal, and sensitive-vegetative. See Eneadas II, Treatise II, IX, 5. In his book *La Philosophie de Plotin*. Paris: Boivin & Cie, 1928, Émile Bréhier states: "The soul extends itself, naturally, because of a necessary procession, from the intelligible world where its superior part remains to the plant that stimulates and animates" (94).

7   *Logos spermatikos* or seminal logos is a very important term in Lezama's work. One can trace the genealogy of this term in Stoic philosophy as well as in Patristic Christianity. About the Stoic conception of this concept Albert Stöckl tells us in paragraph 42 in "Physics of the Stoics" in *Handbook of History of Philosophy I*, London: Longmans, Green & Co, 1914: "The divine nature is, therefore, to be conceived as a rational, artistically working fire, which is at once the Soul and the Reason of the universe. As Universal Reason God contains within Himself, in the rational state, the germs of the objects which constitute the world (λόγος σπερματικός, 'seminal reason'); these germs receive actuality and become manifest in the individual objects of the real world by the action of God as the Soul of the Universe" (137). It was St. Justin Martyr who christianized the term. In his Second Apologia, chapter 13 in "The Logos Sows Seeds in Humanity" he writes: "For each person spoke well, according to the part present in him of the divine logos, the Sower, whenever he saw what was related to him [as a person]. But they who contradict themselves on the more important points appear not to have possessed the hidden understanding and the irrefutable knowledge. Therefore, whatever things were rightly said among all people are the property of us Christians. For next to God, we worship and love the logos who is from the unbegotten and ineffable God, since also he became man for our sakes,

that, becoming a partaker of our sufferings. He might also bring us healings. For all the writers were able to see realities darkly, through the present in them of an implanted seed logos. For the seed and imitation of something, imparted according to capacity, is one thing, and another is thing itself, the part possession and imitation of which is effected according to the grace coming from Him" (*St. Just Martyr. The First and Second Apologies*. New York: Paulist Press, 1997).

8   Here Lezama alludes to the following phrase from Pascal's *Pensées*: "La vraie nature étant perdue, tout devient sa nature; comme le véritable bien étant perdu, tout devient son véritable bien." ["True Nature having been lost, everything becomes natural. In the same way, the true good having been lost, everything becomes the true good" (Trans. Honor Levi. 16, 7)]

9   "Mastaba. An ancient Egyptian tomb consisting of an underground burial chamber with rooms above it (at ground level) to store offerings." (*OED*)

10   Lezama reconstructs his image of Baudelaire's three cats through three poems from *Les Fleurs du Mal*. The reference to the elastic is explicit in poem XXXIX entitled "Le Chat" in verses 5 and 6 in the original French. "Lorsque mes doigts caressent à loisir / Ta tête et ton dos élastique[…]" Richard Howard's translation is as follows: "When my fingers freely caress / your head and supple spine[…]." *Les Fleurs du Mal*. Trans. Richard Howard. Boston: David R Godine, 1985, p. 40). In the poem LI also entitled "Le Chat" in the eighth stanza of the poem we find:

C'est l'esprit familier du lieu;
Il juge, il préside, il inspire

Toutes choses dans son empire;
Peut-être est-il fée, est-il dieu?

Richard Howard translates this verse as follows:

Familiar spirit, genius, judge,
the cat presides-inspires
events that he appears to spurn
half goblin and half god! (p. 56)

Finally, the last poem LXVI entitled "Les chats" says in his second stanza:

[...]Ils cherchent le silence et l'horreur des ténèbres;
L'Érèbe les eût pris pour ses coursiers funèbres
S'ils pouvaient au servage incliner leuer fierté.

Howard translates:

[...]seeks out both silence and the awesome dark...
Hell would have made the cat its courier
could it have controverted feline pride! (p. 69.)

11 In *Paradiso* there is a reference close to this one: "Cat derives from Ka, the most magnetic of animals, which relates
with the tips of its whiskers" (*Paradiso*. Trans. Gregory
Rabassa. New York: Farrar, Strauss and Giroux, 1968, p.
330). The editors of *Paradiso* of the Colección Archivo edition have a footnote about this quote: "When Cemí says
that cat comes from Ka he refers to the symbolic relationship established by the Egyptians between the Double of
the deceased (Ka) and the cat, a wild animal that they do-

mesticated." In the *Book of the Dead*, a book much loved by Lezama that he gave to all his friends with a dedication in the chapter XVII [From the Papyrus of Ani (Brit. Mus. No 10, 470 sheets 7-10, and From the Papyrus of Nebseni (Brit. Mus. No 9, 900 sheets 14, 1. 16. Ff.)].

12 Proton pseudos (Πρῶτον ψεῦδος) means literally "first lie." This term comes from Aristotle's syllogism theory and the relationship that he establishes between false premises and false conclusions. It is of great interest that Lezama associates that false logical connection to the poetic lie. His idea could be related to Freud's use of the proton pseudos concept in his *Psycopathology: Project for a Scientific Psychology* to explain the hysterical processes. The source for Freud as well as Lezama, however, is Aristotle's *Prior Analytics* which is where this concept is defined: "A false argument comes about as a result of its first falsehood." (Book II, Chapter 18, 66a, 16. Indianapolis: Hackett Pub. Co. 1989).

13 In "El secreto de Garcilaso" Lezama includes the following proverb that makes reference to this non-dual one: "He who falls in love with his eyes, says Chinese wisdom in the *Book of Tao*, looks for the hundreds; he who falls in love with his body looks for the non-dual one." We have not found any reference to this proverb in the *Tao Te Ching*.

14 Lezama could be referring to the following fragment [199-72 H] from the *Pensées*: "Que l'homme étant revenu à soi considère ce qu'il est au prix de ce qui est, qu'il se regarde comme égaré, et que de ce petit cachot où il se trouve logé, j'entends l'univers, il apprenne à estimer la terre, les royaumes, les villes, les maisons et soi-même, son juste prix. Qu'est-ce qu'un homme, dans l'infini? […]Car enfin qu'est-ce que l'homme dans la nature? Un néant à l'égard

de l'infini, un tout à l'égard du néant, un milieu entre rien
et tout, infiniment éloigné de comprendre les extrêmes; la
fin des choses et leurs principes sont pour lui invincible-
ment cachés dans un secret impénétrable.[...] Quand on est
instruit on comprend que la nature ayant gravé son image
et celle de son auteur dans toutes choses elles tiennent presque toutes de sa double infinité." Honor Levi's version of
this passage is as follows: "Returning to himself, let man
consider what he is in comparison with all existence: let
him regard himself lost in this remote corner of nature;
and from the little cell in which he finds himself lodged,
I mean the universe, let him estimate at their true value of
earth, kingdoms, cities, and himself. What is man in the
infinite?[...] For in fact what is man in nature? A Nothing in comparison with the Infinite, and All in comparison
with the Nothing, a mean between nothing and everything.
Since he is infinitely removed from comprehending the ex-
tremes, the end of things and their beginning are hopelessly
hidden from him in an impenetrable secret; he is equally
incapable of seeing the Nothing from which he was made,
and the Infinite in which he is swallowed up [...] If we are
well-informed, we understand that, as nature has graven
her image and that of the Author of all Things, they almost
all partake of her double infinity."

15 Lezama refers to the following passage from the Bible:
"But the Lord said unto him, Go thy way: for he is a chosen
vessel unto me, to bear my name before the Gentiles, and
kings, and the children of Israel:" (Acts 9:15) King James
Bible.

16 The novel *Paradiso* closes with the following paragraph:
"*He was coming out of the drowsiness that enveloped him.
The ashes of his cigarette slid down the blue of his tie. He*

put the tie in his hand and blew the ash away. He went to the elevator to go to the coffee stand. He was accompanied by that cold, early-morning feeling as he descended into the depths, to the center of the earth where he would meet smiling Ohnespiegel. A black man in a white uniform was moving along with his shovel, picking up cigarette butts and the surrendered dust. He leaned the shovel against the wall and sat down at the coffee bar. He savored his coffee and milk along with some steaming toast. He began to beat his spoon inside the glass, slowly agitating the contents. Driven by the tinkling, Cemí gave body to Oppiano Licario once again. The syllables that he heard were slower now, but also clearer and more obvious. It was the same voice, but modulated in a different register. Once more he heard, rhythm of hesychasts, now we can begin" (466).

17 "She went over the glass pane, Oppiano's face already showed an impassivity that was not that of his usual discretion, not that of his infinite reply. Like a magic mirror it caught the radiation of ideas, the column of self-destruction of knowledge rose up with the flame's slenderness, was reflected in the mirror, and left its mark" (*Paradiso*, 464-465)

18 "Around the base of the cupola of that temple, in ruins now, there was a small balcony where the monks came out for their midnight prayers; it seems that those ruins of a Christian Church had been built in a period of splendor on top of the ruins of an academy of pagan philosophers. Two centurions came to those ruins to roll dice[...] They began to throw their dice[...] A dice rolled and when it stopped it showed two black dots. The other dice had a more adventuresome roll, it bumped into some small stones and muddy holes; when it finally stopped its march on the creamy surface of the dice three black dots were engraved. Then

the two centurions saw a ghost fly by. The figure of the thinker, compass in hand, jumped into space again. When he fell to earth, the point of the compass hit the surface of the dice that showed the triad. The dice jumped with fury, bumped against a rock of the size of the crab, and retreated toward the other dice, and its surface too now showed the two black dots. The two dice achieved a four, one alongside the other, as if the two surfaces had joined their waters. The four remained under the ruin copula in the center of the crossing of the nave and transept" (*Paradiso*, 404-405)

19 "The spider and the image in place of the body" (465) is a verse in the last text written by Oppiano Licario, and it is a sonnet that is entitled José Cemí. Inaca Eco Licario, Oppiano Licario's sister, gives this sonnet to José Cemí in the last chapter of *Paradiso*.

20 "He was also the first, they say, to build temples to Faith and Terminus, and he taught the Romans their more solemn oath by Faith, which they still continue to use. Terminus signifies *boundary* and to this god they make public and private sacrifice where their fields are set off by boundaries; of living victims nowadays, but anciently the sacrifice was a bloodless one, since Numa reasoned that the god of boundaries was a guardian of peace and a witness of just dealing, and should therefore be clear from slaughter. And it is quite apparent that it was this king who set bounds to the territory of the city, for Romulus was unwilling to acknowledge, by measuring off his own, how much he had taken away from others. He knew that a boundary, if observed, fetters lawless power; and if not observed, convicts of injustice. And indeed the city's territory was not extensive at first, but Romulus acquired most of it later with the spear. All this was distributed by Numa among the indigent

citizens." (Plutarch's Lives I, Numa, XVI, 353. London: W. Heinemann; New York: The Macmillan co, 1914)

21 The references to the comet that announces Julius Caesar's death can be found in *Natural History* by Pliny the Elder as well as in Ovid's Metamorphoses. "On the very day of my Games a comet was visible for seven days in the northern part of the sky. It was rising about an hour before sunset, and was a bright star, visible from all lands. The common people believed that the star signified the soul of Caesar received among the spirits of the immortal gods, and on this account the emblem of a star was added to the bust of Caesar that we shortly afterwards dedicated in the forum." *Rackham, and Rackham, H. Natural History. Harvard University Press, 1938. p. 237*

Ovid, *Metamorphoses*: "Meanwhile, do thou catch up this soul from the slain body and make him a star in order that ever it may be the divine Julius who looks forth upon our Capitol and Forum from his lofty temple.' Scarce had he spoken when fostering Venus took her place within the senate house, unseen of all, caught up the passing soul of her Caesar from his body, and not suffering it to vanish into air, she bore it towards the stars of heaven. As she bore it she felt it glow and burn, and released it from her bosom. Higher than the moon it mounted up and, leaving behind a fiery train, gleamed as a star." *Miller, et al. Metamorphoses. 3rd edition revised / by G.P.Goold. ed., Harvard University Press, Heinemann, 1977. Book XV, p. 425, lines 839-848*

22 "The concept is commonly translated as "leisure with dignity." The meaning is not so simple. The concept can be either a political or a social category. As a political category, 'cum dignitate otium' means "peace with dignity" that the best citizens, optimates, wealthy and powerful statesmen

had in the Roman society of Cicero's times. It was optimates' activity contrasted to other people's activities. Cicero also used the concept 'cum dignitate otium' in a social
sense. It meant "peaceful leisure full of studies" or "peace
in private affairs."[...] Cicero used the concept cum dignitate otium in three of his works: in the oration Pro Sestio
(98), in the rhetoric treatise De oratore (1.1) and in the letter
to Lentulus (Cic. Fam. 1.9.21). Cicero wrote about otium
and dignitasin the 10th Philippic (10.3) as well." (Bragova,
Arina. "The concept cum dignitate otium in Cicero's writings," 45, Studia Antiqua et Archaeologica 22 (1): 45–49)

23 Lezama refers to Whitman's poem "There Was a Child
Went Forth" included in *Complete poetry & selected prose
and letters p. 332.*

24 This poem whose title is "Magnitud de cantidades negati-
vas" is part of the essay "Exámenes" from 1950 included in
his book *Analecta del reloj.*

25 "After that, the room of the most secret person in the big
house—the Colonel. When opened on house-cleaning
days, it had the simplicity of a still life, but night after night
for the children it seemed to float around like a cloud that
could move anywhere, like Pascal's abyss. If on some fur-
tive morning the door was open, little José Cemí would
wander through it with his sister Violante, two years older
than he, looking at his father's field tables, the ones he
used as an engineer during the early years of his military
career. Jacks, played with a ball made of duck tripe, was
not the usual game that occupied the two children; Violante
played them with some servant girl brought to the house
to enliven her moments of boredom or to spare some poor
relation the burden of another mouth to feed or the worry
of another child's change of clothing.The Colonel's books:

the *Encyclopaedia Britannica,* the works of Felipe Trigo, spy novels of World War I in which female spies had to engage in prostitution and the boldest male spies had to acquire wisdom and an ice-coated beard on geological expeditions to Siberia or the Kamchatka. Such books filled up spaces, and were never given a second thought by those liberal-minded, portly people who read a book overnight as soon as they buy it. Their books are always displayed in the same inconvenient and irregular order in which they are acquired, unlike the books of more cultured people, also put on bookshelves, where they must wait two or three years to be read—an immediate and almost unconscious effect, not unlike new trousers of elegant English gentlemen, worn for the first few days by their butlers, until they acquire a stylish simplicity. (Paradiso, p. 5)

26 "He had reached the end of the house. He looked around to master the area. On the right, the kitchen; on the left, the maid's room, with some old furniture. He went into the kitchen; in a crate were the carbon polyhedrons worked by cursed bees, dark honeycombs for the devil's digestion. In one of the ovens, asphyxiated by the ashes, the embers leaped out. From the wooden box he took one of those black polyhedrons. That morning he discovered the rear patio and also how the hand could darken it. His hand stretched the coal across the wall, leaving a black line. He saw the coincidence of his darkened hand and that line; from the slight pressure of the tracing, the whitewash above the line began to rain its ashes down, stopping lightly over the somber divider. The rest of the whitewash, below the line, also felt the coming of the small, compact force and began to creak, crackling with prudery. (Paradiso, 389)

27 A similar motive is recreated in one Lezama Lima's most

famous poems "Rhapsody of the Mule" published in his book of poems *La fijeza* (1942)

28 "Andresito had just played a passacaglia from Bach, they had applauded him, not excessively, but with respectful gravity. He drew away discreetly, for he was bothered by the intemperate congratulations of Don Belarmino, who was chatting with Doña Augusta and his own wife. This lady made much of the merits and the accuracy of the performance... The crowd pressed against the railing, one of whose planks had not been secured because Carlitos had been tugged away by the organist. At the stop on the third floor he looked around to see if he could make out his brother Alberto, but it was no use. He was strolling about on the other floor with the advance guard of the coming invasion, who were the happiest and the loudest of the lot. Burdened by its load, the elevator went up very slowly, and at the third floor still more masked figures got on, laughing and patting each other. Suddenly the plank poorly nailed by Carlitos, who had been tugged away by the organist, gave way, and the chorus broke into a savage cry, and the party stopped, and the fragile figure, in his performer's tuxedo, lay stretched out on the ground, and blood began seeping out of his mouth drop by drop; the antistrophe that fought against the shouts of the chorus imposed the curse of silence. The chorus rose up again very slowly. "Its Don Andrés's boy, it's his son, why did it have to be Don Andrés's son." (*Paradiso*, 59-60)

29 It is in Chapter VII in *Paradiso* where we see recreated with the greatest clarity the influence that tío Alberto's words had on José Cemí, the protagonist of the novel and Lezama's alter ego: "At first, Cemí showed no reaction. His eyes didn't light up, he didn't lean forward in his chair. But

something fundamental had happened and reached him. As if he had been struck by a harpoon of clarity, the family idea of Alberto's demonism finally struck him and wiped him out. What remained of Alberto in his letter to the dentist was the same sign that his vibration gave to his arrival, his laughter, his manner of speaking and writing. Whenever he entered an environment, he modified form from its root up." 165-171)

30 Lezama quotes from a stanza in the poem "Ode to Julián del Casal" also included in this anthology.

31 All these elements, including the verse quoted almost exactly like the original, are part of the poem "Thoughts in La Habana" also included in this anthology.

Interview with José Lezama Lima (1964)
by Armando Álvarez Bravo

1 Text taken from *Órbita de Lezama Lima*, La Habana, 1966, pp. 33-39.

2 In the interview "A Questionnaire for José Lezama Lima" by Salvador Bueno, included in the critical edition of *Paradiso* published by Archivos, Lezama delves deeper and explains this reference: "I believe that it is becoming customary in my work, to repeat the names of Góngora or of Proust. And it is important to clarify my relationship to those figures that represent great moments in poetry or the novel. Neither of the two can be considered a predecessor to my work. Góngora's work is a constant fascination for our poetry. Góngora began with a color, a metal, a sound to which he applied a disproportionate hyperbole in a poetic verb with sufficient aperture so that the new monster surrenders like silk. My friend Fina García Marruz has, as we

all know and like, a great sensibility for creating and as-
sessing poetics, used to say that Góngora turned all things
that were clear into obscure ones and that I turned obscure
ones into clear ones. I begin with an obscure one and with
an obsessive contemplation I am able to establish an irradiant center in the center of that obscurity that gets fragmented with the penetration of the gaze" (729).

3   "An ancient Scandinavian poet. Also sometimes in general
use, a poet." (*OED*)

4   "Giambatista Marino (1569-1625) Neapolitan poet best
known for his *Adone* (1623), a long poem on the love of
Venus and Adonis. The term *marinismo* (or sometimes *se-
centismo*) denotes the flamboyant style of Marino and his
17th-century imitators, with its extravagant imagery, excessive ornamentation, and verbal conceits." (The Oxford
Companion to English Literature (7.ed, published online
2009)

5   Gabriello Chiabrera (1552-1638) was also an italian poet,
often compared to the figure of Marino, for contrast. For
example, the *Encyclopedia of Italian Literary Studies* by
Gaetana Marrone, Paolo Puppa defines him in the following terms: "Chiabrera's poetry, much like that of Giambatista Marino, is innovative and evokes a sense of meraviglia
(wonder) in the reader. Unlike Marino and his followers,
who created this effect through an abundance of extravagant metaphors and witty conceits, Chiabrera's sense of
wonder was based on his use of classical forms" (455-456,
Routledge, 2006).

6   "Il faut avoir une pensée de derrière, et juger de tout par là,
en parlant cependant comme le peuple" (Blaise PASCAL,
Pens. XXIV, 90, éd. HAVET). "*The reason of effects*: We
must keep our though secrets and judge everything by it,

while talking like the people" (*Thoughts*. New York: P.F. Collier & Son, 1909–14, 336).

7   Lezama could be alluding to book 11 of the Odyssey where in the voyage that Odysseus makes to the underworld the spirits are described as "ghosts": "Homer tends to use the term *psyche* to describe his spirits, but we also find *skia*. In later writers, *eidolon* is used (Hdt. 5.92.η¹ and Pl. *Leg.* 959b of the corpse), which can also mean a phantom of the mind, or even just a likeness. Later still, *daimōn*, alone, or combined with other words to evoke particular forms of demon (see below) appears. Other terms (which will appear throughout the entry) evoked the particular ways in which individuals died and became ghosts[...] The first ghost story could be said to appear in Book 11 of the *Odyssey*, when Odysseus makes his way to the edge of the underworld ('where the River Acheron meets the River Styx') and summons the dead, so that he may seek the advice of the dead prophet Tiresias" (Oxford Classical Dictionary)

8   José Martí (1853-1895) was both a renowned Cuban poet, one of the founders of Latin American Modernismo, as well as a leader in the Cuban movement of independence from Spain.

9   The ten prose poems from "La fijeza" are included in this anthology.

10 The narrative *Les amours de Psyché et Cupidon* by Jean de La Fontaine (1621-1695) contains a discussion among four characters who represent La Fontaine and his friends Racine, Molière and Boileau under fictitious names, Polyphile being the one the author chose for himself.

11 "The *Enchiridion* or *Manual of Epictetus* (Ancient Greek: Ἐγχειρίδιον Ἐπικτήτου, *Enkheirídion Epiktḗtou*) (enchiridion is Greek for "that which is held in the hand") is a short

manual of Stoic ethical advice compiled by Arrian, a 2nd-century disciple of the Greek philosopher Epictetus." (Wikipedia)

12 Numas Pompilius is one of the characters recreated in *Plutarch's Lives*. Lezama could be alluding to the following passage: "In like manner Numa's fiction was the love which a certain goddess or mountain nymph bore him, and her secret meetings with him, as already mentioned, and his familiar converse with the Muses. For he ascribed the greater part of his oracular teachings to the Muses, and he taught the Romans to pay especial honours to one Muse in particular, whom he called Tacita, that is, *the silent*, or *speechless one*; thereby perhaps handing on and honouring the Pythagorean precept of silence." (*Plutarch's Lives I. Numa*, VIII, 6. LOEB. London, 1914)

13 "To Numa is also ascribed the institution of that order of high priests who are called Pontifices, and he himself is said to have been the first of them. According to some they are called Pontifices because employed in the service of the gods, who are *powerful* and supreme over all the world; and "potens" is the Roman word for *powerful*. Others say that the name was meant to distinguish between *possible* and impossible functions; the lawgiver enjoining upon these priests the performance of such sacred offices only as were *possible*, and finding no fault with them if any serious obstacle prevented. (Ibid, Numa, IX, 1-2)

14 The complete phrase by Saint Paul is: "caritas omnia suffer, omnia credit, omnia sperat, omnia sustinet" which appears in Cor. XIII. 7, Cor IV 10, in Phil. I 7, in Thess i 3, and in Col, iii 14. See Pelagius's Exposition of Thirteen Epistles of Saint Paul: Introduction. P. 76 by Alexander Souter. Wipf & Stock Pub, 2006

15 "That such as the origin of poetry is finally confirmed by this eternal property of it: that its proper material is the credible impossibility (l'impossible credible) (*The New Science*. Ithaca. Trans. Thomas Goddard Bergin and Max Harold Fisch. Ithaca: Cornell University Press, 2015, 384, p. 120).

16 Blaise Pascal, *Thoughts*, 556,17

17 Lezama refers to the following Stoic doctrine:: "The Stoics say that void is what can be occupied by an existent but is not occupied [...] place is what is occupied by an existent [body] and made equal to what occupies it." (Sextus Empiricus, *Against the Professors*, 10.3–4. Trans. R. G. Bury. Cambridge: Harvard University Press, 1949.)

18 We have corrected a few mistakes that appeared in the original with the use of these German words.

19 Lezama is alluding to "Le Tombeau d'Edgar Allan Poe" by Mallarmé. In its original language the stanza relevant to us goes like this: "Eux, comme un vil sursaut d'hydre oyant jadis l'ange / Donner un sens plus pur aux mots de la tribu / Proclamèrent très haut le sortilège bu / Dans le flot sans honneur de quelque noir mélange" ("They, like an upstart hydra hearing the angel once / purify the meaning of tribal words / proclaimed out loud the prophecy drunk / without honour in the tide of some black mixture," *Stéphane Mallarmé: The Poems in Verse*. Trans. Peter Manson. Miami: Miami University Press, 2012).

20 What is known in the philosophical tradition as a hyperbolic doubt is the metaphysical character that doubt acquires when it takes on the greatest degree of radicalness. Descartes in his Third Meditation of his *Meditations of First Philosophy* explicitly states this problem: "And since I have no cause to think that there is a deceiving God, and

I do not yet even know for sure whether there is a God at all, any reason for doubt which depends simply on this supposition is a very slight and, so to speak, metaphysical one. But in order to remove even this slight reason for doubt, as soon as the opportunity arises I must examine whether there is a God, and, if there is, whether he can be a deceiver. For if I do not know this, it seems that I can never be quite certain about anything else." ("Meditations on First Philosophy," *The Philosophical Writings of Descartes. Vol II.* Trans. John Cottingham, Robert Stoothoff and Douglas Murdorch. Cambridge: Cambridge University Press, 1984, p. 25). The characterization of this type of doubt as "hyperbolic doubt" is linked to the objections that Pierre Gassendi poses to Descartes: "There is just one point I am not clear about, namely why you did not make a simple and brief statement to the effect that you were regarding your previous knowledge as uncertain so that you could later single out what you found to be true. Why instead did you consider everything as false, which seems more like adopting a new prejudice than relinquishing an old one? This strategy made it necessary for you to convince yourself by imagining a deceiving God or some evil demon who tricks us, whereas it would surely have been sufficient to cite the darkness of the human mind or the weakness of our nature." (*The Philosophical Writings of Descartes.* Vol II. *Objections and Replies*, 258, 180. New York: Cambridge University Press, 2009)

21 "The act or process of changing one's mind (in quot. 1577, as a rhetorical device); *spec.* penitence, repentance; reorientation of one's way of life, spiritual conversion." (*OED*)

22 For this reference see the essay "Confluences" also included in this anthology.

23 For the concepts of areté and aristia it is greatly useful to consult *Paideia* by Werner Jaeger:

"Since Pindar conceives *areta* as an aristocratic quality, he believes it to be bound up with the great deeds of heroes of the past. He always sees the victor as the worthy heir to the proud traditions of his family, and honours the great ancestors who have bequeathed some of their glory to him. Yet he does not depreciate the achievement of the victor of today. *Areta* is divine because a god or a demigod was the first ancestor of a family which possesses it: the power descends from him, and is constantly renewed in each succeeding generation. Thus Pindar cannot consider a victor purely as an individual, since his victory was won through his divine blood. Accordingly, almost all his praise of a hero's deeds passes over into praise of the hero's descent" (214) And about *aresteia* he says in another fragment: "The *aristoi* are distinguished by that name from the mass of the common people: and though there are many aristoi, they are striving with one another for the prize of *areté*. The Greek nobles believes that the real test of manly virtue was victory in battle –a victory which was not merely the physical conquest of the enemy, but the proof of hard-won areté. This idea is exactly suited by the word *aristeia*, which was later used for the single-handed adventures of an epic hero. The hero's whole life and effort are a race for the first prize, an unceasing strife for supremacy over his peers. (Hence the eternal delight in poetic accounts of these *aristeia*) In peace-time too, the warriors match their *aretai* against one another in war games: in the *Iliad* we see them in competition even in a brief pause in the war, at the funeral games of Patroclus. It was that chivalrous rivalry which out the motto of knighthood." (7) (*Paideia*, The Ideals of Greek

Culture. Vol I. New York: Oxford University Press, 1945)

24 "τερατεία: the act of relating marvelous occurrences or discoursing on prodigies, portentous preternatural or unnatural appearances, monsters or wonders; hence a marvelous or fictitious narrative[…]" (Donnogan, James. *A new Greek and English lexicon: Principally on the plan of the Greek and German lexicon of Schneider*. Butler & Williams, 1846, pp. 979. 1834).

25 "I am debtor both to the Greeks, and to the Barbarians; both to the wise, and to the unwise." (Romans, 14, King James Bible)

II. ESSAYS AND POEMS ABOUT POETICS

X and XX

1 Spanish text, "X y XX," taken from José Lezama Lima, *Analecta del reloj* (Havana: Orígenes, 1953, pp. 133-150). First published in *Orígenes*, no. 5, Spring 1945, pp. 16-27.

2 Lines 30-32 from Stéphane Mallarmé's poem "Prose pour des Esseintes," which Peter Manson translates as: "all of them in me leapt to see/the family of irises" (*The Poems in Verse*. Oxford: Miami University Press, 113). Lezama also comments on these and other verses from the same poem in his "Prosa de circunstancia para Mallarmé" in *Analecta del reloj*, pp. 266-267, and in the entry for April 25, 1943, in his *Diarios <1939-1949 / 1956-1958>* (Havana: Ediciones Unión, 2001, pp. 59-60).

3 This seems to refer to Apollo's status as principal deity of the Delphic Oracle and to the Pythoness as its priestess. See Robert Graves, *The Greek Myths*, I (Harmondsworth: Penguin Books, 1964, 21. *c*). As for the possibility of such a

deity's death and the role in prophecy of *daimones* or demi-gods, see Plutarch, *The Obsolescence of Oracles*, 10, 19.

4 A paraphrase of lines 21-29 of "Prose pour des Esseintes" immediately preceding those quoted above:

> Oui, dans une île que l'air charge
> De vue et non de visions
> Toute fleur s'étalait plus large
> Sans que nous en devisions.
>
> Telles, immenses, que chacune
> Ordinairement se para
> D'un lucide contour, lacune,
> Qui des jardins la sépara.
>
> Gloire du long désir, Idées….

In Manson's translation:

> Yes, in an island charged by the air
> with sight but not for seers
> every flower loomed extra large
> without our mention it:
>
> All so immense that each one
> ordinarily paraded
> in a lucid contour, lacuna se-
> parating it from the gardens.
>
> Glory of the long desire, Ideas" (p. 113)

5 According to John Gage, *Colour and Culture: Practice*

and Meaning from Antiquity to Abstraction (Boston: Little Brown & Co, 1993, p. 157), the baroque painter Peter Paul Rubens "was the author of a (now lost) treatise on light and colour." We do not know in what source Lezama found his reference.

6 André Lhote was a 20th century French painter, sculptor and art critic whose mature painting was cubist in manner.

7 Concerning the relation between sunbeams, prophetic power and Apollo's status as solar deity, see Plutarch, 39, 42. Concerning Zeus's punishment of Apollo for having killed the Cyclopes by making him tend for a year the sheep-folds of King Admetus of Pherae, see Graves, 21. *n, o,* an episode discussed in greater detail by Roberto Calasso, *The Marriage of Cadmus and Harmony* (New York: Vintage Books, 1994, pp. 71-77).

8 Actually, it was Boreas, the North Wind, that was believed to have this fecundating power. See Graves, 48.2. Euphorion could be the short-lived son of either Achilles and Helen in Greek myth or Faust and Helen in Goethe's *Faust Part Two*.

9 This same dream, in almost the same words, is told in the entries for November 7, 1939, in Lezama's *Diarios*, México: Ediciones Era, 1994, p. 24, including the remark about reading and rereading Descartes.

10 This dream is also told, in almost the same words, in the entry for January 3, 1940, of the *Diarios*, pp. 34-35, prefaced by these remarks: "My dear friend Concha Albornoz tells me she has dreamt about me. I tell her it must have been an awful nightmare. She tells me her delightful story."

11 See M. R. Wright, *Empedocles: the Extant Fragments* (London: Duckworth, 1995, p. 240): "The relevant fragment is given by Aristotle [*Physics*] with a brief comment

that Empedocles at one time, apparently, explains vision by an issue of light from the eye and at another by effluences from the objects seen."

12 See Stendhal, *Le rouge et le noir*, Book Two, Chapter VII, "Une attaque de goutte" (An attack of gout), where the protagonist Julien Sorel, after a trip to London, reports that "the wisest man in England is mad for an hour daily; he is visited by the demon of suicide, who is the national deity" (*The Red and the Black*. Trans. C. K. Scott Moncrieff. New York: Modern Library, 1925).

13 In both Elias Rivers's *Renaissance and Baroque Poetry of Spain* (New York: Dell, 1966) and José Manuel Blecua's *Poesía de la Edad de Oro: II, Barroco* (Madrid: Clásicos Castalia, 1987), these lines from the "Epístola moral a Fabio" by the baroque Spanish poet Andrés Fernández de Andrada read as follows: "…usó como si fuera vil gaveta / del cristal transparente y luminoso," which Rivers translates (p. 257) as "he used as if it were a common cup / bright transparent crystal."

14 These lines, also from the "Epístola moral a Fabio," Rivers translates (p. 254) as "Oh, if I could only, seeing how I die, / finish learning to die…."

15 An allusion to the opening words of Mallarmé's "Prose pour des Esseintes": "Hyperbole! de ma mémoire / Triomphalement ne sais-tu / Te lever, aujourd'hui grimoire / Dans un livre de fer vêtu…." In Hartley's translation (p. 62): "Hyperbole! from my memory / Can you not triumphantly / Arise, today like an occult language / Copied into a book bound in iron…." In his comments here on these lines, Lezama disregards the exclamation point after "hyperbole" which indicates that that noun is being apostrophized and that the following "de" doesn't connect "hyperbole"

to "mémoire" in a genitive construction but instead goes with the later verb "te lever" to indicate the source of the "hyperbole" being called forth. For an instance of the same misreading, see Lezama's interview with Armando Álvarez Bravo in *Órbita de Lezama Lima* (Havana: UNEAC, 1966, pp. 40-41) also included in this anthology.

16 A reference to Lezama's "Coloquio con Juan Ramón Ji-ménez," published first in *Revista Cubana*, vol. 11, no. 31, Jan. 1938, pp. 73-95, then as a booklet (Havana: Dirección de Cultura, 1938) and later included in *Analecta del reloj*, pp. 40-61

17 The combination of "Príncipe de las Flores" with "Dama de las Serpientes" reappears in Lezama's later poem "Re-cuerdo de lo semejante" again in a Minoan context. But these same designations also apply to the ancient Aztec dei-ties Xochipilli and Coatlicue, which fact, given the context here of "cultural synthesis," Lezama may have implied as well.

18 See Plato, *Phaedrus* §237-241

19 See entry for May 4, 1940 in *Diarios* (p. 39): "In Victor Bro-chard's excellent book on Socrates and Plato is given, inci-dentally, a definition of science that we find very pleasing. 'Science—Brochard says, with acute insight into Greek culture—, in other words, *knowledge of the real quantity of pleasure*, cannot be defeated.'" This was probably taken from a volume of Brochard's essays on those philosophers in Spanish translation which we have not seen. But the cor-responding words occur in his essay "L'Oeuvre de Socrate" in his *Études de philosophie ancienne et de philosophie moderne* (Paris: Librairie Philosophique J. Vrin, 1954, p. 41): "la science, c'est-à-dire la connaissance de la quantité réelle de plaisir, ne peut-être vaincue."

20 The text of "X y XX" in *Analecta del reloj* here says "constructed" but we prefer the more plausible "constituted" found in the text in *Orígenes*.

21 "No te asotiles tanto, que te despuntarás" are words spoken to Preciosa by the old gypsy woman in Cervantes's exemplary novel "La gitanilla." Harriet de Onís (*Six Exemplary Novels*, Great Neck NY: Barron's Educational Series, 1961, p. 110) renders them as "don't put such a fine point on things or they will break," a translation which, however, obscures the fact that in the original it's the person and her words that are too "pointed" and may "break" like the point of a pencil. To understand Lezama's comments here on this quotation, it's well to keep in mind that (1) "agudeza" or "sharpness" includes the sense of "wit" and (2) for "point" Spanish has two words, "punto" (a point in space, a dot, a period) and "punta" (the point of a sharp instrument or weapon or the tip of one's finger or tongue) and it's the latter that recurs here and in later passages

22 The *Orígenes* text here says "is his resistance" but we prefer the more plausible "in his resistance" found in *Analecta*. The references to "side" and "lance" evoke the accounts in John 19: 34-37 and 20: 20-29 telling how, while still on the cross, Christ was wounded in his side by a soldier with a lance and how, later, upon meeting with his disciples, he points to that wound and the others in his hands and feet as proof of his resurrection.

23 The phrase "aristocratie discontinue" appears in Paul Valéry's essay "Je disais quelquefois à Stéphane Mallarmé…" (I would sometimes say to Stéphane Mallarmé…). See Valéry's *Oeuvres*, I, Paris: Bibliotèque de la Pléiade, 1957, p. 651, in a passage that speaks of the poetic gift as testifying to a kind of noble descent.

24 Spanish has two words for "fish": "pez" (live fish) and "pescado" (the participle of the verb "pescar," to fish, which means fish that's been caught for food). In the original, the line added here asks: "¿el pensamiento pescado tiene que ser un pez muerto?," which may mean either "does the thought that's fished have to be a dead fish?" or "does the thought 'fish' have to be a dead fish?."

25 The phrase "ein eigener Tod" ("a death of one's own") and similar ones are emphasized toward the beginning of Rainer Maria Rilke's *Die Aufzeichnungen des Malte Laurids Brigge* (1910). See, for ex., the translation by Stephen Mitchell, *The Notebooks of Malte Laurids Brigge* (New York: Vintage Books, 1985), pp. 8-16.

26 *Narrative of A. Gordon Pym*, in Edgar Allan Poe, *Poetry and Tales* (New York: The Library of America, 1984), p. 1040.

27 *Ibid.*, p. 1049.

28 *Ibid.*, p. 1090.

29 *Ibid.*, p. 1138.

30 *Ibid.*, pp. 1140-1141.

31 *Ibid.*, p. 1149

32 See Michel de Montaigne, *Essais*, Chapter 55, "Des senteurs" (Of smells).

33 Pierre de Bérulle was a 17th century French cardinal and Ernest Héllo a 19th century French writer on religious subjects, but we have not located the latter's reference to the former. As told in Luke 2: 22-38, when Mary and Joseph brought the newborn Jesus to the temple for his and his mother's purification, among those present were Simeon and the prophetess Anna, who had long anticipated the advent of Christ and now saw their faith confirmed. This moment has subsequently been celebrated on February 2

as the Ceremony of the Candles or Candlemas, also known as the Presentation of Jesus at the Temple or Feast of the Purification of the Virgin.

34 Pedro Antonio Iturriondo and his son Ignacio are characters in Miguel de Unamuno's novel *Paz en la guerra* (1897).

35 From the last line of Charles Baudelaire's poem "Le Voyage": "Au fond de l'inconnu pour trouver le nouveau!" ("Deep in the unknown to find the new!" Trans. Richard Howard, 157).

Coronation of Formlessness

1 First published in *Diario de la Marina* (Havana), January 2, 1955, 4-A. Text taken from *Tratados en la Habana* (Havana: Universidad Central de las Villas, 1958), pp. 69-71.

2 The phrase "chosen vessel" forms part of God's reply to Ananias concerning Saul in Acts 9: 15-16 (King James Version): "But the Lord said unto him, Go thy way: for he is a chosen vessel unto me, to bear my name before the Gentiles, and kings, and the children of Israel: For I will shew him how great things he must suffer for my name's sake." In the Revised Standard Version the corresponding phrase is "chosen instrument."

3 After quoting in his journal entry for April 10, 1933, a passage from Montaigne ("Il ferait beau vieillir, si nous ne marchions que vers l'amendement: c'est un mouvement d'ivrogne, titubant, vertigineux, informe" (III, chap. 9), Gide remarks: "Je doute si le 'informe' ne signifie pas, ici, dans l'esprit de Montaigne, plutôt 'sans beauté' que 'sans forme'; mieux justifié ainsi:in-formosus, la négation in convenant bien davantage du reste a une épithète qu'à un substantif (où je ne parviens pas à trouver d'autre ex-

emple qu'elle y soit jamais accolée). Littré ne donne point d'exemple de cette acception.Mais le mot, dans l'exemple de Boileau, qu'il cite: 'La tragédie informe et grossière en naissant…' laisse entrevoir le glissement qui put se produire d'un sens à l'autre.Je sais bien qu'il y a le 'inform-is' latin d'où le français découle directement; mais précisé-ment ce mot, lorsque Virgile ou Horace l'emploie, signifie bien plutôt 'sans beauté' que 'sans contour,' et Montaigne, nourri de ces auteurs, s'en souvient." *Journal 1889-1939*, Paris: Gallimard, 1951, pp. 1164-1165) ["I wonder if the last word, *informe*, does not signify in Montaigne's mind, rather 'without beauty' than 'without form'; better justi-fied thus: *in-formosus*, the negation in- being more suitable to an epithet than to a substantive (I cannot find any other example where it is so linked) Littré gives no example of that acceptation. But the word in the example from Boileau that he quotes: 'Tragedy, *informe* and coarse at its birth…' allows one to glimpse the passage that might have taken place from one meaning to the other. I am well aware that there is the Latin *informis*, from which the French comes directly; but it just happens that this word, when Virgil or Horace uses it, means rather 'without beauty' than 'with-out contour,' and Montaigne, raised on those authors, re-member this"] (*Journals. Vol. 3: 1928-1933*. Trans. Justin O'Brien. Urbana and Chicago: University of Illinois Press, 2000, p. 266).

4   Having come to Nemea, of which Lycurgus was king, they sought for water; and Hypsipyle showed them the way to a spring, leaving behind an infant boy Opheltes, whom she nursed, a child of Eurydice and Lycurgus. For the Lemnian women, afterwards learning that Thoas had been saved alive, put him to death and sold Hypsipyle into

slavery; wherefore she served in the house of Lycurgus as a purchased bondwoman. But while she showed the spring, the abandoned boy was killed by a serpent. When Adrastus and his party appeared on the scene, they slew the serpent and buried the boy; but Amphiaraus told them that the sign foreboded the future, and they called the boy Archemorus. They celebrated the Nemean games in his honor; and Adrastus won the horse race, Eteoclus the foot-race, Tydeus the boxing match, Amphiaraus the leaping and quoit-throwing match, Laodocus the javelin-throwing match, Polynices the wrestling match, and Parthenopaeus the archery match. [Apollodorus. *The Library I*. Trans. J. G. Frazer. Cambridge: Harvard University Press, 1921, Book III. 3.6.4)

5   See Gide, op. cit., entry for December 5, 1921, p. 705. Commenting on a statement by Amiel ("L'expression unique est une intrépidité qui implique la confiance en soi et la clairvoyance. Pour arriver à touche unique, il ne faut pas douter, et tu doutes toujours."), Gide remarks: "Et cela est excellent; mais pas toujours juste, il me semble. La 'touche unique' n'est pas forcément preuve d'intrépidité; elle peut résulter aussi bien d'un *consentement au sacrifice*. Tout choix implique un sacrifice; et l'on ne dessine pas bien sans choisir" ["'The single expression is an intrepidity that implies self-confidence and clairvoyance. To achieve the unique touch, one must not doubt, and you are always doubting.' That is excellent, but not always correct, it seems to me. The 'unique touch' is not necessarily a proof of intrepidity; it can result just as well from an *acceptance of sacrifice*. Every choice implies a sacrifice; and it is impossible to draw well without choosing"] (*Journals. Vol. 2: 1914-1927*. Trans. Justin O'Brien. Urbana and Chicago:

University of Illinois Press, 2000, p. 277).

Complex and Complicated

1   First published in *Diario de la Marina* (Havana), 4-A, August 14, 1954. Text taken from *Tratados en la Habana* (Havana: Universidad Central de las Villas, 1958), pp. 49-52.

2   See *Thus Spoke Zarathustra*, Part Two, Section Two, "Upon the blessed isles": "But let me reveal my heart to you entirely, my friends: *if* there were gods, how could I endure not to be a god! *Hence* there are no gods. Though I drew this conclusion, now it draws me" (*The Portable Nietzsche*. Trans. by Walter Kaufmann. London: Penguin Books, 1982, p. 198).

3   "Vacate et videte" are the first words of verse 11 of Psalm 45 in the Vulgate: "Vacate et videte quoniam ego sum Deus exaltabor in gentibus exaltabor in terra," which corresponds to verse 10 of Psalm 46 in the Revised Standard Version: "Be still and know that I am God. I am exalted among the nations, I am exalted in the earth!."

4   See 1 Corinthians 13: 12. In the Vulgate: "Videmus nunc per speculum in aenigmate: tunc autem facie ad faciem. Nunc cognosco ex parte: tunc autem cognocam sicut et cognitus sum." In the Revised Standard Version: "For now we see in a mirror dimly, but then face to face. Now I know in part; then I shall understand fully, even as I have been fully understood."

Ten Prose Poems

1   Text taken from La fijeza: La Habana: 1949, pp. 71-90.

Thoughts in Havana

1   Spanish title: "Pensamientos en la Habana"taken from José Lezama Lima, *Poesía completa*. Madrid: Sexto piso, pp. 234-244. First published in *Revista Orígenes*, 1944. Vol. 3. It belongs to the book of poems *La fijeza*, 1949

The Dance of Jargon

1   Spanish title: "La danza de la jerigonza" taken from José Lezama Lima, *Poesía completa*. Madrid: Sexto piso, pp. 340-349. First published in *Revista Orígenes*, 1947. Vol 7. It belong to the books of poems *La fijeza*, 1949

III. ESSAYS ON POETS: LEZAMA AS A READER OF MALLARMÉ, GÓNGORA AND VALÉRY

New Mallarmé

1   Text taken from José Lezama Lima, Tratados en la Habana (Havana: Universidad Central de las Villas, 1958), pp. 135-144. First published in Diario de la Marina (Havana), February 26, 1956, p. 4-D, and March 4, 1956, p. 11-D.

2   French for "raspberry liqueur" and "cherry juice."

3   Sebastian I, king of Portugal, after whose disappearance in battle in Morocco in 1578 it was long believed he would one day return to reclaim his throne and save his country in time of need, a belief called sebastianismo.

4   Thierry Maulnier, Introduction à la poésie française (Paris: Galllimard, 1939), p. 74, speaking of Maurice Scève (c. 1501-c.1564) and his poems collected in Délie: "d'une intensité mallarméenne," but not using the word "pensée"

5   The School of Lyon was a group of poets in the French city of Lyon in the mid-16th century inspired by Italian Renaissance thought and poetry, whose most celebrated member was Maurice Scève.

6   Tournon was the provincial city where Mallarmé first taught English; during his three years there, he began work on his *Hérodiade* and "L'Après-Midi d'un Faune." The night of Idumea echoes a line in his poem "Don du poëme," "Je t'apporte l'enfant d'une nuit d'Idumée!" ("I bring you the child of a night in Idumea!"), by which he alluded to two births: those of his *Hérodiade* and of his daughter Geneviève while he lived in Tournon. According to legend, Idumea or Edom was, before Adam and Eve, a land whose kings reproduced themselves asexually. Valvins was a village near Fontainebleau where Mallarmé had a vacation cottage. The Rue de Rome was the street in Paris where he settled in 1875; the Tuesday gatherings of artists and writers at his apartment there became famous.

7   In his book *Les mots anglais*, Mallarmé discusses the English language's hybrid mixture of elements of Anglo Saxon and Old French resulting from the Norman conquest of England, to which these fires on the respective coasts seem to allude.

8   Valéry, "Sorte de préface" ("A Kind of Preface") (*Oeuvres, Tome I*. Paris: Gallimard, 1957, p. 686): "Le livre *Les Mots anglais* est peut-être le document le plus révélateur que nous possédions sur le travail intime de Mallarmé?" ("*Les mots anglais* may well be the most revealing document we possess concerning his secret research." *Collected Works of Paul Valery, Volume 8: Leonardo, Poe, Mallarme*. Trans. James R. Lawler and M. Lowry. Princeton: Princeton University Press, 1972, p. 306.)

9   "Il me semblait quelquefois qu'il eût examiné, pesé, miré
    tous les mots de la langue un à un, comme un lapidaire ses
    pierres, tant la sonorité, l'éclat, la couleur, la limpidité, la
    portée de chacun, et je dirais presque son *orient…*" (*Ibid.
    loc.cit.*) ["Sometimes it seemed to me that he had exam-
    ined, weighed, help up to the light all the words of the lan-
    guage, one by one as a lapidary his precious stones: the
    sound, the brilliance, the colour, the limpidity, the meaning
    of each of them, I would almost say his orient luster" (Ibid,
    p. 305)]

10 "Il parla, un soir, des différences qu'il percevait entre les
    effets possibles des mots abstraits selon qu'ils se termi-
    nent en *té* (comme *verité*), en *tion* (comme *transition*) ou
    en *ment* (comme *entendement*). Il ne lui paraissait pas in-
    différent d'avoir observé ces nuances…." (*Ibid., loc. cit.*)
    ("One evening he spoke of the differences he perceived
    between the possible effects of abstract words according
    to whether they end with the syllable *té* [as in *vérité*], with
    tion [as in *transition*], or with *ment* [as in *entendement*]. It
    did not seem to him a trifling matter to have noticed these
    nuances…." Ibid, pp. 305-306)

11 These two lines belong to one of Unamuno's *Cancionero*
    poems. The poem is the number 1529 and begins with the
    following two verses: "Salamanca, Salamanca / renaciente
    maravilla." The two verses quoted by Lezama are the fol-
    lowing: "Hechizo salmanticense / de pedantesca dulzura."

12 Mallarmé's *Les dieux antiques* is his edited and annotated
    translation of the English author George W. Cox's *Mythol-
    ogy of the Aryan Nations*, a work that frequently traces
    myths back to natural phenomena, but we have not found
    this exact quotation in Mallarmé's text.

13 See Mallarmé, *Les dieux antiques*: "Nous parlons

aujourd'hui du Soleil qui se couche et se lève avec la certi-
tude de voir ce fait arriver, mais, eux, les peuples primitifs,
n'en savaient pas assez pour être sûrs d'une telle régularité;
et quand venait le soir, ils disaient: 'Notre ami le Soleil est
mort, reviendra-t-il?'" (*Oeuvres Complètes*. Paris: Gallimard, 1945, p. 1,169) ("We nowadays speak of the Sun's rising and setting with the certainty of seeing that happen, but
primitive peoples didn't know enough to be sure of such
regularity, so when evening came, they would say: 'Our
friend the Sun has died, will he return?.'") (<fr.wikisource.
org/wiki/Les_Dieux_antiques/origine_et_developpement_
de_la_mythologie>)

14 The Italian artist Benvenuto Cellini (1500-1571) sculpted a
bronze relief in Florence depicting Perseus' rescue of Andromeda after he had beheaded the Medusa.

15 See the final tercet of Baudelaire's poem "Parfum exotique"
("Exotic perfume"): "Pendant que le parfum des verts tam-
ariniers, / Qui circule dans l'air et m'enfle la narine, / Se
mêle dans mon ame au chant des mariniers" ["While the
aroma of green tamarinds / dilates my nostrils as it drifts
to sea / and mingles in my soul with sailors' song" (Trans.
Richard Howard, p. 30)]

16 Lines 6-7 from Mallarmé's poem "Brise marine" ("Sea
breeze"): "…la clarté déserte de ma lampe / Sur le vide pa-
pier que la blancheur défend…." (Translation by Anthony
Hartley: "…the desolate light of my lamp / On the empty
paper, defended by its own whiteness….")

17 The phrase "temptation of the devil" occurs in a January
1866 letter to Mallarmé from his friend the writer Villiers
de l'Isle-Adam (1840-1889), but in a context rather different
from the one suggested here by Lezama. In his admiration
for an early version of Mallarmé's "Don du poëme" and

wanting to see how simpler souls might react to it, Villiers claims he himself yielded to such a temptation by marching down the stairs in the building where he lived and declaiming the poem while beating a drum, so as to observe the effects on his cook and the neighbors. See *Correspondance générale de Villiers de l'Isle-Adam et documents inédits*, ed. Joseph Bollery, vol. 1 (Paris: Mercure de France, 1962), pp. 82-84.

18 From Part II, "Scène," of Mallarmé's *Hériodiade*: "Je m'apparus en toi comme une ombre lointaine, / Mais, horreur! des soirs, dans ta sévère fontaine, / J'ai de mon rêve épars connu la nudité!" ("I appeared to myself in you as a distant shadow/But horror! some evenings in your austere fountain,/I have known the nudity of my scattered dream" (*The Poems in Verse*. Trans. Peter Manson. Miami: Miami University Press, 2012, p. 72)

19 The Russian dancer Vaslav Nijinsky (1889 or 1890-1950), known especially for his performances with Serge Diaghilev's Ballet Russes between 1909 and 1913, choreographed and danced the main role in a ballet set in 1912 to the music of Claude Debussy's tone poem "Prélude à l'après-midi d'un faune" of 1894, inspired by Mallarmé's poem.

20 In his essay "Stéphane Mallarmé" (*Oeuvres*, I, pp. 660-680), Valéry calls these lines from "L'Après-Midi d'un Faune" "les plus beaux vers su monde." The sonnets mentioned are "Les grenades" ("The Pomegranates") and "L'abeille" ("The Bee") in *Charmes*.

21 "Pan and Syrinx" was a painting by the French artist François Boucher (1703-1770) inspired by Ovid's account in the *Metamorphoses* of Pan's attempt to seduce the nymph Syrinx.

22 Valéry, "Je disais quelquefois à Stéphane Mallarmé..." ("I

Would Sometimes Say to Mallarmé...") (*Oeuvres*, I, p. 646): "Celui-là donc qui ne repoussssait pas les textes complexes de Mallarmé se trouvait insensiblement engagé à réapprendre à lire." (Translation by Malcolm Cowley: "So anyone who did not put aside Mallarmé's involved texts found himself engaged by slow degrees in the task of re-learning how to read.") (Trans. M. Cowley and James R. Lawler. p. 274)

23 Mallarmé in his text about Hamlet included in *Divagations* refers to the Shakespearean character in the following terms: "mais avance le seigneur latent qui ne peut devenir, juvénile ombre de tous, ainsi tenant du mythe. Son solitaire drame! et qui, parfois, tant ce promeneur d'un labyrinthe de trouble et de griefs en prolonge les circuits avec le suspens d'un acte inachevé." ("[...]but there steps forth the latent lord who cannot become, the juvenile shadow of us all, thus partaking of myth. His solitary drama! and who, sometimes, so much does this wanderer of his labyrinth of trouble and grief lengthen its circuits through the suspension of an accomplished act." *Divagations*. Trans. Barbara Johnson. Cambridge: Harvard University Press, 2007, p. 125.)

24 The Spanish poet Juan José Domenchina in his edition of "The Fifth Duino Elegy" by Rilke published in Mexico in 1945 added the following note to Rilkes' enigmatic expression ("Subrisio saltat"): "'The smile dances'. Subrisio, onis was introduced in Latin during the fourth century by San Jeronimus." Domenchina refers as a source for this information the book of J. F. Angelloz *Rainer Maria Rilke; l'évolution spirituelle du poète* published in 1936. It is very probable that Lezama knew these two books.

25 See, in Albert Thibaudet's *La poésie de Stéphane Mal-*

larmé: étude littéraire (Paris: Gallimard, 1926), the chapter entitled "La Prose (pour des Esseintes)," pp. 403-416.

26 Valéry, "Je disais quelquefois...," p. 651: "Tout médiocre qu'était sa condition dans le monde qui mange, gagne et griffonne, cet homme faisait songer de ces êtres semi-rois, semi-prêtres,—semi réels, semi légendaires, auxquels nous devons de croire que nous ne sommes point tout animaux." (Translation by Malcolm Cowley and James R. Lawler: "Modest as was his situation in the world of those who eat, earn, and scribble, he somehow suggested those beings, half kings and half priests, half real and half legendary, to whom we owe the belief that we are something more than animals." p. 282.)

27 Concluding lines from Mallarmé's sonnet which begins "Toute l'âme résumée..." ("The entire soul summed up..."): "Too precise a meaning scratches out / Your mysterious literature." The names mentioned are all of Cuban writers of the 19th century: Tristán de Jesús Medina (1833-1886), Ramón Zambrana Valdés (1817-1866) and his wife Luisa Pérez de Zambrana (1835-1922), Julián del Casal (1863-1893), Ricardo del Monte (1828-1909) and José Martí (1853-1895).

28 "Un coup de dés jamais n'abolira le hasard" ("A throw of the dice will never abolish chance"), Mallarmé's last major poem, written in 1897, broke with traditional verse form and typographical arrangement by omitting conventional punctuation and scattering its words and phrases in different sized type and irregular spacing over its several pages.

Compliment for Mallarmé

1 Text taken from José Lezama Lima, *Analecta del reloj* (Ha-

vana: Orígenes, 1953), pp. 241-243. First published in *Grafos*, 9 (99); [14]; mayo 1942.

2   Here and in the following three paragraphs Lezama quotes phrases from a passage in Mallarmé's essay "Crise de vers" ("Crisis of Verse"): "L'oeuvre pure implique la disparition élocutoire du poëte, qui cède l'initiative aux mots, par le heurt de leur inégalité mobilisés; ils s'allument de reflets réciproques comme une virtuelle traînée de feux sur des pierreries, remplaçant la respiration perceptible en l'ancien souffle lyrique ou la direction personelle enthousiaste de la phrase." ("The pure work implies the disappearance of the poet speaking, who yields the initiative to words, through the clash of their ordered inequalities; they light each other up through reciprocal reflections like a virtual swooping of fire across precious stones, replacing the primacy of the perceptible rhythm of respiration or the classic lyric breath, or the personal feeling driving the sentences." *Divagations*. Trans. Barbara Johnson. Cambridge: Harvard University Press, 2007, p 208.) Lezama reads "heurt" ("shock," "clash") as "joy," apparently taking it as akin to "heureux" ("happy").

3   From the "Scène" in Mallarmé's poem "Hérodiade": "Mirror! / Cold water frozen in your frame by boredom / how many times, and for hours, distressed" (Trans. Peter Manson, p. 73).

4   From Valéry's poem "Fragments du Narcisse": "Fontaine, ma fontaine, eau froidement présente, / Douce aux purs animaux, aux humains complaisante / Qui d'eux-mêmes tentés suivent au fond la mort, / Tout est songe pour toi, Soeur tranquille du Sort!" (Translation by David Paul: "Fountain, my fountain, water coldly present, / Sweet to the purely animal, compliant to humans / Who self-tempted pursue

death into the depths, / To you all is dream, tranquil Sister of Fate!")

5   Here and in the following sentence Lezama refers to Mallarmé's sonnet which begins "Une dentelle s'abolit / Dans le doute du Jeu suprême / À n'entr'ouvrir comme un blasphème / Qu'absence éternelle du lit." (Trans. Peter Manson. "Lace cancels itself out / in doubt of the supreme Game / to half-reveal like a blasphemy only / eternal absence of bed" p. 187.)

6   See opening lines of Valéry's sonnet "Les grenades": "Dures grenades entr'ouvertes / Cédant à l'excès de vos grains…." (Ibid. Trans. by David Paul: "Tough pomegranates half-opening / Yielding to your intemperate seeds…." p. 207.)

Circumstantial Prose for Mallarmé

1   Text taken from José Lezama Lima, *Analecta del reloj* (Havana: Orígenes, 1953), pp. 263-270. First published as "El Pen Club y Mallarmé," *Orígenes*, año 5, no. 19 (1948), pp. 36-40.

2   "Stéphane" refers, of course, to Mallarmé and "don Luis" to the Spanish writer Luis de Góngora (1561-1627), the difficulty of whose poetry has sometimes been compared with that of Mallarmé's.

3   In section 27 of the 1891-'92 edition of his "Song of Myself," Walt Whitman asks: "To be in any form, what is that?."

4   "Le blanc souci de notre toile" is the last line of Mallarmé's sonnet "Salut" ("Toast"). This last line, and the whole poem, is translated to English in disparate ways: "the white disquiet of our cloth" (Peter Manson), "And plumped the

naked canvas of our craft" (Blake Bronson-Barlett and Robert Fernandez) "Concerns born of our blank white chart" (David Scott), "of our sail's white preoccupation" (E. H. and A. M. Blackmore).Alex Ross in an article published in the New Yorker describes the divergence of the translators in the following manner: "Consider the sonnet "Salut," which addresses a gathering of poets. Rival English translations of the last three lines […] almost form a poem in themselves, in the manner of Stevens's "Thirteen Ways of Looking at a Blackbird" ("Encrypted. Translators confront the supreme enigma of Stéphane Mallarmé's poetry." *The New Yorker*, April 11, 2016)

5   The lines quoted here are from Mallarmé's sonnet that opens with "Au seul souci de voyager / Outre une Inde splendide et trouble…" ("To the sole concern of journeying / Beyond a splendid and troubled India…") and closes with "Par son chant reflété jusqu'au / Sourire du pâle Vasco" ("By its song reflected all the way / To the pale Vasco's smile").

6   See Mallarmé's letter of April 20, 1868, to François Coppée: "…voici deux ans que j'ai commis le peché de voir le Rêve dans sa nudité idéale, tandis que je devais amonceler entre lui et moi un mystère de musique et d'oubli. Et maintenant, arrivé à la vision d'une Oeuvre pure, j'ai presque perdu la raison et le sens des paroles les plus familères." ("it's been two years now since I committed the sin of seeing the Dream in its ideal nakedness, whereas I should have been amassing between it and me a mystery of music and oblivion. And now, since I've reached the terrible vision of a pure work of art, I've almost lost my reason and the sense of the most familiar words" (*Selected Letters of Stephane Mallarmé*. Trans. Rosemary Lloyd. Chicago: Uni-

versity of Chicago Press, 1988, p. 84) The phrase "tribal sense" echoes a line in Mallarmé's poem "Le Tombeau d'Edgar Poe": "Donner un sens plus pur aux mots de la tribu…" ("To give a more pure meaning to the words of the tribe….")

7   See "Magie" in Mallarmé's *Divagations*: "Je dis qu'existe entre les vieux procedés et le sortilège, que restera la poésie, une parité secrète… […] Le vers, trait incantatoire! et on ne déniera au cercle que perpétuelle ferme, ouvre la rime une similitude avec les ronds parmi l'herbe, de la fée ou du magicien." (Translation by Barbara Johnson: "I claim that, between the old procedures and the magic spell that poetry will always be, a secret parity exists… […] Verse is an incantation! And one cannot deny the similarity between the circle perpetually opening and closing with rhymes and the circles in the grass left by a fairy or magician." p. 284.)

8   "For I install, by science, / the heartfelt spiritual / in the labour of my patience / atlas, herbal and ritual." (Trans. Peter Manson, p. 110)

9   Mallarme's poem "Don du poème" begins with the following verse: "Je t'apporte l'enfant d'une nuit d'Idumée!" ("I bring to you the child of an Idumean night!" Translation by Peter Manson.)

10 Lines 30-36 from "Prose pour des Esseintes": "Everything in me was exalted to see / the family of irises / rise to this new duty, // but this sensible, tender sister / carried her glance no further / than to smile, and to understand her is an old care of mine." (Translation by Anthony Hartley.)

11 See "Ballets" in *Divagations*: "…ainsi qu'avant un pas elle invite, avec deux doigts, un pli frémissant de sa jupe et simule une impatience de plumes vers l'idée." (Translation by Barbara Johnson: "…as when, before taking a step, she

invites one, with two fingers, into the trembling folds of her skirts, and simulates an impatience of plumes toward the idea." p. 132.)

12 See the second stanza of Mallarmé's sonnet that opens "Une dentelle s'abolit / Dans le doute du Jeu suprême..." ("Lace cancels itself out / in doubt of the supreme Game..." Trans. Peter Manson, p. 187): "Cet unanime blanc conflit / D'une guirlande avec la même, / Enfui contre la vitre blême / Flotte plus qu'il n'ensevelit." (Trans. Peter Manson: "This unanimous white conflict / of a garland with the same, rushing against the pale glass / floats more than it shrouds." p. 187.)

13 This "tetralogy" is the cycle of Richard Wagner's four operas comprising *The Ring of the Nibelung* (*The Rhine Gold*, *The Valkyrie*, *Siegfried* and *Twilight of the Gods*), at the end of which the magical gold ring, coveted by so many, is retrieved by the Rhine maidens and returned to its origins in the river.

14 Lezama is alluding to Heidegger's inaugural lecture at the University of Freiburg. "Was ist Metaphysik?" "All the same, we shall try to ask about the nothing. What is the nothing? Our very first approach to this question has something unusual about it. In our asking we posit the nothing in advance as something that "is" such and such; we posit it as a being. But that is exactly what it is distinguished from. Interrogating the nothing—asking what and how it, the nothing, is—turns what is interrogated into its opposite. The question deprives itself of its own object.// Accordingly, every answer to this question is also impossible from the start. For it necessarily assumes the form: the nothing "is" this or that. With regard to the nothing question and answer alike are inherently absurd." ("What is Metaphys-

ics?," *Pathmarks*. Trans. David Farrell Krell. Cambridge: Cambridge University Press, 1998, p. 85.)

15 A line from Valéry's "La Jeune Parque": "Tant de mes visions parmi la nuit et l'oeil, / Les moindres mouvements consultent mon orgueil." ("So much do the slightest stirrings of my visions / Between night and the eye defer to my pride." Trans. David Paul, p. 75.)

16 Two lines from Valéry's poem "Palme," which in the original read somewhat differently: "Chaque atome de silence / Est la chance d'un fruit mûr!" (Translation by David Paul: "Every atom of silence / Is a chance of ripened fruit!" p. 233).

17 The *Grandes Heures* of Anne of Brittany (1477-1514) was a book of hours illuminated by Jean Bourdichon between 1503 and 1508. The Limbourg brothers (Herman, Paul and Johan) illuminated another famous book of hours, *Les Très Riches Heures du Duc de Berry*, between 1412 and 1416. "The Fouqués" perhaps refers to a single artist, Jean Fouquet (1420-1481), who illuminated yet another book of hours, the *Livre d'Heures d'Étienne Chevalier*, completed around 1460.

About Paul Valéry

1 Spanish text, "Sobre Paul Valéry," taken from José Lezama Lima, *Analecta del reloj* (Havana: Orígenes, 1953, pp. 98-115). First published in *Orígenes*, no. 7, Autumn 1945, pp. 16-27.

2 Lines 67-68 from "Le Cimetière marin": "Ici venu, l'avenir est paresse. / L'insecte net gratte la sécheresse...." ("Once here, the future is an idleness, / The clear-cut insect scratches at the dryness." *Collected Works of Paul Valéry, Vol I.*

Trans. David Paul. Princeton: Princeton University Press, 2015, p. 217)

3 See the tercets of Valéry's sonnet "Baignée" in *Album de Vers Anciens* (*Oeuvres*, I, p. 79): "Un bras vague inondé dans le néant limpide / Pour une ombre de fleur à cueillir vainement / S'effile, ondule, dort par le délice vide, // Si l'autre, courbé pur sous le beau firmament, / Parmi la chevelure immense qu'il humecte, / Capture dans l'or simple un vol ivre d'insecte." (trans. David Paul: "A vague arm submerged in that limpid non-being / Uselessly to cull the reflection of a flower / Grows thin, undulates, dozes in the delicious void, // While the other, purely curved under the clear heaven, / Amid the immense coiffure it be-sprinkles, / Arrests a crazy insect's flight in the pure gold." p. 17.)

4 Lezama evokes here a passage from Mallarmé's essay "Crise de vers" referring to the mysterious origins of metrical verse: "Arcane étrange; et, d'intentions pas moindres, a jailli la métrique aux temps incubatoires. Qu'une moyenne étendue de mots, sous la compréhension du regard, se range en traits definitifs, avec quoi le silence." (trans. Barbara Johnson: "What a strange mystery: and, from no lesser intentions, metrics appeared, during incubatory times. What caused a medium extent of words, under the gaze's comprehension, to take on definitive traits, surrounded by silence?" p. 206) Here, as in some later quotations in this essay, Lezama misconstrues the sense of certain words in the French original.

5 "…l'idée se fait sensation sous le regard…." See "Eupalinos ou l'Architecte" in *Oeuvres*, II, p. 81.

6 "Le Dessin n'est pas la forme, il est la manière de voir la forme." See "Degas Danse Dessin" in *Oeuvres*, II, p. 1224.

7 This "acute critic" is Ezra Pound. See "How to Read" in

Literary Essays of Ezra Pound (New York: New Directions, 1968, p. 26): "By using several hundred pages of prose, Flaubert, by force of architectonics, manages to attain an intensity comparable to that in Villon's *Heaulmière*, or his prayer for his mother. This does not invalidate my dissociation of the two terms: poetry, prose."

8 See Albert Thibaudet, *Histoire de la littérature française de 1789 à nos jours* (Paris: Librairie Stock, 1936, p. 254): "Ainsi donc tous les poètes romantiques se sont posé la question du roman, ont écrit des romans importants. Les précurseurs et les poètes du Parnasse, eux, ou n'y ont pas touché, comme Baudelaire et Leconte de Lisle, ou en ont fabriqué sans conviction comme Banville [...]. Le vrai roman parnassien, c'est le roman antique qui dérive plus ou moins de ce Tétrarque honoraire que fit Flaubert.» (trans. Charles Lam Markmann: "So, then, all the romantic poets faced the question of the novel, wrote important novels. As for the forerunners and the poets of Parnassus, either they avoided the novel, like Baudelaire and Leconte de Lille, or they attempted it without conviction—like Banville [...]. The real Parnassian novel was the antique novel that derived more or less from that titular tetrarch, Flaubert." *French Literature from 1795 to Our Era*. New York: Funk & Wagnalls, 1968)

9 "As the fruit dissolves into pleasure...," line 25 from "Le Cimetière marin" (*Oeuvres*, I, p. 148).

10 First three lines of stanza #25 of Lorenzo de' Medici's poem *Ambra (Descriptio hiemis)*: "Come le membra virginali entrorno / nella acqua bruna e gelida sentìo, / e, mosso da leggiadro corpo adorno...." (Continuation: "...della spilunca uscì l'altero iddio, / dalla sinistra prese el torto corno, / e nudo el resto, acceso di disio, / difende el capo

inculto a' febei raggi / coronato d'abeti e montàn' faggi.")
(trans. Jon Thiem: "When she immersed her maiden members in / His dark, cold stream, Ombrone felt them, and, /
Excited by her body's grace and lightness, / The haughty
godling issued from his cave. / His left hand taking up his
twisted horn, / He stands quite naked, ardent with desire. /
And crowned with fronds of fir and mountain beech, / He
shields his tousled head from Phoebus's rays." *Lorenzo De'
Medici: Selected Poems and Prose*. Pennsylvania: University of Pennsylvania Press, 1991, p. 132)

11 Last words of "L'amateur de poèmes," the concluding
poem in *Album de Vers Anciens*: "…une pensée singulière-
ment achevée" (*Oeuvres*, I, p. 95).

12 Compare this with a passage in Valéry's *Choses tues* (*Oeuvres*, II, p. 476): "La musique m'ennuie au bout d'un peu de
temps, et d'autant plus court qu'elle a eu plus d'action sur
moi. C'est qu'elle vient gêner ce qu'elle vient d'engendrer
en moi, de pensées, de clartés, de types et de prémisses. //
Rare est la musique qui ne cesse d'être ce qu'elle fut; qui
ne gâte et ne traverse ce qu'elle a créé, mais qui nourisse
ce qu'elle vient de mettre au monde, en moi." (trans. Stuart
Gilbert: "After a short time music gets on my nerves—a
time that's all the shorter the more the music has affected
me. Because it now tends to obstruct all that, to start with,
it had called to life: thoughts, insights, archetypes, and
premises. // Rare indeed is music that does not cease being
what it was, that does not spoil and counteract what it has
created, but nourishes what it had brought to birth within
me." *Collected Works of Paul Valery, Vol. 14*. Princeton:
Princeton University Press, 1970, p. 8)

13 See Valéry's "Préface" to *Monsieur Teste* (*Oeuvres*, II, p.
11): "Je suspectais la littérature, et jusqu'aux travaux assez

précis de la poésie. L'acte d'écrire demande toujours un certain 'sacrifice de l'intellect'. On sait bien, par exemple, que les conditions de la lecture littéraire sont incompatibles avec une précision excessive du langage." (Trans. Jackson Mathews: "For me literature was suspect, even the fairly precise works of poetry. The act of writing always requires a kind of 'sacrifice of the intellect.' We know very well, for instance, that our way of reading literature is incompatible with any excessive precision of language." *The Collected Works of Paul Valéry. Vol. VI*. Princeton: Princeton University Press, 1973, pp. 3-4)

14 Compare this with the Doctor's statement in Valéry's dialogue *L'Idée fixe ou deux hommes à la mer*: "…*la fatigue m'excite. Plus je suis fatigué, plus je veux en faire.*" (*Oeuvres*, II, p. 203). (Translation by David Paul: "…fatigue stimulates me. The more tired I am, the more I want to do." *Idée Fixe*. New York: Pantheon Books, 1956, p. 16.)

15 "Tant de mes visions parmi la nuit et l'oeil…," line 95 from *La Jeune Parque* (*Oeuvres*, I, p. 98) (Trans. Peter Manson. "So much do the slightest stirrings of my visions / Between night and the eye defer to my pride." p. 75).

16 See *Oeuvres*, II, p. 13: "…l'existence d'un type de cette espèce no pourrait se prolonger dans le réel pendant plus de quelques quarts d'heure…" (trans. Jackson Mathews: "…a character of this kind could not survive in reality for more than a few quarters of an hour…" *Collected Works of Paul Valéry, Vol 6*. Princeton University Press, 1973, p. 5).

17 See the fragment entitled "L'homme de verre" in the "Extraits du Log-Book de Monsieur Teste" of *Monsieur Teste* (*Oeuvres*, II, p. 44): "Si droite est ma vision, si pure ma sensation, si maladroitement complète ma connaissance, […] je me reflète et me répercute, je frémis à l'infini des

miroirs—je suis de verre." (trans. Jackson Mathews: "So direct is my vision, so pure my sensation, so clumsily complete my knowledge, [...] I reflect and reverberate myself, I quiver to the infinity of mirrors—I am glass." Ibid. pp. 44-45.)

18   *Oeuvres*, II, p. 14: "Donner quelque idée de'un tel monstre, en peindre les dehors et les moeurs; esquisser du moins un Hippogriffe, une Chimère de la mythologie intellectuelle, exige,—et donc excuse,—l'emploi, sinon la création, d'un langage forcé, parfois énergiquement abstrait." (trans. Jackson Mathews: "To give some idea of such a monster, to describe his appearance and his habits, to sketch at least a Hippogryph, a Chimera of the mind's mythology, requires—and therefore excuses—the use if not the creation of a forced language, at times vigorously abstract." Ibid. p. 7.)

19   The Euphorion evoked here is the son of Faust and Helen in Act III, Part Two of Goethe's *Faust*, the boisterous and aspiring spirit of poetry who, like Icarus, plunges to his death. See, in particular, lines 9596-9906.

20   Words addressed by Eupalinos to his own body in "Eupalinos ou l'Architecte" (*Oeuvres*, II, p. 99): "Instrument vivant de la vie, vous êtes à chacun de nous l'unique objet qui se compare à l'univers. La sphère tout entière vous a toujours pour centre; ô chose réciproque de l'attention de tout le ciel étoilé! Vous êtes bien la mesure du monde, dont mon âme ne me présente que le dehors." (trans. William McCausland Stewart: "Instrument, thou, of life, thou art for each one of us the sole being which can be compared with the universe. The entire sphere always has thee for a center; O mutual object of the attention of all the starry heavens! Thou art indeed the measure of the world, of which my soul

presents me with the shell alone." *Dialogues*. New York: Pantheons Books, 1956, p. 91.)

21 This echoes one of Valéry's assertions about Teste. See *Oeuvres*, II, p. 14: "Dans cette étrange cervelle, où la philosophie a peu de crédit, où le langage est toujours en accusation, il n'est guère de pensée qui ne s'accompagne du sentiment qu'elle est provisoire; il ne subsiste guère que l'attente et l'exécution d'opérations definies." (trans. Jackson Mathews: "In that strange head, where philosophy has little credit, where language is always under indictment, there is rarely a thought free of the sense that it is provisional; very little remains but expectation and the performance of definite operations." p. 8)

22 "No one meditates," Teste's reply at the theater to his companion's remark "Je voudrais voir un théâtre inspiré de vos méditations" (*Oeuvres*, II, p. 21: "I would like to see a theater inspired by your meditations" p. 16).

23 After leaving the theater, Teste's companion observes (*Oeuvres*, II, p. 22): "Nous marchions, et il lui échappait des phrases presque incohérentes. Malgré mes efforts, je ne suivais ses paroles qu'à grand'peine, me bornant enfin à les retenir. L'incohérence d'un discours dépend de celui qui l'écoute. L'esprit me paraît ainsi fait qu'il ne peut être incohérent pour soi-même." (trans. Jackson Mathews: "As we walked along, he was uttering almost incoherent phrases. Although I tried, I could barely follow his words, and in the end merely recalled them. The incoherence of speech depends on the one listening to it. The mind seems to me so made that it cannot be incoherent to itself." *ibid., loc. cit.*)

24 Speaking of the effect on him of the music they've just heard at the theater, Teste's companion remarks (*ibid., loc. cit.*): "'Pourtant, *répondis-je*, comment se soustraire à une

musique si puissante! Et pourquoi? J'y trouve une ivresse
particulière, dois-je la dédaigner? J'y trouve l'illusion d'un
travail immense, qui, tout à coup me deviendrait possible…
Elle me donne des *sensations abstraites*, des figures délicieuses de tout ce que j'aime,—du changement, de mouvement, du mélange, du flux, de la transformation.…'" (trans.
Jackson Mathews: "'And yet, *I replied*, how can we escape
a music of such power! And why should we? I find a special excitement in it; must I reject it? I find in it the illusion
of a tremendous work that might suddenly become possible
for me… an illusion that gives me *abstract sensations*, delightful images of everything I love—change, movement,
mixture, flow, transformation…'" p. 17)

25 To his companion's above cited exclamations, Teste replies
(*ibid.*, *loc. cit.*): "'Je suis chez MOI, je parle ma langue, je
hais les choses extraordinaires. C'est le besoin des esprits
faibles. Croyez moi à la lettre: le génie est *facile*, la *divinité*
est *facile*… Je veux dire simplement—que je sais comment
cela se conçoit. C'est *facile*.'" (trans. Jackson Mathews: "'I
am at home in MYSELF, I speak my own language, I hate
extraordinary things. Only weak minds need them. Believe
me literally: *genius* is *easy*, *divinity* is *easy*… I mean simply…that I know how it is to be conceived. It is *easy*.'"
ibid., *loc. cit.*).

26 Teste remarks to his companion (*ibid.*, p. 23): "Vous con-
naissez un homme sachant qu'il ne sait ce qu'il dit!" (trans.
Jackson Mathews: "You know a man who knows that he
doesn't know what he's saying!" p. 18).

27 At his lodging, after he has gotten into bed, Teste remarks to
his companion (*ibid.*, p. 24): "Rappelez-vous!—Quand on
est enfant on se *découvre*, on découvre lentement l'espace
de son corps, on exprime la particularité de son corps par

une série d'efforts, je suppose? On se tord et on se trouve ou on se retrouve, et on s'étonne! on touche son talon, on saisit son pied droit avec sa main gauche, on obtient le pied froid dans la paume chaude! … Maintenant, je me sais par coeur. Le coeur aussi." (trans. Jackson Mathews: "Remember! When we are children we *discover* ourselves, we learn little by little the extent of our body, we express our body's particularity by a series of movements, I suppose? We twist and discover or rediscover ourselves, and are amazed! We touch our heel, or hold the right foot in the left hand, we take a cold foot into a warm palm! … Now, I know myself by heart. My heart included." p. 19)

28 Lines 27-28 from Baudelaire's poem "Les Phares," which allude to engravings by Goya: "De vieilles au miroir et d'enfants toutes nues, / Pour tenter les démons ajustant bien leurs bas…" ("Crones at a mirror served by naked girls / who straighten stockings to entice the Fiend." *Les Fleurs du Mal*. Trans. Richard Howard. Boston: David R Godine, 1985)

29 For Aristotle, the soul is one, but endowed with five groups of faculties (*dunámeis*): the "vegetative" faculty (*threptikón*), concerned with the maintenance and development of organic life; the appetite (*oretikón*), or the tendency to any good; the faculty of sense perception (*aisthetikón*); the "locomotive" faculty (*kinetikón*), which presides over the various bodily movements; and reason (*dianoetikón*). The Scholastics generally follow Aristotle's classification. For them body and soul are united in one complete substance. The soul is the *forma substantialis*, the vital principle, the source of all activities." (*The Catholic Encyclopedia*. Dubray, C. (1909). "Faculties of the Soul")

30 Lines 372-374 from *De rerum natura*, which we trans-

late from Lezama's quotation in Spanish. In the original: "cedere squamigeris latices nitentibus aiunt / et liquidas aperire vias, quia post loca pisces / linquant, quo possint cedentes confluere undae." (trans. W. H. D. Rouse: "They say that water yields to the pressure of scaly creatures and opens liquid ways, because fish leave room behind them for the yielding waves to run together." *De Rerum Natura*. Cambridge: Harvard University Press, 1982)

31 Words spoken by Phaedrus in "Eupalinos ou l'Architecte" referring to the way the ship builder Tridon viewed the forms of fish (*Oeuvres*, II, p. 137): "On eût dit qu'il sentait par lui-même, leurs formes favorables conduire, de la tête vers la queue, par le chemin le plus rapide, les eaux qui se trouvent devant eux, et qu'il s'agit, pour avancer, de remettre derrière soi...." (trans. William McCausland Stewart: "It was as though he himself felt their well-adapted forms conducting from head to tail, by the quickest way, the waters which lie in front of them, and which must be put behind them that they may advance...." p. 139)

32 We restore here a part of this sentence included in the original version of the essay in *Orígenes* but omitted in the versions in *Analecta del reloj* and *Obras completas,* which is the phrase "...un pozo progresivo, un punto ridículo en el pozo..." ("...a progressive well, a ridiculous point in the well...").

33 For this quote of Cézanne see Ambroise Vollard, *Paul Cézanne*, Paris: Crès, 1924, p. 135

34 See "L'enseignement de la poétique au Collège de France" (*Oeuvres*, I, p. 1442): "...la partie essentielle d'une *Poétique* devrait consister dans l'analyse comparée du mécanisme (c'est-à-dire, de ce que l'on peut, *par figure*, appeler ainsi) de l'acte de l'écrivain, et des autres conditions moins dé-

finies que cet acte semble exiger ("inspiration," "sensibili-
té," etc.).)." (trans. Ralph Manheim: "…the essential part of
a doctrine of *Poetics* should consist in a comparative analysis of the mechanics (that is, of what might *figuratively* be
so called) of the writer's act and of the other less clearly
defined conditions that it seems to call for ('inspiration,'
'sensibility,' etc.)." *Collected Works of Paul Valery, Vol. 13*.
Princeton: Princeton University Press, 1971, p. 88)

35 Lines 93-96 from Valéry's *La Jeune Parque*, which we
translate from Lezama's quotation in Spanish. In the original (*Oeuvres*, I, p. 98): "Et brisant une tombe sereine, /
Je m'accoude inquiète et pourtant souveraine, / Tant de mes
visions parmi la nuit et l'oeil, / Les moindres mouvements
consultent mon orgueil." (trans. David Paul: "And breaking
a tomb serene, / I lean on my arm, uneasy and supreme, /
So much do the slightest stirrings of my visions / Between
night and eye defer to my pride." *Collected Works of Paul
Valéry, Vol I*. Trans. David Paul. Princeton: Princeton University Press, 2015, p, 75.) Lezama renders as "I reduce myself" the verb "je m'accoude" ("I lean on my elbow") and
makes masculine the feminine adjectives the speaker of the
poem uses in referring to herself.

Conversation about Paul Valéry

1 Notes found among Lezama's papers after his death. Text
taken from *Lezama disperso*. Prologue, compilation and
notes by Ciro Bianchi Ross. Havana: Ediciones Unión,
2009, pp. 122-129.

2 "Foolish peacock" in English in the original.

3 See "Les broderies de Marie Monnier" in Valéry's *Oeuvres*,
II, pp. 1244-1245. Marie Monnier (1894-1976) was a noted

French embroiderer.

4 See, in *Conversations of Goethe with Johann Peter Ecker-mann*, entries for early March 1832 (young counselor von Spiegel), Sept. 24, 1822 (lithographs from Stuttgart and violet vapors of iodine), Feb. 25, 1822 (medal sent from Bohemia) and Dec. 17, 1822 (discovery of salt springs).

5 An echo of Valery's remark about Leonardo da Vinci in "Léonard et les philosophes": "...il semble lui-même avoir dispensé son ardeur aux sujets les plus variés, selon l'humeur du jour et les circonstances; jusqu'à donner l'impression, que je ne hais pas, d'une sort de condottière au service de toutes les Muses tour à tour" (trans. Malcolm Cowley: "...Leonardo himself seems to have lavished his ardor on the greatest variety of subjects, depending on circumstances and the mood of the hour—so much so that he gives the not unpleasant impression of being a sort of condottiere in the service of all the Muses turn by turn" *Collected Works of Paul Valéry, Vol 8*. Princeton: Princeton University Press, 2015, pp. 132-133). *Oeuvres*, I, p. 1251.

6 A famous poem of Valéry's first published in 1920 and later included in *Charmes*, which Lezama quotes later in these notes.

7 "Green, how I want you, green" ("For the love of Green" by Federico García Lorca. *The Selected Poems of Federico García Lorca*. trans. William Logan. New York City: New Directions, 1955.)

8 Lezama is referring to the poem "Verde Verderol" by Juan Ramón Jiménez.

9 Another famous poem of Valéry's, "La Jeune Parque," in the form of a long dramatic monologue spoken by Clotho, the youngest of the Fates, was first published in 1917. "Narcisse" may refer to either "Narcisse parle" in *Album*

de vers anciens or "Fragments du Narcisse" in *Charmes*, which also includes "Les grenades." The French medievalist Gustave Cohen's commentary on "Le Cimetière marin" was published as *Commentaire du Cimetière marin* (Paris: Gallimard, 1933). The Megarian school of philosophy was founded in the 4th century BC by Euclid of Megara, a disciple of Socrates.

10 An echo of words spoken by Teste's companion in the chapter of Valéry's *Monsieur Teste* entitled "La soirée avec Monsieur Teste": "Elle [une musique] me donne des *sensations abstraites*, des figures délicieuses de tout ce que j'aime,—du changement, du mouvement, du mélange, du flux, de la transformation…" *Oeuvres, II*, p. 22. (trans. Jackson Matthews: "It [a piece of music] gives me *abstract sensations*, delightful images of everything I love—change, movement, mixture, flow, transformation" p. 17)

11 "Doing the opposite, doing otherwise." And yet, in his essay "Situation de Baudelaire," Valéry claims Baudelaire set about to do precisely that: "Dans le domaines de la création, qui sont aussi les domaines de l'orgueil, la necessité de se distinguer est indivisible de l'existence même. Baudelaire écrit dans son projet de préface aux *Fleurs du mal*: '*Des poètes illustres s'étaient partagé depuis longtemps les provinces les plus fleuries du domaine poétique*, etc. Je ferai donc autre chose…'" *Oeuvres, I*, p. 600. (trans. James R. Lawler: "In the domain of creation, which is also the domain of pride, the need to come out and be distinct is part of life itself. Baudelaire wrote in the preface he planned for *Les Fleurs du Mal*: 'Illustrious poets had long shared among themselves the most abundantly flourishing provinces of the domain of poetry… *I shall therefore do otherwise*…'" p. 195.)

12 This echoes a passage in Albert Thibaudet's *Histoire de la littérature française de 1789 à nos jours* (Paris: Librairie Stock, 1936, pp. 321-322): "La fleur du jour, c'est la fleur de la veille plus la floraison. La poésie de Baudelaire, c'est la poésie de Saint-Beuve plus la poésie. Je veux dire que la matière de cette poésie plus le rayon et le génie de la poésie pure, aliment de lumière, réservé aux dieux, et auquel Sainte-Beuve n'a pas goûté. On distinguera dans les *Fleurs du mal* cette matière et ce rayon." (trans. Charles Lam Markmann: "Today's flower is yesterday's flower plus efflorescence. Baudelaire's poetry is Sainte-Beuve's poetry plus poetry. I mean the matter of that poetry plus the radiance and the genius of pure poetry, the aliment of light reserved to the gods, which Sainte-Beuve never tasted. This manner and this radiance will be found in *Les Fleurs du Mal*." *French literature from 1795 to our era*. New York: Funk & Wagnalls, 1968)

13 See Stéphane Mallarmé, "Richard Wagner: Rêverie d'un poète français," in his *Divagations*: "…un auditoire éprouvera cette impression que, si l'orchestre cessait de déverser son influence, le mime resterait, aussitôt, statue" (trans. Barbara Johnson: "…an audience should feel the impression that, if the orchestra stopped playing, the mime would immediately become a statue" p. 109).

14 See lines 45-46 of "Le Cimetière marin": "Entre le vide et l'événement pur, / J'attends l'écho de ma grandeur interne…." For Valéry's "pure event," Lezama substitutes "dream."

15 This echoes a passage in T. S. Eliot's essay "Tradition and the Individual Talent": "The poet's mind is in fact a receptacle for seizing and storing up numberless feelings, phrases, images, which remain there until all the particles

which can unite to form a new compound are present to-gether. // If you compare several representative passages of the greatest poetry you see how great is the variety of types of combination, and also how completely any semi-ethical criterion of 'sublimity' misses the mark. For it is not the 'greatness', the intensity, of the emotions, the components, but the intensity of the artistic process, the pressure, so to speak, under which the fusion takes place, that counts." *Selected Essays: 1917-1932*. New York: Harcourt, Brace and Company, 1932, p. 9.

16 See Valéry's essay "Je disais quelque fois à Stéphane Mallarmé…" (I Would Sometimes say to Stéphane Mallarmé…): "Mais cent instants divins ne construisent pas un poème, lequel est une durée de croissance et comme une figure dans le temps…" *Oeuvres*, I, p. 648 (trans. Malcolm Cowley: "The fact remains that a hundred divine moments do not compose a poem, which is a temporal unit of development and might be called a structure in time…" p. 277).

17 An echo of the second stanza of Mallarmé's poem "Prose pour des Esseintes": "Car j'installe, par la science, / L'hymne des coeurs spirituels / En l'oeuvre de ma patience, / Atlas, herbiers et rituels." (trans. Peter Manson. "for I install, by science, / the heartfelt spiritual / in the labour of my patience, / atlas, herbal and ritual." p. 111)

18 See Jean-Henri Fabre, *The Life of the Grasshopper*, chap. XI: "The White-Faced Decticus: His Habits."

19 Lines 75-76 from "Le Cimetière marin." ["And Noon up there, Noon the motionless" (*Collected Works of Paul Valery. Vol I*. Trans. by David Paul. Princeton University Press, 2015. p. 217)]

20 An allusion to Valéry's dialogue "Eupalinos ou l'architecte," in which the souls of Socrates and Phaedrus converse after

their death and at one point mention "the very admirable Stephanos, who appeared so many centuries after us," a reference to Stéphane Mallarmé. The fact that Lezama places Valéry among them implies he took these notes after Valéry's own death on July 20, 1945.

21 In the myth of the construction of lower Thebes, Amphion was able to lift and place the stones with the aid of music played on a lyre given to him by Hermes. See Graves 76. *c*. On this subject Valéry wrote a "mélodrame" first performed in 1931, with music composed by Arthur Honegger. Its text is found in *Oeuvres*, I, pp. 166-181, and Valéry's later lecture, "Histoire d'Amphion (Mélodrame)," in *Oeuvres*, II, pp. 1277-1283.

The Poetic Act and Valéry

1 Spanish text, "El acto poético y Valéry," taken from *Analecta del reloj* (Havana: Orígenes, 1953), pp. 253-255.

2 See Ezra Pound, *The Spirit of Romance* (NY: New Directions, 1952), p. 14: "Poetry is a sort of inspired mathematics, which gives us equations, not for abstract figures, triangles, spheres, and the like, but equations for the human emotions."

3 The ancient Greek mathematician Eratosthenes (c. 276 BC - c. 195 BC) devised a simple algorithm for finding prime numbers known as "the Sieve of Eratosthenes."

4 In his *Studies in the History of the Renaissance* (1873), Walter Pater (1839-1894) said: "all art constantly aspires towards the condition of music."

5 Valéry's *Introduction à la Poétique* (1938) contains the text of the opening lecture of his course on poetics at the Collège de France in December 1937, under the title "Pre-

mière leçon du cours de poétique," along with a briefer
text entitled "L'enseignement de la poétique au Collège de
France." Both are included in vol. I of his *Oeuvres* (Paris:
Bibliotèque de la Pléiade, 1957), pp. 1340-1358 and 1438-
1443.

6   Valéry distinguishes between "l'action qui fait" (the action
that makes or does) and "la chose faite" (the thing made or
done). See *Oeuvres*, I, p. 1343.

7   "…considérer le Langage lui-même comme le chef-
d'oeuvre des chefs-d'oeuvre littéraires…" (*ibid.*, pp. 1440-
1441). (trans. Ralph Manheim: "…consider language itself
as the masterpiece of literary masterpieces…" *Collected
Works of Paul Valery, Vol. 13*. Princeton: Princeton University Press, 1971, p. 88).

8   "Le poète qui multiplie les figures ne fait donc que re-
trouver en lui-même le langage à l'état naissant" (*ibid.*,
p. 1440). ("The poet who makes repeated use of figurative
speech is only rediscovering, within himself, the *nascent
state* of language" *Ibid. loc.cit*).

9   "Religation" as "binding together," from the Latin *religare*,
one of the possible etymologies for "religion."

10 "…les raisonnements délicats dont les conclusions pren-
nent l'apparence des divinations…" (*ibid.*, p. 1347).

11 See, in one of the sections entitled "A Memorable Fancy"
in William Blake's *The Marriage of Heaven and Hell*, the
dialogue between the Angel "whose works are only Analytics" and the "pitiable foolish young man," which culminates in a void "between saturn & the fixed stars."

Lezama's Diary Entries on Descartes and Valéry

1   Text taken from pp. 22-24 of José Lezama Lima, *Diarios:*

1939-1949 / 1956-1958. Compilación y notas de Ciro Bianchi Ross. Havana: Ediciones UNIÓN, 2001.

2   Lezama is referring to the following stanza of "Le Cimetière marin" by Paul Valéry:

> Ô pour moi seul, à moi seul, en moi-même,
> Auprès d'un coeur, aux sources du poème,
> Entre le vide et l'événement pur,
> J'attends l'écho de ma grandeur interne,

> Ah for myself, to my own self within,
> Close by a heart, at the sources of the poem,
> Between emptiness and the pure event,
> I await my grandeur's echo from within

[*Collected Works of Paul Valery. Vol I*. Trans. David
Paul. Princeton University Press, 2015.]

3   Lezama is referring to the following passage in *Meditation
on First Philosophy* by Descartes: "I realize that I am, as
it were, something intermediate between God and nothingness, or between supreme being and non-being." *The
Philosophical Writings of Descartes. Vol II*. Trans. John
Cottingham, Robert Stoothoff and Douglas Murdorch.
Cambridge: Cambridge University Press, 1984, p. 39.

4   Lezama is referring here to the following passage in Meditation on First Philosophy by Descartes: "But this is still
not entirely satisfactory. For error is not a pure negation"
(*Ibid. loc.cit*)

5   I am aware of a certain weakness in me, in that I am unable
to keep my attention fixed on one and the same item of
knowledge at all times; but by attentive and repeated medi-

tation I am nevertheless able to make myself remember it as often as the need arises, and thus get into the habit of avoiding error." (Ibid. 43)

6 when the mind understands, it in some way turns towards itself and inspects one of the ideas which are within it; but when it imagines, it turns towards the body and looks at something in the body which conforms to an idea understood by the mind or perceived by the senses." (Ibid. 51)

7 Lezama is referring to the following stanza of *Charmes.* "Fragments du Narcisse" by Paul Valéry.

> *J'aime... J'aime*!… Et qui donc peut aimer autre
> chose
> Que soi-même?…
> Toi seul, ô mon corps, mon cher corps,
> Je t'aime, unique objet qui me défends des morts

> [*I love, I love.* And who can love any other
> Than himself?…
> You only, body mine, my dear body
> I love, the one alone who shields me from the
> dead!"

> *Collected Works of Paul Valery. Vol I.* Trans. David
> Paul. Princeton University Press, 2015, 159.]

Serpent of Don Luis de Góngora

1 Text taken from *Analecta del reloj*: La Habana: Orígenes, 1953, pp. 183-214.

2 The second half of this opening paragraph (from "with the invasive fatigue…" down to "…causing it to disappear and

be concealed") refers most immediately not to events narrated in the main body of the poem, but rather to its preliminary "Dedicatoria" addressed to the poem's dedicatee, the Duke of Béjar, which envisions him as a hunter resting alongside animals he has killed. However, the phrase "… which prepares the beginning of sleep inducing metamorphoses…" points to later sequences in the *Soledad primera* which evoke the descent of sleep upon various characters.

3   These quoted phrases are taken from three different letters of Góngora to Francisco de Corral dated December 18, 1618; January 1, 1619 and September 1, 1620.

4   The historical references in this paragraph pertain mostly to the years Góngora spent in Madrid cultivating connections at court in hopes of improving his financial situation. Mentioned here, along with the famous painters El Greco and Velázquez, are: Hortensio Félix Paravicino, poet and religious orator; Felipe IV's powerful favorite Gaspar de Guzmán, Count-Duke of Olivares; and Góngora's friend the poet and libertine Juan de Tassis, Count of Villamediana. A fire during a court performance of the latter's allegorical masque *La gloria de Niquea* was rumored to have been set by Villamediana himself so he could rush in and bodily carry the Queen to safety because he lusted after her. This and other indiscretions, including his mordant satires, are said to have motivated Villamediana's assassination on a Madrid street in 1622, possibly at the King's or Olivares' orders.

5   In the book of Tobit in the Apocrypha (12: 6), Tobit's and Tobias's companion, as yet not having identified himself as the angel Raphael, says to them: "Bless God, praise him, and magnify him, and praise him for the things which he hath done unto you in the sight of all that live. It is good

333

to praise God, and exalt his name, and honourably to shew forth the works of God; therefore be not slack to praise him." Here, as well as later in the passage marked by note 77, the adjective "somber" is more in keeping with Lezama's view of Góngora than with Tobias.

6   See Leonardo da Vinci, *Notebooks*. Arranged, rendered into English and introduced by Edward MacCurdy (NY: Reynal & Hitchcock, 1939), p. 876: "When you make a figure and wish to see whether the shadow corresponds to the light, and is neither redder nor yellower than is the nature of the essence of the colour which you wish to show in shadow, you should do as follows: with a finger make a shadow upon the illuminated part, and if the accidental shadow made by you is like the natural shadow made by your finger upon your work, it will be well then by moving the finger nearer or further off, to make the shadows darker or lighter, comparing them constantly with your own."

7   An allusion to Calderón's well-known play *El alcalde de Zalamea* (The Mayor of Zalamea) which tells how civil law prevails over military transgression.

8   Lines 9-14 from Góngora's sonnet "Tonante monseñor, ¿de cuándo acá…?."

9   [Author's Note] "In the Icelandic *skalds* too much clarity is considered a technical fault. The Greeks also required the poet's word to be dark. Among the troubadours, in whose art the play-function is more in evidence than in any other, special merit was attributed to the *trobar clus*—the making of recondite poetry." J. Huizinga, *Homo Ludens*, translated by R. F. C. Hull, Boston: Beacon Press, 1955, p. 135. [Lezama quotes the corresponding passage in the Spanish translation by Eugenio Ímaz, México: Fondo de Cultura Económica, 1943, p. 207. *Trobar clus* or "closed

poetry" was the enigmatic mode of the poetry of medieval troubadours.]

10 An echo of fragment 93 of Heraclitus: "The lord whose oracle is that at Delphi neither speaks nor conceals, but indicates."

11 After his landfall early in the *Soledad primera*, the protagonist goes in the darkness toward a distant light characterized in various ways: "vacilante / breve esplendor de mal distinta lumbre" (lines 57-58), "piedra, indigna tiara /…/ de animal tenebroso, cuya frente / carro es brillante de nocturno día" (lines 73-76) and "carbunclo, Norte de su aguja" (line 82). Edith Grossman's translation: "vacillant / brief gleam of a distant, an indistinct light," "gem, undeserved coronet / … / of a tenebrous gloom-loving beast, whose brow / the brilliant carriage is of nocturnal day," "carbuncle, polestar to his compass." (*The Solitudes: A Dual-Language Edition with Parallel Text*. New York: Penguin Books, 2011, pp. 10-12). On this basis Lezama forms his "animal carbunclo" and treats it as a recurrent entity in the poem, on the same level of literal reference as the protagonist himself and the persons he encounters.

12 "Stroke in the side" refers to how Christ while still on the cross was wounded in the side by a soldier with his spear, a moment which John 19: 35 emphasizes by adding the words: "He who saw it has borne witness—his testimony is true, and he knows that he tells the truth—that you also may believe. For these things took place that the scripture might be fulfilled."

13 San Juan de la Cruz, *Subida del Monte Carmelo*, II, xvii, 6, which speaks in the singular of "ejercicio de pequeñuelo," rendered in E. Allison Peers's translation as "the business of a child": "We have already explained how the things of

sense, and the knowledge that spirit can derive from them, are the business of a child." *Ascent of Mount Carmel*. Mineola: Dover Publications Inc, 2008, pp. 141-142.

14 San Juan de la Cruz, *op. cit.*, II, xvii, 5. E. Allison Peers' translation.

15 "La media luna del blanco" may also be translated as "the half moon of the white one." "Half moon" echoes the allusion at the opening of the *Soledad primera* to the horns of Zeus in his guise as a bull in order to ravish Europa (lines 2-3: "…el mentido robador de Europa / (media luna las armas de su frente…)." (Grossman's translation: "Europa's false-hearted abductor /—a half moon the weapons of his brow….") "White one" would refer to the fact that he took the form of a white bull, while the sense of "blanco" as "target" would be justified by Lezama's immediately preceding mention here of "hunts."

16 St. Ignatius of Loyola, *Spiritual Exercises*, First Week, first paragraph of Principle and Foundation. Translation by Father Elder Mullan SJ. NY: P. J. Kennedy & Sons, 1914. <www.ccel.org/ccel/ignatius/exercises.xii.i.html> We have included a few words in brackets to complete the sense of the phrase Lezama quotes in Spanish.

17 The goat Amaltheia, who suckled the infant Zeus, was later transformed by him into the constellation Capricorn and one of her horns into the Cornucopia of endless bounty (see Graves, 7*b*). In the *Soledad primera*, lines 202-205, she is explicitly named as part of an extended metaphor for the fruitful banks of the mountain stream observed by the protagonist: "…orladas sus orillas de frutales, / quiere la Copia que su cuerno sea, / si al animal armaron de Amaltea / diáfanos cristales…." In the *Soledad segunda*, lines 303-308, she is alluded in another metaphor describing a hill covered

with grazing goats: "…un cerro elevado, / de cabras estrel-
lado, / iguales, aunque pocas, / a la que, imagen décima
del cielo, / flores su cuerno es, rayos su pelo." Grossman's
translation: "with its banks ornamented by fruit trees, / Copia herself desires it for her horn /—if the creature of Amal-
thea had been armed / with crystal transparency," (p. 21) "a
high hill / studded and starred with she-goats, / just like the
one, though fewer, / tenth image in the heavens—/ whose
horn is flowers, whose hair is made of beams." (p. 103)
Lezama objectifies the figurative Amaltheia as a recurrent
entity in the poem much as he treats the "carbuncle beast."

18 "The pilgrim" ("el peregrino") is one of several designations for the anonymous protagonist of the *Soledades*,
termed "hidden" here because of his tactful concealment
before introducing himself to members of the rustic wedding party (see *Soledad primera*, lines 267-269 and 350-
356). For "the old leader of the fishermen," see below note
42.

19 During the marriage celebration in the *Soledad primera*, the procession of the bride joined by other maidens
is evoked in an extended passage of complex figuration
which includes references to the Phoenix, ancient Egypt
and the pyramids (lines 946-957: "…la novia sale de vil-
lanas ciento / a la verde florida palizada, / cual nueva Fénix
en flamantes plumas / matutinos del Sol rayos vestida, /
de cuanta surca el aire acompañada / monarquía canora,
/ y, vadeando nubes, las espumas / del Rey corona de los
otros ríos, / en cuya orilla el viento hereda ahora / pequeños
no vacíos / de funerales bárbaros trofeos / que el Egipto
erigió a sus Ptolomeos." Grossman's translation: "…the
bride, at the head of countless peasant girls, / goes to the
enclosure green and flowering, / like a new phoenix dressed

in plumes as brilliant / as rays of the morning sun, accompanied / by the lyric monarchy / that cuts through air and, fording clouds, crowns with foam / the king of all the rivers: / on its banks now the wind inherits trophies / deserted and not small / of barbarous funeral rites / erected by Egypt for her Ptolomies." pp. 71-72) As in the cases of the "carbuncle beast" and "the goat Amaltheia," Lezama reads this extended metaphor as a literal change of scene.

20 Lines 357-360 from Góngora's poem "Panegírico al Duque de Lerma."

21 There aren't any "nymphs of charcoal" ("ninfas de carbón") in the *Soledades*, but this may refer to a kind of disguise, in view of the essay's reference a bit earlier to the procession requiring that "all besmear and mask themselves," like carnival celebrants

22 The New World turkey is evoked in lines 309-312 of *Soledad primera*, but the words quoted here are *not* from the poem

23 The *Primero sueño* ("First dream") was a philosophical poem of nocturnal vision by the 17th century Mexican nun Sor Juana Inés de la Cruz. "*Amateur* of scholasticism" alludes to Sor Juana's depiction of herself as autodidact in her autobiographical essay "Response to the most illustrious poetess Sor Filotea de la Cruz."

24 Lines 884-886 from the *Primero sueño*, in Margaret Sayers Peden's translation (modified): "…feigns solid form / adorned with all dimensions / though not deserving even to be a surface." (*Poems, Protest, and a Dream: Selected Writings*. New York: Penguin Classics, 1997)

25 See Leonardo da Vinci, *op. cit.*, p. 863: "…the first picture was nothing but a line which surrounded the shadow of a man made by the sun upon a wall."

26 See Góngora's poem *Fábula de Polifemo y Galatea*, line 290: "la brújula del sueño vigilante," "the compass of his vigilant sleep."

27 During the wedding celebrations, the old man complains that the number of fireworks lit might cause a devastating fire (see *Soledad primera*, lines 645-658).

28 When Proserpina went back to the world of the living, Ascalaphus was the gardener who revealed she had tasted a pomegranate in Tartarus and thus would have to return there. He was then punished by Jupiter by being transformed into an owl (see Graves, 24 *j*, *k*, *l*, where Proserpina and Jupiter are designated by their Greek names Core and Zeus). Ascalaphus is evoked as owl and as mythical personage in both *Soledades* (in the first, lines 990-991; in the second, lines 791-798, 886-892 and 974-979).

29 Lines 781-782 of the *Soledad segunda*. Grossman's translation: "...vulgar deceit, not bountiful industry, / granted dominion over / the eagle, the butterfly." (p. 137)

30 Lezama takes advantage of how Góngora deals with the "American osprey" to criticize, like he did in other instances in his work, the image that Hegel gives of the American continent in his book *Lectures on the Philosophy of World History*. Hegel defined the American continent with these words: "America has always shown itself physically and spiritually impotent, and it does so to this day. For after the Europeans had landed there, the natives were gradually destroyed by the breath of European activity. Even the animals show the same inferiority as the human beings." (*Lectures on the Philosophy of World History*. Trans. by H. B. Nisbet. Cambridge: Cambridge University Press, 1975, p.163). Lezama dedicates many pages of his book *La expresión americana* to refute the idea that Hegel has of the

American continent.

31 Lines 753-754 of the *Soledad segunda*: Grossman's translation: "brave wonder of the air."

32 See Calderón, *La vida es sueño*, I, lines 304-308: "…o aquesta pistola, áspid / de metal, escupirá / el veneno penetrante / de dos balas, / cuyo fuego / será escándalo del aire" ("…or this pistol, metal / asp, will spit / the venom of two bullets, / whose fire / will be a scandal of the air").

33 See Calderón, *El postrer duelo de España*, I, lines 497-498: "estimate the counterbasses / of all your contretemps."

34 Concluding line of John Donne's poem "The Sun Rising."

35 A reference to the French professor of philosophy Victor Brochard's essays "Les arguments de Zénon d'Elée contre le mouvement" and "Les prétendus sophismes de Zénon d'Elée."

36 The epigraph for the first edition of Valéry's *L'Idée fixe ou deux hommes à la mer* (Paris: Laboratoires Martinet, 1932), taken from Góngora's poem "La toma de Larache," instead of the correct citation "En roscas de cristal serpiente breve" ("In crystal coils brief serpent"), gives "En rocas de cristal serpiente breve" ("On crystal rocks brief serpent"), an error emended in later editions.

37 [Author's Note] Verse cited by Américo Castro, in *España en su historia*, p. 399. See also, on the same page, the reference to *irradiation* in Arabic poetry. [Full title and reference: *España en su historia: Cristianos, moros y judíos* (Buenos Aires: Editorial Losada, 1948). The lines quoted, "La belleza resplandeciente en el rayo de su frente, / y de ella viene una brisa de almizcle y de alcanfor," are from the Arabic poem *Historia de los amores de Bayad y Riyad*, prior to 13th century.]

38 A repeated refrain in the pilgrim's hymn of gratitude upon

being welcomed by the goatherds in *Soledad primera* (lines
94-95, 106-107, 122-123, 134-135). Grossman's translation:
"Oh fortunate, oh happy / shelter at any hour!" (p. 39)

39 References to various moments early in the *Soledad primera*: the fire lit by the goatherds which the pilgrim glimpses
from afar (lines 92-93), their whistling to their herds (line
105), their staffs (line 121) and the melting of the wax secur-
ing Icarus' wings (line 132-133), which the pilgrim evokes
as a symbol of the danger of excessive ambition in his
hymn to having found "fortunate…happy shelter" among
these humble people.

40 Cambay was an ancient trading port in India (now called
Khambhat) mentioned in lines 370-374 of the *Soledad segunda*: "…y la humedecida, / o poco rato enjuta, / próxima
arena de esa opuesta playa / la remota Cambaya / sea de
hoy más a vuestro leño ocioso…" (Grossman's translation:
"…and let the ever damp / or only briefly dry / sand of that
nearby beach in terra firma / be from now on far Cambay
/ to your idle bark…"), words spoken by the pilgrim ex-
pressing his wish that the old fisherman and his sons never
venture far from their native shore, as explorers and traders
did before. Lilybaeum is the ancient name of the port in
Sicily now called Marsala, evoked in lines 25-26 of the *Polifemo*: "Donde espumoso el mar Siciliano / el pie argenta
de plata al Lilibeo…" (Rivers's translation: "Where foam-
ily the sea of Sicily / silvers the foot of Mt. Lilybaeum…"
Renaissance and Baroque Poetry of Spain. Long Grove:
Waveland Press, 1988, p. 165). "La remota Cambaya" is
also a line in Lezama's own poem "Los ojos del Río Tinto"
in *La fijeza*.

41 See lines 407-413 of *Soledad segunda*, spoken by the old
fisherman to the pilgrim: "Bárbaro observador (mas dili-

gente) / de las inciertas formas de la Luna, / a cada con-
junción su pesquería, / y a cada pesquería su instrumento, /
más o menos nudoso, atribuído, / mis hijos dos en un bajel
despido, / que el mar cribando en redes no comunes…"
Grossman's translation: "An observer not learned but diligent / of Luna's changeable forms, / to each conjunction
a kind of fishing, / to each kind of fishing its own imple-
ments /—more knots or fewer—accord, / I bid farewell to
my two sons in their boat, / who sieve the sea with uncom-
mon nets…." (pp. 109-110)

42 San Juan de la Cruz, *Noche oscura*, II, ix, 4. Peers' translation.

43 *Op. cit.*, II, ix, 5. Peers' translation.

44 *Ibid.*

45 See the opening lines of San Juan de la Cruz's poem "La
noche oscura": "En una noche oscura, / con ansias en
amores inflamada…" Rivers' translation: "On a dark night,
/ inflamed with the passions of love…." (p. 138)

46 *Noche oscura*, II, xvi, 13. Peers' translation. This is also a
passage from Psalms 31: 20.

47 [Author's Note] "Now that we have explained the reasons
why the soul called this contemplation a 'secret ladder',
it remains for us to explain likewise the word 'disguised',
and the reason why the soul says also that it went forth
by this 'secret ladder' in 'disguise'. "For the understanding
of this it must be known that to disguise oneself is naught
else but to hide and cover oneself beneath another garb and
figure than one's own—sometimes in order to show forth
under that garb or figure, the will and purpose which is in
the heart to gain the grace and will of one who is greatly
loved; sometimes, again, to hide oneself from one's rivals
and thus to accomplish one's object better. At such times a

man assumes the garments and livery which best represent and indicate the affection of his heart and which best conceal him from his rivals.

"The soul, then, touched with the love of Christ the Spouse, and longing to attain to His grace and gain His goodwill, goes forth here disguised with that disguise which most vividly represents the affections of its spirit and which will protect it most securely on its journey from its adversaries and enemies, which are the devil, the world and the flesh. Thus the livery which it wears is of three chief colours—white, green and purple...." San Juan de la Cruz, *Noche oscura*, II, xxi, 1-3, Peers' translation. See the whole of chapter xxi.

Frazer emphasizes that the colors used by the druids in their ceremonies were white, green and red. San Juan de la Cruz surely was familiar with that antecedent.

48 [Author's Note] A phrase of Amiel's.

49 [Author's Note] "Lu ce matin à Paule le Préambule—ébauché hier au soir—de mon étude pour la *Revue de Genève*—sur la thèse de Jean Baruzi. Je citais à Paule le mot que Brunschwicg disait l'autre jour à Jean—et dans lequel Jean voyait avec raison un vrai mot de philosophe: 'Quel est le oui qui est derrière ce non?'. Jean de la Croix, en effet—autant qu'un tout premier contact me permet de m'en rendre compte—c'est la souveraineté du non—du non, acquiérant un maximum de positivité, devenant comme Jean le dit fort bien quelque part 'l'Affirmation d'un univers nocturne'. J'ai grande impatience de lire ce chapitre sur la critique des appréhensions distinctes, car je sens que tout tourne autour de cela."—Charles Du Bos, *Journal*, p. 139, vol. II. Passage dated Monday, June 9, 1924, in Du Bos' *Journal 1924-1925*, Paris: Corrêa, 1948. (Translation: "Read to Paule this

morning the Preamble—drafted last night—of my study for the *Revue de Genève*—on Jean Baruzi's thesis. I quoted to Paule the words that Brunschwicg said to Jean the other day—and which Jean rightly found to be truly a philosopher's phrase: 'What is the yes that lies behind this no?'. Indeed, John of the Cross, in so far as this first contact allows me to see—is the sovereignty of negation—of a negation that takes on the greatest positive value, becoming, as Jean says so well somewhere, 'the Affirmation of a nocturnal universe'. I am very eager to read this chapter about the critique of distinct apprehensions, for I sense that everything revolves around that." Jean Baruzi's doctoral dissertation *Saint Jean de la Croix et le problème de l'experience mystique* was published in 1924.)

50 Line 374 of Garcilaso de la Vega's "Égloga tercera": "[The nymphs] all plunged together into the shallows," (p. 82) Rivers' translation.

51 Line 345 of Garcilaso's "Égloga segunda": "dark disheveled sisters," Rivers' translation.

52 Lezama is quoting from Euripides' *Heracles*. "the fields unsown over plains wide-spreading" ("Madness of Hercules", *Euripides* III. Trans. Arthur S. Way. London: William Heinemann, 1930, v. 369 p. 157)

53 Next to last line of Luis Carrillo de Sotomayor's poem "Fábula de Acis y Galatea": "…and this the beautiful fountain and cold crystal…."

54 The *manjuarí* or Cuban gar fish (*Atractosteus tristoechus*), a species peculiar to that country, has been called a living fossil because its primitive traits represent a transitional stage between fish and reptile, which would account for its mention in this context of metamorphoses.

55 Lines 497-500 of the *Polifemo*, in Rivers's translation:

"Hardly were his limbs lamentably oppressed by the fatal rock when the feet of the biggest trees were shod in the liquid pearls of his veins." (p. 184)

56 *Ibid.*, lines 503-504: "He reached Doris, who, with pitying tears, greeted him as a son in law, acclaimed him as a river." (p. 185)

57 Concluding lines of Pedro Espinosa's poem "Fábula de Genil": "…because the nymph, seeing her plight was dire, and her virginity thus oppressed, was, as she wept, transformed into water."

58 See the old fisherman's account in the *Soledad segunda*, lines 418-444, of how two of his daughters hunted a seal, called "escamada fiera" or "peña escamada" ("scaly animal," "scaly crag").

59 All these references are to the *Soledades*: the murex as source of dye indirectly alluded in *Soledad segunda* (line 558: "…ni del que enciende el mar tirio veneno…"), the half moon and sunbeams in Taurus in the evocation of Zeus at the very beginning of *Soledad primera* (lines 3-4: "…media luna las armas de su frente / y el Sol todos los rayos de su pelo…"), and Pallas and Arachne later in *Soledad primera* (lines 835-839: "De errantes lilios unas la floresta / cubran, corderos mil que los cristales / vistan del río en breve undosa lana; / de Aracnes otras la arrogancia vana / modestas acusando en blancas telas…"). Grossman's translation: "nor venom that fires the Tyrian sea," "a half moon the weapons of his brow, / the Sun's rays all the strands of his hair," "Let some cover the woods with errant lilies: / thousands of lambs, dressing the river crystal / in short tightly curling wool; / let others, modest, depict the arrogance / of Arachne on white cloth…."

60 Nereus, though not explicitly named there, is the "ancient

seagod" or "old man of the sea" whose daughters, the Ne-
reids, in the final book of the Odyssey, help prepare the
immolation of the remains of Achilles. "Marine mutations"
refers to his powers of metamorphosis, featured prominent-
ly in the eleventh labor of Hercules.

61 The mention of Pallas Athene here evokes the moment in
the first book of the Odyssey when the goddess, in the guise
of a family friend named Mentes, speaks to Telemachus of
trading voyages and assures him that his father Odysseus
will eventually return home.

62 This seems to echo a passage in the pilgrim's lament addressed to the sea in verses 137-143 of the *Soledad segunda*:
"Audaz mi pensamiento / el Cenit escaló, plumas vestido, /
cuyo vuelo atrevido, / si no ha dado su nombre a las espumas, / de sus vestidas plumas / conservarán el desvaneci-
miento / los anales diáfanos del viento." Grossman's translation: "With audacity my thought / scaled the heights, clad
in feathers, / whose daring incautious flight /—if it has not
given thy foam its name—/ of its well-feathered raiment /
the diaphanous annals of the wind / will preserve the van-
ishment." (p. 91)

63 In verses 365-502 of the *Soledad primera*, the old mountain
man, detecting in the pilgrim's clothing signs of his recent
shipwreck, delivers a long discourse on the perils of ocean
trade and exploration, which includes figurative allusions
to the heliotrope (verse 372) and the polestar (verses 379-
394).

64 In the *Soledad primera*, the young shepherd who has pointed out to the pilgrim the ruins of a castle where he had
served as a soldier is seen by the pilgrim as "armado a Pan,
o semi capro a Marte / en el pastor mentidos" (verses 233-
235). Grossman's translation: "fully armed Pan or semicap-

rine Mars / the shepherd seemed to him…." (p. 23)

65 Among the offerings brought to the rustic wedding banquet by the mountain people in the *Soledad primera* are young goats, rabbits and honey (verses 297-308 and 321-328).

66 In the *Soledad primera*, the pilgrim observes several young mountain women on their way to the wedding, of whom Lezama here focuses upon three who share the motifs of music or dance: "…canoro instrumento, que pulsado / era de una serrana junto a un tronco, / sobre un arroyo de quejarse ronco…" (verses 239-241); "Negras pizarras entre blancos dedos / ingeniosa hiere otra…" (verses 251-252); and "Al son pues deste rudo / sonoroso instrumento, / lasciva el movimiento / mas los ojos honesta, / altera otra bailando la floresta" (verses 254-258). Grossman's translation: "…a melodious instrument strummed / by a mountain girl sitting under a tree, / beside a stream, made hoarse by its complaining…"; "Pieces of black slate between white fingers / another, ingenious, strikes…"; and "To the sound, then, of this crude / and sonorous instrument /—lascivious the movement, but modesty in her eyes—/ another disquiets, dancing, the greensward."

67 Lezama says this plant with a "veined aquatic leaf, a favorite of Goethe's" is called "amelo." But the English equivalent of that is the amellus or amellus aster, a flowering garden plant which doesn't correspond to the description here. We have not been able to locate this reference in Goethe.

68 The Laetrygonians, led by Antiphates, are a tribe of man-eating giants who destroy all but one of Odysseus' ships in the tenth book of the Odyssey. In the old mountain man's discourse on the perils of ocean trade and exploration in the *Soledad primera*, the Carib Indians of the New World are compared to them (see verses 419-424).

69 See verses 1483-1488 of *La Chanson de Roland* in Gerard
J. Brault's translation: "There was a Saracen there from
Saragossa, / Half the city is his, / It is Climborin, who was
not a man of honor. / He took Count Ganelon's oath, / He
kissed him on the mouth as a sign of friendship, / He also
gave him his helmet and carbuncle." (*La Chanson de Roland: Student Edition*. Pennsylvania: Penn State University
Press, 1990, p. 93). This is a moment in the Saracens' and
the French traitor Ganelon's conspiracy that leads to the
death of Roland.

70 This refers to an incident related in the chapter entitled "Introduction to the Pains of Opium" in Thomas de Quincey's
Confessions of an English Opium-Eater.

71 According to Genesis 1: 20-22, on the fourth day of creation
"…God said, 'Let the waters bring forth swarms of living
creatures, and let birds fly above the earth across the firmament of the heavens.' / So God created the great sea monsters and every living creature that moves, with which the
waters swarm, according to their kinds, and every winged
bird according to its kind. And God saw that it was good.
/ And God blessed them, saying 'Be fruitful and multiply
and fill the waters in the seas, and let the birds multiply on
the earth.'"

72 Refrain to Góngora's poem "Al nacimiento de Cristo
Nuestro Señor": "Who has heard? / Who has heard? / Who
has seen what I have seen?"

73 See lines 135-136 of the *Polifemo*: ""¡Oh cuánto yerra /
delfín que sigue en agua corza en tierra!" Rivers' translation: "Oh how mistaken / is the dolphin that pursues in the
water a deer on land!" (p. 169)

74 The Count of Niebla was the dedicatee of the *Polifemo*,
invoked as hunter in its opening stanzas.

75 [Author's Note] See the following sonnet, attributed to the Count of Villamediana:

A C Ó R D O B A

Gran plaza, angostas calles, muchos callos;
obispo rico, pobres mercaderes;
buenos caballos para ser mujeres,
buenas mujeres para ser caballos.

Casas sin talla, hombres como tallos;
aposentos colgados de alfileres;
Baco descolorido, flaca Ceres;
muchos Judas y Pedros, pocos gallos.

Agujas y alfileres infinitos;
una puente que no hay quien la repare;
un vulgo necio, un Góngora discreto;

un San Pablo entre muchos Sambenitos:
Esto en Córdoba hallé; quien más hallare,
póngaselo por cola a este soneto.

See also this epitaph for the Count, attributed to Góngora:

Aquí yace, aunque a su costa,
un monstruo en decir y hacer;
por la posta vino a ser
y dejó de ser por la posta.
Puerta en el pecho no angosta
le abrió el acero fatal.
Pasajero, el caso es tal

que da luz con su vaivén,
y no importa correr bien
si se ha de parar en mal.

Ode to Julián del Casal

1   Spanish text, "Oda a Julián del Casal" taken from José
Lezama Lima, *Poesía completa*. Madrid: Sexto piso, 2016,
pp. 850-858. First published in *Revista de la Biblioteca Na-
cional José Martí*, 1963.

GREEN INTEGER
Pataphysics and Pedantry
Douglas Messerli, *Publisher*

Essays, Manifestos, Statements, Speeches, Maxims,
Epistles, Diaristic Notes, Narrative, Natural Histories,
Poems, Plays, Performances, Ramblings, Revelations and
all such ephemera as may appear necessary to bring society
into a slight tremolo of confusion and fright at least.

Individuals may order through
www.greeninteger.com
Bookstores and libraries should order through our distributor
Consortium Book Sales & Distribution / Ingram Books
(800) 283-3572 / www.cbsd.com

*

SELECTED NEW TITLES

<u>2016</u>

Jim Gauer *Novel Explosives* [978-1-55713-433-2] $15.95
Douglas Messerli *My Year 2001: Keeping History a Secret* [978-1-55713-428-8] $15.95
   My Year 2009: Facing the Heat [978-1-55713-429-5] $15.95
F. T. Marinetti *The Untameables* [978-1-933382-23-4] $12.95

<u>2017</u>

Régis Bonvicino *Beyond the Wall: New Selected Poems* [978-1-55713-431-8] $12.95
Lee Seong-Bok *Ah—Mouthless Things* [978-1-55713-440-0] $12.95
Lucebert *The Collected Poems: Volume 2* [978-1-55713-434-9] $17.95
Ern Malley *The Darkening Ecliptic* [978-1-55713-439-4] $12.95
Douglas Messerli *My Year 2010: Shadows* [978-1-55713-432-5] $15.95
Steven Moore *My Back Pages* (hardcover) [978-1-55713-437-0] $30.00

2018

Paul Celan *Lightduress* [1-931243-75-1] $19.95 [REPRINT]
Maria Irene Fornes *Abingdon Square* [1-892295-64-4] $19.95 [REPRINT]
Jean Grenier *Islands: Lyrical Essays* [1-892295-95-4] $19.95 [REPRINT]
Atilla Jozsef *A Transparent Lion* [978-1-933382-50-0] $19.95 [REPRINT]
Ko Un *Songs for Tomorrow: A Collection of Poems 1960-2002* [978-1-933382-70-8] $19.95 [REPRINT]
  Ten Thousand Lives [1-933382-06-6] $19.95 [REPRINT]
Vladimir Mayakovsky *Vladimir Mayakovsky: A Tragedy* [978-1-55713-444-8] $19.95
Douglas Messerli *My Year 2000: Leaving Something Behind* [978-1-55713-443-1] $15.95
  My Year 2011: No One's Home [978-1-55713-442-4] $15.95
  Stay [978-1-55713-447-9] $12.95
Steven Moore *My Back Pages* [978-1557134387] $23.00
Toby Olson *The Life of Jesus: An Apocryphal Novel* [978-1-55713-441-7] $19.95
Gertrude Stein *Tender Buttons* [1-931243-42-5] $19.95 [REPRINT]
  Three Lives [1-892295-33-4] $19.95 [REPRINT]
Paul Verlaine *The Cursed Poets* [1-931243-15-8] $19.95 [REPRINT]

2019

Adonis *If Only the Sea Could Sleep: Love Poems* [978-1-931243-29-2] $19.95 [REPRINT]
Richard Kalich *The Assisted Living Facility Library* [978-1-933382-29-6] $13.95
José Lezama Lima *A Poetic Order of Excess: Essays on Poets and Poetry* [978-1-892295-98-9] $13.95
Douglas Messerli *My Year 2012: Centers Collapse* [978-1-55713-445-5] $15.95
  My Year 2013: Murderers and Angels [978-1-892295-83-5] $15.95
Jean Renoir *An Interview* [978-1-55713-330-4] $19.95 [REPRINT]
Rainer Maria Rilke *Duino Elegies* [978-1-931243-07-0] $19.95 [REPRINT]
Oscar Wilde *The Critic as Artist* [978-1-55713-368-7] $19.95 [REPRINT]

CPSIA information can be obtained
at www.ICGtesting.com
Printed in the USA
LVHW050124010819
626069LV00002B/2/P